FIGHTING TECHNIQUES
OF THE EARLY MODERN WORLD
AD 1500 ~ AD 1763
EQUIPMENT, COMBAT SKILLS, AND TACTICS

FIGHTING TECHNIQUES

OF THE EARLY MODERN WORLD

AD 1500 ~ AD 1763

EQUIPMENT, COMBAT SKILLS, AND TACTICS

CHRISTER JÖRGENSEN MICHAEL F. PAVKOVIC ROB S. RICE FREDERICK C. SCHNEID CHRIS L. SCOTT

THOMAS DUNNE BOOKS
ST. MARTIN'S PRESS ≈ NEW YORK

THOMAS DUNNE BOOKS
An imprint of St. Martin's Press

www.stmartins.com

Library of Congress Cataloging-in-Publication Data
on file at the Library of Congress

ISBN: 0-312-34819-3

EAN: 978-0-312-34819-9

First U.S. Edition 2006

Editorial and design by
Amber Books Ltd
Bradley's Close
74–77 White Lion Street
London N1 9PF
United Kingdom
www.amberbooks.co.uk

Project Editors: Michael Spilling and Tom Broder
Design: Zoe Mellors
Picture Research: Natasha Jones and Terry Forshaw

Printed in Singapore

10 9 8 7 6 5 4 3 2 1

CONTENTS

CHAPTER 1

THE ROLE
OF
INFANTRY

Through much of the European Middle Ages, mounted warriors were the single most important component of the majority of field armies. But by the middle of the fifteenth century changes in European warfare led to the creation of large standing armies. These armies came to rely on ever-increasing numbers of highly trained and well-equipped infantry.

Over the next three centuries infantry would once again be the dominant force on the battlefield. Two overarching factors contributed to the increasing role of infantry on the battlefield. First, and perhaps most important, was the development of administrative structures that would allow the early modern state to recruit and eventually maintain ever larger forces of standing foot soldiers. While states initially relied on military contractors and mercenary soldiers to

AFTER THE ROUT *of the Austrians, Frederick the Great searched for shelter in the village of Leuthen. Some of the troops following him struck up a hymn, 'Now thank we all our God', which became known as the Leuthen Chorale. The hymn was soon taken up by virtually every man in the Prussian army.*

staff their new infantry units, improving administrative and financial organization soon allowed states to retain soldiers with the colours for longer periods of time. This in turn provided opportunities for the development of unit identities, cohesion and discipline.

Second was the introduction of a new weapons system, based on the combination of the pike, a weapon of great antiquity, and the hand-held firearm – referred to as 'shot' – based on the new technology of gunpowder. The widespread introduction of infantry polearms, especially the pike, in the hands of disciplined mercenary foot soldiers, or the standing units of the early modern state, allowed infantry to keep even the most heavily armoured horseman at bay. When combined with the range and stopping power of gunpowder weapons, disciplined infantry forces became a formidable battlefield instrument.

Swiss, *Landsknechts* and *Tercios*

In the Valois-Hapsburg Wars at the beginning of the fifteenth century, bodies of infantry armed with pikes and firearms came to play an increasingly important role in battle. While both close-order infantry armed with pike and other polearms and firearm-equipped infantry appear during this time and are usually considered in tandem as 'pike and shot', it is important to recognize that they developed independently of one another and drew on very different traditions. The result was that the evolution of pike-and-shot tactics reflected constant experimentation and adaptation over the period of nearly two centuries.

Although there had been pike-armed foot soldiers during the thirteenth and fourteenth centuries, often based on urban militias, particularly in the Low Countries, the model for

'When they engaged the fight, the Swiss pressed so hard upon the enemy with their pikes that they soon opened their ranks, but the Spaniards, under the cover of their bucklers, nimbly rushed in with their swords and fought them so furiously that they slaughtered the Swiss and gained a complete victory.'

— MACHIAVELLI (ON BARLETTA)

such troops from 1500 onwards were the companies of Swiss mercenaries who were to become a fixture in French armies of the period. The Swiss had earned a formidable reputation during the fifteenth century, defeating the Burgundians at Grandson and Murten in 1476 and again at Nancy in 1477. These victories were won by the Swiss' aggressive use of columns of infantry armed primarily with the pikes, supported by men wielding the halberd. The Swiss pike was a long spear, up to six metres (18 feet) long. The halberd was a polearm mounting a combination of axe blade and spear point, with a hooked blade or spike opposite the axe blade on a two-metre (six-foot) shaft of hardwood. The pike allowed infantry to form in deep ranks that could be closely packed together, sometimes with only 15 centimetres (six inches) separating files, and with four or five pike heads protruding before each foot soldier in the front rank.

Standing ready on the defensive, pikemen were an intimidating obstacle, to cavalry especially. The halberd's weight and reach made it a potent weapon against infantry or even armoured horsemen. It did, however, require a large amount of space to be wielded effectively and so was not suitable for closed ranks. Up until about 1450, the Swiss were primarily armed with the halberd, but after a defeat at the hands of some Milanese heavy cavalry some 20 years earlier, the Swiss quickly began to field a preponderance of pikemen. Men armed with the halberd were still used to guard the units' colours and as separate detachments to support the pike units. Many troops would have worn a breastplate and helmet, although some seem to have foregone armour altogether. Those in the front ranks had heavier armour, usually adding tassets (plates protecting the front of the thigh), as well as armour for the upper arms and perhaps the forearms as well.

But the success of the Swiss cannot be attributed to their weapons or formations alone. Their social organization played a major role in the effectiveness of their fighting techniques. Although the pike is a reasonably easy weapon to master, especially on the defensive in closed ranks, since there is not a great deal of individual weapon-handling, the pike in and of itself did not make a pike unit successful on the battlefield. Rather, the cohesion of the pike unit was the critical factor, and the Swiss form of social organization re-inforced the cohesion of their units.

Swiss pikemen were organized into *Haufen* (companies), of approximately 200 men each. The *Haufen* was composed of men from the same region, recruited from both urban centres and outlying rural communities. The company was commanded by a *Hauptmann*, or captain, who was an appointed representative of the town council; other officers in the unit were elected by the men. The *Haufen* was therefore a tightly knit unit with strong ties to the community and the canton of which it was a part. This made Swiss foot soldiers willing to make incredible sacrifices for their communal comrades, with units often fighting to the last man.

Moreover, the importance of maintaining the *Haufen*'s integrity on the battlefield may have played a role in the Swiss not giving quarter to the enemy since the unit would need to detach some of its members to guard the captives. The communal nature of Swiss units also reinforced training since communities could train men from their youth onwards. Indeed, by the end of the fifteenth century a formal school teaching pike drill had opened in Bern.

AN ARRAY OF INFANTRY *polearms of the 16th and 17th centuries shown here includes, from left to right, three varieties of pike, halberd, bill hook, glaive and military hammer. The lengthy iron sleeve extending down the length of the shaft of the weapons, especially the pikes, made it difficult for the enemy to hack off the head of the weapon.*

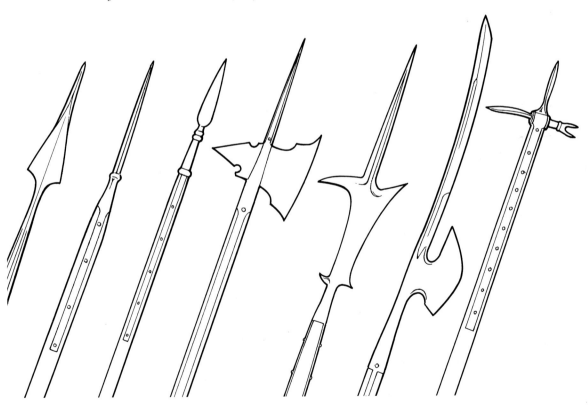

Swiss Halberdier

These typical Swiss halberdiers from the late 15th or early 16th century do not wear any significant armour, except for the soldier on the left, who is protected by a sallet-style helmet. They are armed with a simple form of halberd that has a long, heavy cleaver-like blade that could hack its way through armour or the shaft of an enemy polearm. The halberd is also equipped with a point on the opposite side of the staff. This could be used to pierce even plate armour, as well as being useful as a spear tip for thrusting. The length of these weapons made them effective against both infantry and cavalry. In addition, each is provided with a sword. The soldier on the left carries a shortsword known as a Katzbalger, meaning cat-gutter, while the soldier on the right has a longer broadsword.

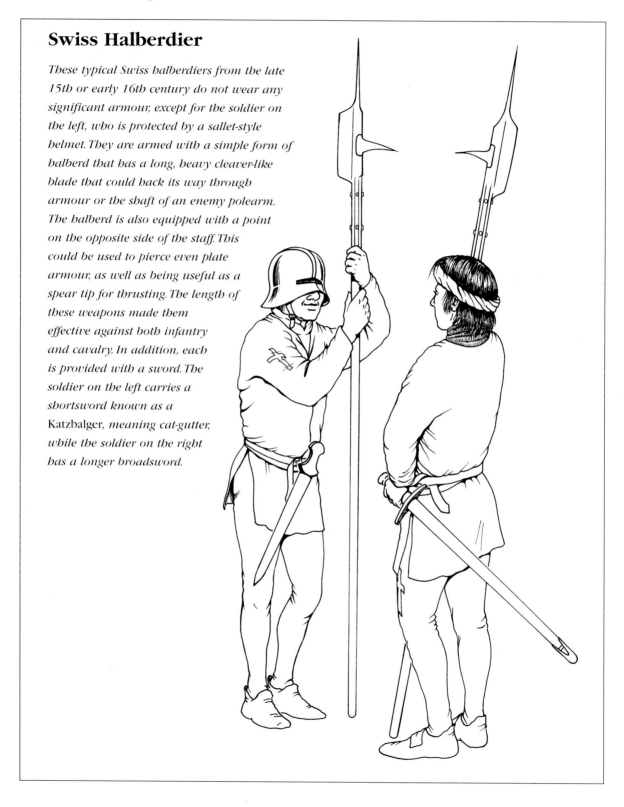

On the battlefield, the *Haufen* were traditionally grouped into three deep columns. These formations were descended from the medieval practice of organizing an army into three 'battles': the vanguard, main body and rearguard. The Swiss in general had these three columns move in echelon. Moreover, Swiss tactics were characterized by very quick and aggressive charges across the battlefield in order to bring the enemy to hand-to-hand combat. Their reputation for speed was such that it was said they could charge enemy artillery before the cannon could get off a second shot.

The *Landsknechts*

The great success of the Swiss infantry at the end of the fifteenth century produced tremendous demand for units of Swiss mercenaries. Unfortunately, the very close social structure that gave the Swiss *Haufen* such incredible unit cohesion on the battlefield made it unlikely that there would be large numbers of Swiss for hire. Moreover, of the major employers, it was the French, rather than the Hapsburgs, who tended to secure the services of most available Swiss mercenary units. Initially this was no doubt due to the Swiss struggle for independence from Hapsburg domination. The near monopoly of Swiss soldiers enjoyed by the French in was formalized with the signing of the 'Perpetual Peace' between France and the Swiss Confederation in 1516. As a result, the Hapsburgs and most other states had to find alternative sources for their infantry forces. To exacerbate matters further, Swiss troops had the unfortunate habit of leaving their employer whenever they perceived their homeland to be in danger, adding another factor contributing to the paucity of Swiss mercenaries.

As a result, states who wished to be able to compete militarily had to develop alternatives. The Hapsburg Holy Roman Emperor sought a solution by creating his own force of disciplined infantry, raised within the empire and trained in the use of the pike. Thus in 1486, Emperor Maximilian I began raising the first units of *Landsknechte*. The term translates as 'servants of the land'. They were to provide the empire with a standing body of disciplined foot soldiers. Maximilian came to realize that the only way to compete with the Swiss was to adopt as much of their system as was practical. In terms of organization, equipment and training this was feasible. It was more difficult to replicate the iron discipline that came from the cohesion of the Swiss' unit.

In his attempt to re-create the ties of the Swiss *Haufen*, Maximilian ordered that a company of *Landsknechts*, known as a *Fähnlein*, be mustered according to the Swiss system. A *Kriegsherr* (gentleman of war) received a recruiting commission to raise a company or regiment of *Landsknechts*. Officers were selected, recruiting parties sent out and potential recruits gathered at an appointed place. Famous or successful commanders, like the Imperialist commander Georg von Frundsberg, could gather several thousand volunteers in a matter of a few weeks. The troops would then be lined up and marched through an arch made from two halberds supporting a pike. As they reached this gateway, they were examined by an officer in order to determine if the man was fit for service. Upon successfully passing inspection the recruits received a month's pay, formed a circle and were read the 'Letter of Articles'. These were the rules and regulations that defined their commission and conduct. Finally, the assembled *Landsknechts* swore an oath to obey their officers and to follow all the regulations laid out in the articles.

From 1490, in order to strengthen the bonds of loyalty to the emperor, all *Landsknechts* swore a

> *'I conclude, therefore, that a good infantry must be able not only to withstand cavalry but also to confront any other sort of infantry fearlessly; and this, as I have often said before, must be entirely a result of their discipline and arms.'*
>
> — MACHIAVELLI, THE ART OF WAR

personal oath of allegiance to Maximilian as 'the father of the *Landsknechts*'. In theory, *Landsknechts* were not to fight against the empire, but since *Kriegsherren* were allowed to raise forces for service in the pay of other states, this was not always the case.

Once recruited, men were assigned to a *Fähnlein*, which had a theoretical strength of 400

LANDSKNECHT ARQUEBUSIERS *of the 16th century wore dress typical of mercenaries of the period, with brightly coloured 'slashed' coats and legwear worn over colourful undergarments. These men also wear breastplates and carry the short 'cat-gutter' sword in addition to their firearms.*

men. One-quarter of the men were to be more experienced men who held the most dangerous positions in battle and, as their name *Doppelsöldner* implies, they received double pay. Most *Doppelsöldner* were equipped with halberds or large two-handed swords, but a small proportion of each company's *Doppelsöldner,* usually 25 to 50, were equipped with firearms, initially the *arquebus*. A number of companies, usually ten, would then be formed into a regiment numbering roughly 4000 men.

The standard *Landsknecht* formation was the *gevierte Ordnung,* or pike block. This formation was more defensive in nature than the three columns of the Swiss. It consisted of a solid block of pikemen with *Doppelsöldner* armed with halberds and especially two-handed swords formed in the very front and at the rear. *Doppelsöldner* armed with *arquebuses* were stationed along the sides of the block and often in four small detachments near the four corners to act as skirmishers. When threatened, these *arquebusiers* retired to shelter between the files of pikemen. When the pike block advanced, it was preceded by a *verlorne Haufe,* literally the 'lost outfit', but usually translated as 'forlorn hope' since many of the men were not expected to survive the battle. The forlorn hope was composed of volunteers, men chosen by lot, or even prisoners given the opportunity to redeem themselves (or die trying) and was deployed in a thin line in order to use halberds and two-handed swords to cut their way into the enemy's formation, making a gap that could be exploited by their own pikemen.

Most *Landsknechts* were armed and armoured in a manner similar to the Swiss they hoped to imitate. The pikemen often wore breastplates and helmets for protection and carried a pike and a short sword, the *Katzbalger* (cat gutter). The pike favoured by the *Landsknechts* was generally shorter than that of the Swiss, sometimes only 4.2 metres (14 feet) in

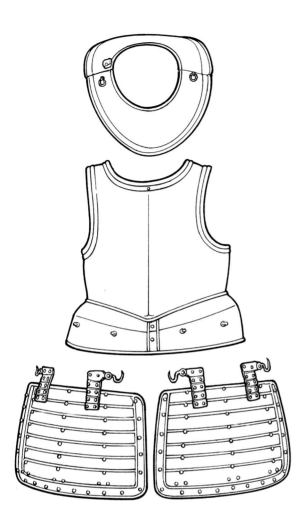 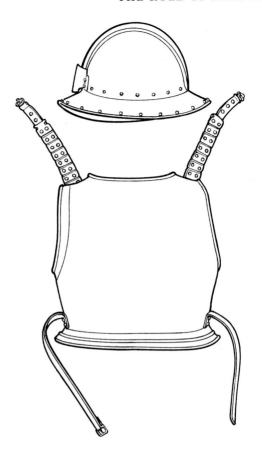

ARMOUR WORN BY *a well-equipped infantryman of the 17th century might include the gorget (on the top left), used to protect the throat, the breastplate and a pair of tassets worn over the upper thighs. On the right is the soldier's backplate and helmet. This type of armour would have been typical of a pikeman of the period, especially one expected to fight in the front ranks.*

length. *Doppelsöldner* and pikemen in the front ranks were usually better armoured, adding tassets and arm protection to their panoply.

The Spanish *Tercios*

The Spaniards also formed a major element in the Imperial armies that fought in the Valois-Hapsburg wars. But unlike the *Landsknechts*, who copied the Swiss, Spanish armies of the period were a reflection of the armies of the *Reconquista*, who fought the epic struggle to liberate the Iberian Peninsula from the Moors. Spanish armies of this period were forged in the final stage of the *Reconquista,* in particular the last two decades of the fifteenth century. Given the duration and nature of this conflict, the Spaniards had engaged

in a style of frontier warfare with the Moors and as a result, Spanish armies were generally composed of lighter armed troops suitable for such conditions.

By the last decade of the fifteenth century, the *Reconquista* had created a standing army in Spain. Like the French (and their Swiss mercenaries) and the Imperialists in Central Europe, the Spaniards did have forces of heavily armoured men-at-arms and pikemen, the latter descended from spear-armed militia of Spanish towns, but these were in the minority. In the Spanish infantry, only about

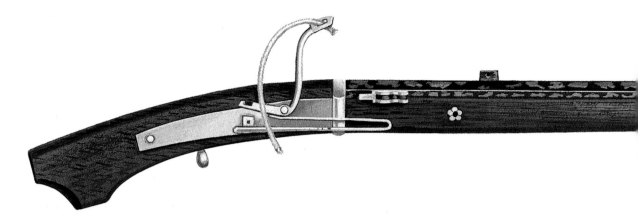

one-third were pikemen, the remainder being roughly divided between sword- and buckler-armed light infantry and skirmishers armed with missile weapons including crossbows and, increasingly, *arquebuses*. Machiavelli records how the Spanish were able to use these light skirmishers to good effect at Barletta in 1502:

'When they engaged the fight, the Swiss pressed so hard upon the enemy with their pikes that they soon opened their ranks, but the Spaniards, under the cover of their bucklers, nimbly rushed in with their swords and fought them so furiously that they slaughtered the Swiss and gained a complete victory.'

The lightly-armed swordsmen and skirmishers were not just suited to the hit-and-run warfare of the *Reconquista*, they were useful when Spanish troops were deployed to Italy. The Lombard plain was criss-crossed with rivers and numerous canals and the Italians had begun making use of field fortifications. In such conditions the lightly armed Spanish troops were very valuable.

The equipment of the Spanish pikemen was comparable to others of their ilk, many wearing helmet and cuirass. The men in the front rank frequently wore extra protection for their arms and thighs. The more lightly armed sword-and-buckler troops, crossbowmen and *arquebusiers* wore various armour including leather jerkins, studded brigantines and some plate cuirasses.

At the beginning of the Italian Wars, Spanish infantry were organized *colunelas,* or columns. Initially, these units numbered approximately 600 men but by 1505 the number had increased to

1000 men. The 20 *colunelas* of in Italy in 1505 were in turn brigaded in four or five larger units called *banderas.* The *colunelas* were mixed formations composed primarily of pikemen and *arquebusiers*, supported by a smaller number of soldiers armed with sword and buckler.

In 1534, the Spaniards undertook a major reorganization of their infantry forces when they introduced the *tercio.* The *tercio* was a larger formation, theoretically numbering almost 3000 men and was probably formed through the amalgamation of three *colunelas* (the allusion to three in the term *tercio* probably refers to its resemblance to one of the three battles used in the traditional organization rather than the formation of the *tercio* from three *colunelas*). The *tercio* generally consisted of 12 companies, ten of pikemen and two of *arquebusiers*. A pike company had 219 pikemen while a company of *arquebusiers* had 224 men. *Arquebusier* companies had an additional 15 men and pike company 20 men armed with the musket.

The musket was a heavier form of firearm, introduced in 1521, that fired a ball twice the weight of that fired from the *arquebus* (roughly 10 balls per pound against the 20 balls per pound for the *arquebus*). This gave the musket greater penetration, but the weapon was so heavy – as much as 9 kilogrammes (20 pounds) – it needed to be rested on a forked rest when being fired. This gave the *tercio* a ration of nearly three and a quarter pikemen for each soldier armed with a firearm. But muster rolls show that *tercios* were usually more like 1500 strong and had a ratio close

WHEN THE TRIGGER OF *a typical early matchlock* arquebus *was pulled, the lighted match was lowered into the pan holding the black powder. The powder would ignite, sending a spark through an adjacent hole in the barrel, causing the powder there to ignite in turn, propelling the ball from the barrel.*

to two and a quarter pikemen for each firearm-equipped soldier, thus being smaller and relying more heavily on firepower than the table and organization and equipment indicates.

The Sixteenth Century:
An Age of Experimentation

In the early phase of the pike-and-shot period, the development of tactics reflects an effort to determine the best way to integrate the two weapons systems. The main problem centred on how to protect the vulnerable *arquebusiers* on the battlefield. In order to be truly effective, these men needed to be employed in mass, but the slow

loading time of the matchlock *arquebus*, and later the even slower musket, made them vulnerable, especially to charges by heavy cavalry. Managing the heavy weapon, forked rest and black powder in an open container while holding the lighted slow-burning match was an awkward task.

The answer developed by the Imperialists, in particular the Spaniards, was to employ firearms behind field fortifications. This may have developed from the identification of firearms with crossbows, which had been at their best in siege warfare: both had good penetration but were slow to reload. Moreover, many of the *arquebusiers* employed in Italy had their origins in urban militias and so were familiar with fighting from behind fixed defensive positions. The Spaniards were aided by their French enemies, who frequently obliged by charging the field fortifications with their impetuous noble heavy cavalry, the gendarmes, and their aggressive Swiss infantry. An early example of this occurred at the Battle of

A MATCHLOCK MUSKETEER *prepares to fire his weapon. Once he has loaded his weapon, the musketeer goes through several motions in order to fire the heavy and cumbersome weapon. Care was necessary due to the difficulty of working with a burning match in the close quarters of the ranks and the need to fire the heavy musket from a forked stand.*

IMPERIAL LANDSKNECHTS *and Swiss in French employ engage in 'push of pike' at the Battle of Pavia, 1525. Note the halberdiers and* arquebusiers *who are supporting the main body of pike-armed infantry.*

Cerignola in April of 1503. Here the Spanish commander Gonzalo Fernández de Córdoba deployed his troops behind a trench backed by a parapet. The centre of his line was held by some 2000 *arquebusiers* deployed four ranks deep supported by pikes and artillery. The French under the Duc de Nemours launched a headlong charge at the Spanish line. An explosion of gunpowder stores at a Spanish battery silenced their artillery, but the *arquebusiers* held their ground and fired volley after volley into the French cavalry, who were milling around in front of the trench, and caused heavy casualties, including the Duc de Nemours. An assault by the French infantry was also driven off by the firepower of the *arquebusiers*.

The Spaniards tried to repeat this success nine years later at the Battle of Ravenna (April 1512). The Spanish and Papal army under Pedro Navarro, who had commanded the *arquebusiers* at Cerignola, deployed units of pikemen and *arquebusiers* behind a trench supported by

artillery, including some light-calibre pieces and heavy handguns mounted on carts. The French gendarmes and their commander, Gaston de Foix, did not, however, charge the trench unsupported as they had at Cerignola. Instead, the French opened an artillery bombardment which was answered by the guns of the Spaniards and their Italian allies. The French guns not only silenced the Spanish artillery but goaded the Spanish and Italian heavy cavalry into a disordered charge. The French gendarmes routed the Spanish and Italian cavalry and followed them back through gaps in the Spanish lines. At the same time the French

infantry, including some *Landsknechts* now fighting for France, were assaulting the Spanish infantry behind the trench. At this moment, the French gendarmes ceased pursuing the allied cavalry and attacked the Spanish infantry from the rear. Many Spaniards were killed although some 3000 infantry managed to retreat in good order.

For the next decade, the French, Swiss and Spaniards all experimented with the best way to employ the various types of troops that made up their armies. At the Battle of Bicocca in April of 1522, the Spaniards once again found a recipe for success. This time, they deployed along a relatively wide sunken road and strengthened it with entrenchments. Although the French had hoped to repeat their victory at Ravenna by weakening the Spanish positions with an artillery barrage, their Swiss infantry refused to wait in reserve and charged towards the Spanish lines. Weakened by Spanish artillery, the Swiss reached the sunken road only to find the entrenchments were too high for them to reach with their pikes. As they formed at the base of the parapet for an assault, Spanish *arquebusiers* fired into the densely packed formations. A few Swiss were able to mount the rampart but were driven back by *arquebusiers* and *Landsknecht* pikemen. The Swiss were shattered and the French were forced to withdraw.

The Spaniards made a dramatic change in the way in which they employed firearm-equipped infantry during the French invasion of 1524. At the end of April, a French army led by Guillaume de Bonnivet, admiral of France, was retreating before a numerically superior Imperialist army, having been defeated in the previous month near Milan. The French were pursued by an Imperialist force under the Italian condottiere Giovanni de Medici, and the Marquis de Pescara. The Imperialist troops included a number of *arquebusiers* and musketeers, who were mounted on horseback but fought on foot. The Imperialist troops harried the French forces composed of Swiss pikemen and gendarmes by constantly firing at them from their flanks. Whenever the Swiss or French cavalry turned to charge, the *arquebusiers*, led by Pescara, simply used their mobility to withdraw and reform at another point along the French line of march. The French suffered very heavy casualties

Battle of Pavia

1525

The Imperialist forces attacked the French army of Francis I besieging Pavia, taking advantage of some key desertions amongst the Swiss mercenaries in French pay. The Imperialists launched their attack after a complicated night manoeuvre that allowed them to breach the wall of the ducal hunting park that served as the French camp. As the Imperial forces entered the park and deployed into battle order, the Imperialist forces in Pavia also sallied forth from the town, complicating the French predicament. Caught by surprise, Francis was forced to commit his forces in uncoordinated attacks on a number of fronts. Moreover, the Imperialist forces made use of the terrain in the park to protect their infantry, especially those armed with firearms, which permitted them to be used offensively while minimizing casualties. This proved instrumental in the defeat of the French army.

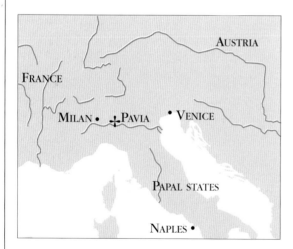

King Francis I of France laid siege to the strategically important town of Pavia in northern Italy in October, 1524. The purpose was to secure his lines of communication before proceeding to attack Naples.

2 Led by Italian pioneers, the Imperialists breach the wall to the Park of Mirabella, entering the French encampment and deploying for action.

5 The Swiss and *Landsknechts* of the French are driven off by the musketry of Spanish and Italian troops who make use of the cover provided by the park.

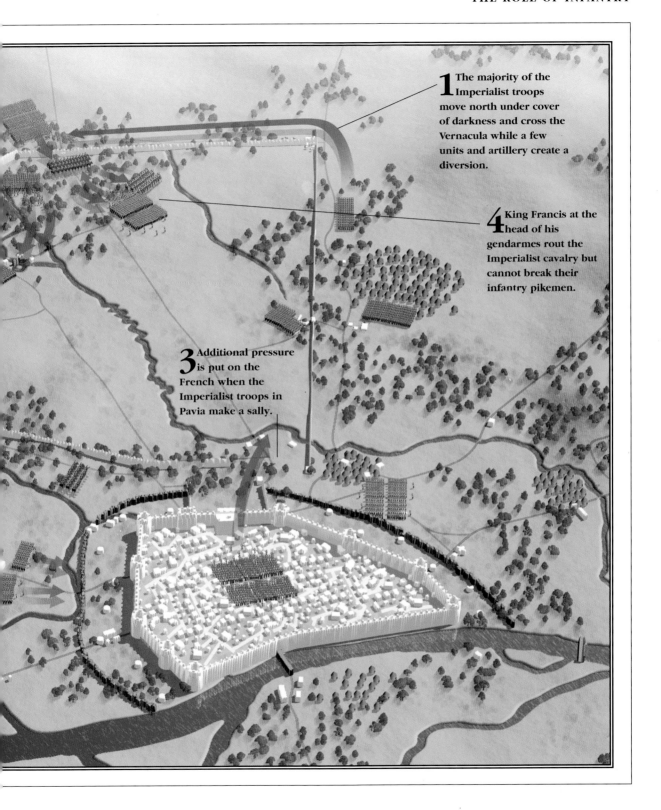

1 The majority of the Imperialist troops move north under cover of darkness and cross the Vernacula while a few units and artillery create a diversion.

4 King Francis at the head of his gendarmes rout the Imperialist cavalry but cannot break their infantry pikemen.

3 Additional pressure is put on the French when the Imperialist troops in Pavia make a sally.

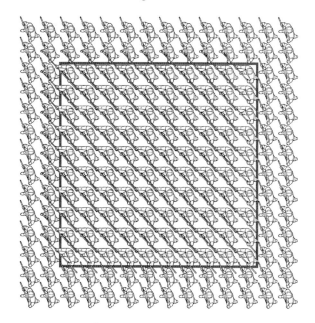

THE FORMATION OF A PIKE SQUARE *surrounded by* arqubusiers *allowed troops armed with firearms to shelter themselves from the enemy, especially cavalry, while deployed in the open and without the benefit of protection from fortifications.*

THE FORMATION OF A PIKE SQUARE *surrounded by* arqubusiers *allowed troops armed with firearms to shelter themselves from the enemy, especially cavalry, while deployed in the open and without the benefit of protection from fortifications.*

too. Moreover, an invasion of southern France led by Charles Bourbon, constable of France, who had joined the Imperialists after a quarrel with Francis, had been unsuccessful and the army was forced to make a costly retreat across the Alps. Shortly after the new papal alliance, Francis divided his forces, sending ahead John Stuart, duke of Albany with nearly 11,000 troops, one-third of his men.

Unfortunately the siege of Pavia did not proceed as Francis had hoped. The initial attempt to carry the town by storm failed and the French undertook a more deliberate siege, slowly but steadily moving their batteries forward. In November, French engineers began to build a dam to hold back the River Ticino so that the army could assault Pavia from a side where it had no defences. Unfortunately, heavy rains in December swelled the river and the dam was washed away. Given the lack of success to this point, it was suggested to Francis that he withdraw to winter quarters, to preserve the army from bad weather and disease. But Francis was not inclined to do so, especially when he learned that the garrison was greatly discontented due to a lack of pay and the conditions of the siege and so he continued the siege through February.

The Imperialists did not remain idle through the winter. In January, Charles Bourbon returned to Germany where he was given permission and money by the emperor to raise additional forces. He gathered a force of 500 horsemen and 6000 *Landsknechts* under the command of the legendary Georg von Frundsberg and marched to join the Imperialist army in Italy. With the addition of Bourbon's troops the Imperialists mustered some 17,000 foot and 1000 horse under the command of Charles de Lannoy, Viceroy of Naples and his lieutenant Pescara. At this point they determined to march to Pavia and raise the siege.

The Imperialists hoped to lure Francis away from Pavia by threatening his lines of communication, but Francis was determined to

including their commander. This affair, known as the 'Rout of the Sesia' demonstrated the offensive potential of firearms, which up to this point had relied on defensive fire from prepared positions.

In the following year, the tactical developments of the Valois-Hapsburg wars in Italy culminated at the Battle of Pavia. At this battle, the Spaniards demonstrated how steady pike-and-shot units could be used without prepared fortifications by improvising their own obstacles.

Pavia 1525: Tactical Surprise

On 28 October, 1524, King Francis I of France and his large army began a siege of the town of Pavia. The town was held by an Imperialist garrison under the command of Don Antonio de Leyva. The plan was to secure the town before embarking on a campaign to retake Naples. The French army invested the town and Francis made preparations for the invasion of Naples. These included strengthening his army with the addition of 6000 Swiss from Grisons and 2000 more from Valais. He also acquired perhaps 200 men through the services of Giovanni de Medici and his Black Bands. In December, Francis made a diplomatic coup when he signed a treaty with the Pope, who had abandoned the Imperialist cause. He hoped that Florence and perhaps Venice would join the alliance

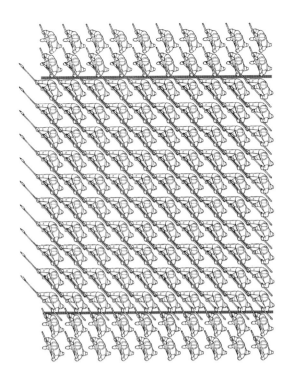

WHEN VIEWED FROM ABOVE *in this formation the pikemen appear to be the 'torso' and the firearm-equipped musketeers the 'sleeves' of a coat. This formation concentrated the fighting power of the pikemen and musketeers but still provided good protection for the shot so long as the ratio of pike to shot favoured the former.*

maintain the siege. As they approached, Francis took up a position along the Vernacula Brook and strengthened his position with earthworks and artillery. His entrenchments ran along the Vernacula from the Ticino north to the wall of the Park of Mirabella, the large ducal hunting reserve five kilometres (three miles) north of the town. Lannoy moved his forces to the opposite bank of the Vernacula Brook and put up entrenchments.

For three weeks the two armies engaged in an exchange of artillery fire from their respective field fortifications, but neither was able to gain a real advantage. Neither was inclined to attempt an assault. Instead each hoped the other side would be weakened by other factors. In the case of the Imperialists, many of the *Landsknechts* in the field army had not seen pay for several months and so

were coming dangerously close to mutiny or desertion. For the French, the main threat came from the sickness that was common in a long winter siege. But on 17 February news reached Lannoy that changed the situation significantly. First, Giovanni de Medici had been wounded during a sortie and was rendered *hors de combat*. Without their commander to hold them together, the mercenaries of the Black Bands melted away, reducing Francis' army by nearly 2000 men. Another piece of news was even more encouraging: the 6000 Swiss from Grisons were recalled to deal with a problem on their own border. Thus, without a blow being struck, Francis had lost 8000 men, reducing his army to 1300 gendarmes, 4500 *Landsknechts* including the infamous Black Legion that had remained in French service since Ravenna, 5000 Swiss, and 9000 French and Italian troops.

Given the substantial losses to the French forces and the mutinous murmuring of his own troops, Lannoy decided to launch a surprise attack through the night of 23 February. Moving his army north along the Vernacula under the cover of darkness, he found a suitable point to ford and crossed over to the French side of the brook. He then formed his troops into five divisions of infantry, supported by two small divisions of cavalry. The Imperialist artillery began a bombardment to cover the movement of the army and some infantry stayed in the fieldworks to support the deception. Some 2000 Italian pioneers began to dismantle the north-eastern section of wall that enclosed the Park of Mirabella and formed the northernmost defences of the French encampment. The wall was breached, the Imperialist troops poured through and began to form in a line of battle.

But it was not possible to form a conventional line given the copses and hedge-lined boulevards of the ducal hunting park. On the left was the division of the Marquis del Vasto, formed of perhaps 1500 Spanish and Italian *arquebusiers* and musketeers and 200 light horse. The next division was led by Pescara and consisted of Spanish foot soldiers. The third division was the main body of *Landsknechts* under Lannoy, flanked by the two small cavalry units. Next came Bourbon

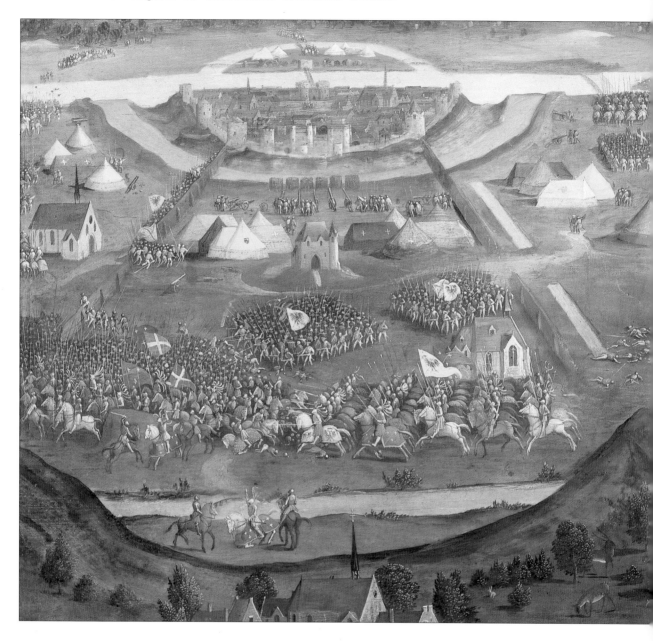

leading his own *Landsknechts*. The last division was the rearguard composed of an assortment of Italian and Spanish infantry. The rain and fog had helped the Imperialists achieve near total surprise, the only resistance being a small body of Italians who were easily brushed aside.

At this point Francis learned that the enemy had not only breached his lines but were now forming up within his own encampment. To make the situation worse, his forces were scattered all along the French lines, facing both Pavia as well as the Vernacula. Matters were further complicated by Imperialist troops making a sally from the town (de Leyva had received word the day before of the impending attack when a messenger slipped through the French lines). The troops in the best position to launch a counter-attack were those encamped near the king's headquarters, who

A PAINTING OF THE BATTLE OF PAVIA, *fought in 1525, depicts the Imperialist forces as they breach the wall of the Park of Mirabella and have deployed for battle. Units of Imperialist infantry and cavalry are clearly shown.*

effectively preventing them from firing any further, and charged into one of the Imperialist cavalry units, scattering them and killing their commander. Francis then turned to attack the columns of Imperialist infantry but was unable to break through the pike blocks of *Landsknechts* in the centre. The superb French heavy cavalry could bowl over any cavalry opponents on the field but they could not defeat the pike blocks without support, and Francis failed to organize his attacks to provide that support. Having been checked, his gendarmes seem to have lost their cohesion and became disordered.

Meanwhile two columns of infantry, the Swiss and the *Landsknechts* in French service, moved up to join the attack. The Swiss moved towards del Vasto's *arquebusiers* and musketeers, but their experiences at Bicocca and the Sesia seem to have blunted the legendary Swiss audacity. The Swiss closed with del Vasto's men but did not press home the charge. It seems as if the *arquebusiers* and musketeers were making use of whatever cover was available in the hunting park and then falling back as the Swiss drew near, but constantly firing and causing casualties. The Swiss were unwilling to suffer the heavy casualties of the earlier battles: they had already learned the lesson that firearm infantry were a dangerous enemy. After some brief 'push of pike' with Pescara's Spaniards, the Swiss withdrew from the battle.

On the French right, the *Landsknechts* including the Black Legion came to grips with the *Landsknechts* forming Lannoy's division. The hand-to-hand fighting was grim between these two groups and the French *Landsknechts* fought well until taken in the flank by Georg von Frundsberg's *Landsknechts* in Bourbon's division. The French *Landsknechts* stood their ground and were wiped out in the fierce melee that followed.

The withdrawal of the Swiss column opened the way for the Spanish and Italian *arquebusiers* and musketeers to move in support of the troops

included the great majority of the *gendarmerie* and a small artillery reserve. Moving up in support were the Swiss pikemen and the *Landsknechts* including the Black Legion. Francis led his gendarmes forwards, while the artillery deployed and began firing on the Imperialist rearguard. These troops suffered from the French artillery and were broken by a charge of some French gendarmes. Francis then led a charge across the front of his artillery, thus

in the centre. They repeated the tactics they had used the previous year at the 'Rout of the Sesia.' These tactics have become institutionalized since we are told by a contemporary that they fought 'in small units all over the field without a definite battle line according to the long experience and the new precepts of Pescara.' Using available cover

A DEPLOYMENT OF A PIKE SQUARE surrounded by shot and supported by 'horns' of shot at each of its four corners allowed for a substantial volume of fire from the shot in every direction. However, it was primarily a defensive formation since it was not easy to move while maintaining its cohesion.

they began to fire at the French gendarmes at point-blank range. The disordered French gendarmes found themselves unable to charge into the copses or across hedges and found their predicament further complicated by blocks of Imperialist pikes who further hampered any attempts at manoeuvre or escape. These firearms caused very heavy casualties among the French cavalry with both *arquebus* and musket capable of penetrating armour at such close range. Francis soon found himself surrounded, unhorsed and wounded. He was nearly killed by a Spanish infantryman but was rescued by a French knight who had followed Charles Bourbon into exile.

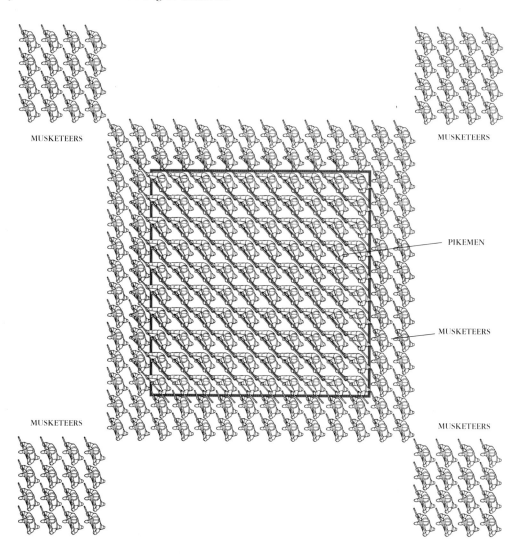

MUSKETEERS

MUSKETEERS

PIKEMEN

MUSKETEERS

MUSKETEERS

MUSKETEERS

The Battle of Pavia represents the epitome of early pike-and-shot tactics. It reflects and evolution in the use of firearms, which allowed them to be transformed from a purely defensive role to a more offensive one. But as yet there was no fully integrated system of tactics to allow the pikemen and the infantry equipped with firearms to work in close cooperation.

The Dutch Reforms

In 1568 the Dutch began their long battle for independence from Spain and would remain at war intermittently for 80 years. The problems faced by the young Dutch republic played an important role in the military reforms that would take place there over several decades to come. Although many of these reforms centred on infantry organization, drill and tactics, the nature of warfare in the Netherlands would be one of many more sieges than battles.

The name most often associated with the Dutch reform movement is Maurice of Nassau (1567–1625). He was the son of William the Silent who had been one of the main leaders of the Dutch revolt. In 1684, at the age of only 17, he became *Stadthalter* of Holland and Zeeland. In 1590, he was made captain-general of all of the Dutch forces and was then in a position to undertake his reforms.

Like many of the military men of his age, Maurice hoped to emulate the military establishments of antiquity, in particular the Romans. Maurice read military manuals from antiquity, in particular those of Vegetius, Aelian, and the *Taktika* of the Byzantine emperor, Leo, as well as the works of contemporary commentators such as Justus Lipsius. What emerged for Maurice was an emphasis on regular standing forces and the importance of discipline and drill. But within the context of classical antiquity, Maurice also saw the importance of making more effective use of the constantly improving technology of gunpowder weapons.

One of the most important changes instituted by Maurice was the creation of a standing army. The army was still made up primarily of foreigners serving for pay. Some of these were mercenaries in the traditional sense, while others were foreign troops sent by their monarchs to serve under Dutch command and at Dutch expense (notably from England). In 1603, for example, the Dutch army consisted of a total of 132 companies. Of that number there were 43 English, 32 French, 20 Scottish, 11 Walloon, 9 German and a mere 17 Dutch. The main reason for the preponderance of foreigners was the relatively small population of the Netherlands, combined with the need to keep an army in the field almost constantly for 80 years. Maurice recognized that keeping these companies in his service all year round, rather than discharging them in the off-season or at the end of a campaign, would make the Dutch army a more effective fighting force in the long run.

The maintenance of this standing army also allowed Maurice to initiate new standards of discipline and drill. In this, Maurice was aided by his cousins William Louis and John, counts of Nassau. Maurice and his cousins oversaw the standardization of drill, and equipment, so that all the troops in Dutch service would be using the same methods regardless of their origin. The length of the pike and the armour of the pikemen, as well as the length and calibre of firearms were all standardized. Perhaps more important was the codification of drill at this time in the 'Dutch Discipline'. All words of command as well as the manual of arms for both the pike and *arquebus* and musket were regularized. In 1607 Jacob de Gheyn's *Wapenhandelinghe* was published – a complete manual of arms for pike, *arquebus* and musket illustrated with 116 plates, accompanied by the appropriate commands and a commentary.

Maurice also modified the military organization and tactics of the Dutch infantry. Once again Maurice turned to antiquity for inspiration. He hoped to replicate the flexibility of the Roman legion by creating units based upon the cohort to replace the large unwieldy regiments and *tercios* of his own time. To that end, he reorganized each Dutch regiment into two or more battalions. In theory, each battalion was to be 550 men, the same size as a cohort in Vegetius' *antique legio,* and was made up of 250 pikemen and 300 men armed with firearms, 60 of which were to form a line of skirmishers. The pikes were to form in the centre of the battalion with *arquebusiers* and musketeers on the wings.

Moreover, these units drew up in fewer ranks than the earlier regiments and *tercios*; figures vary but the pikes seem to have been between five and ten deep and the shot between eight and 12 ranks deep. The shot were trained to use countermarch fire, a tactic inspired by Aelian. In this formation the files of shot had intervals between them wide enough for a man to march.

The first soldiers in the file would fire a volley and then do an about face, marching back through the intervals and join the rear rank, all the while going through the drill to reload their weapons. This would be followed by the men of the second rank and then the third and so on. By the time men from the front rank returned to their original position, they would be reloaded and ready to fire another volley and start the drill all over again.

This method of firing required great discipline but created a constant volume of fire from the unit. When threatened by cavalry, the *arquebusiers* and musketeers would retire behind the pikes without disrupting the formation. In battle, the Dutch usually formed their battalions in three lines of battle. These lines could be staggered to resemble a chequerboard so that the battalions in the individual lines could support one another. This bears a striking resemblance to the Roman *acies triplex* of a legion drawn up in similar formation. Maurice laid the foundations for the early modern standing army based on constant drill and a high standard of discipline. He also developed a system of tactics that truly integrated pike and shot in a coherent fashion. Ironically, throughout the two decades of conflict with Spain, Maurice was only twice able to take his army into battle (both were victories), yet found himself participating in no fewer than 29 sieges.

The Thirty Years' War: the Swedish Synthesis

The system initiated by Maurice of Nassau and his reforms almost reached perfection with the

Swedish army of Gustavus Adolphus during the Thirty Years' War (1618–1648). Under Gustavus Adolphus the standing army founded upon a combination of drill and discipline – and in the Swedish case re-inforced by religious devotion – with the more flexible small units and tactics of the Dutch System. This made the Swedes a formidable power in the seventeenth century.

Gustavus Adolphus was clearly influenced by the Dutch reformers. In 1601 his father, Charles IX, had been contact with Maurice's cousin John of Nassau in order to import the Dutch System to Sweden and had arranged for the young Gustavus Adolphus to have a Dutch tutor, John Skytte, who introduced to him the military writings of both the ancients and the contemporary Dutch. Later he received instruction from a Dutch commander and met John of Nassau himself in 1620.

As king of Sweden, Gustavus Adolphus did much more than import the Dutch military system, he improved upon it. Probably the most

significant improvement centred on the emphasis on firepower as an instrument of offence as well as defence. He shortened and lightened the muskets carried by Swedish soldiers, allowing them greater mobility and the ability to load and fire somewhat faster. He further augmented the firepower of his infantry by attaching light and mobile artillery pieces directly to his infantry units. These three-pounders could keep up with the infantry and, especially with improvements in ammunition, add substantially to the unit's offensive firepower. The Swedish army of the seventeenth century, like that of the previous

A PIKE-DRILL SEQUENCE *illustrated in a 17th-century manual shows the various positions of the pike. You can see the 'push of pike' second from the right and the manoeuvre for receiving cavalry in the final panel. The introduction of such manuals were important in standardizing drill in the increasingly large standing armies of the period.*

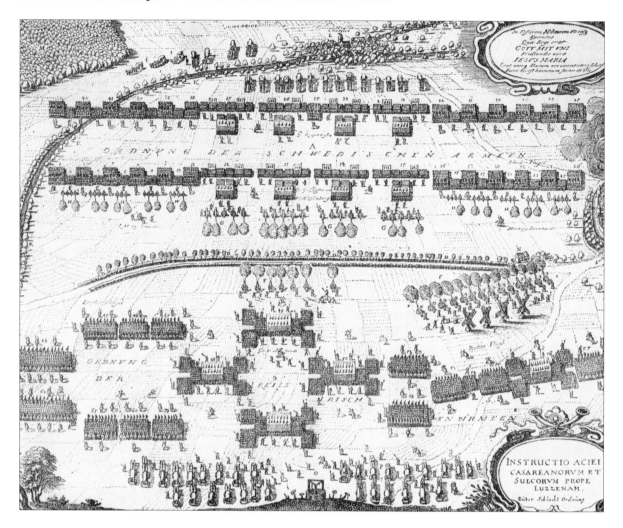

GUSTAVUS ADOLPHUS WAS KILLED *at the Battle of Lützen in 1632. The Swedish positions are shown at the top and Imperialist dispositions are at the bottom of the illustration. The more linear formations of Swedes are easily distinguished from the deeper tercio-style formations of the Imperialist infantry.*

century, was built on a national levy, in which one peasant in ten could be taken into the army. These men would be formed into provincial *Landsregements,* each of which would in turn provide three field regiments to the army. These field regiments were composed of eight companies, but like the Dutch, they were deployed into smaller units called squadrons (analogous to the battalion in the Dutch System).

At full strength a squadron consisted of 216 pikemen organized into 12 corporalships of 18 men each and 288 musketeers into 12 corporalships of 24 men each. It was common to detach four of the corporalships of musketeers to serve separately, often in support of the Swedish cavalry.

The Swedes were incapable of supporting a very large standing army from the native population alone and therefore hired mercenaries to supplement the men from the *Landsregements.* The Swedes made use of mercenaries from two main sources. The first was Germany which had a long tradition of mercenary service. The second was Scotland. Gustavus Adolphus recruited extensively among the Scots, not only enlisted men (some 13,000 during the Thirty Years' War), but also officers: they accounted for no fewer than 30 colonels and six generals. The mercenaries were organized and drilled according to Swedish regulations, the 'Swedish Discipline', which would soon be copied by many European armies. Like the Dutch, the Swedes kept both their native troops and mercenaries with the colours year round and so could expect a high degree of discipline. This included mandatory attendance at religious services. Punishment for excessive absenteeism could even result in the death penalty.

On the battlefield squadrons were grouped together in a formation known as a brigade. The Swedish brigade normally numbered three or four squadrons. These squadrons deployed in two mutually supporting lines and were placed in a chequerboard formation. Attached to each of the brigades were as many as 12 three-pounder battalion guns. These light cannon could be dragged forwards with the infantry and added to

the brigade's firepower. This was especially true since Gustavus Adolphus introduced ammunition in wooden cases. The use of cased ammunition for these light artillery pieces actually enabled them to fire more quickly than the musketeers (about eight rounds to every six fired from a musket). These brigades were made permanent formations during the Thirty Years' War and so developed a high level of cohesion and *esprit de corps*. They were referred to by colour, based on the colour of the coats worn by one or more of the regiments that formed the unit, for example, the Blue Brigade, Yellow Brigade or Green Brigade.

Swedish tactics emphasized firepower and so the Swedes deployed in even shallower formations than the Dutch. The standard formation for the squadron was six ranks deep, with the pikemen formed in the centre and the musketeers on the wings or even some in front of the unit. In this formation, the musketeers would employ

A LIGHT, MAN-HANDLED *'leather' battalion gun of this type, shown in a reconstruction, was deployed with the infantry of the Swedish squadrons under Gustavus Adolphus. Supplied with pre-cased ammunition, they significantly added to the firepower of the Swedish foot.*

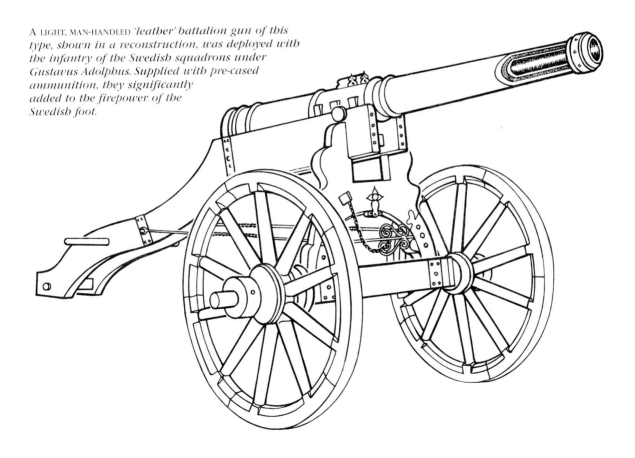

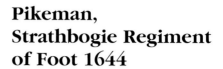

Pikeman, Strathbogie Regiment of Foot 1644

The Strathbogie Regiment was raised in March, 1639, by George Gordon, 2nd Marquis of Huntly to support the Royalist cause. The regiment was raised primarily from Lowland Scots and was both well trained and well equipped. At the time of the Bishop's War, the regiment mustered some 600 men, about one-third of whom were pikemen, and was provided with arms purchased in England. At this time, the pikemen may have been armoured since the supplies from England included '1000 pikes with harness and armour'. The regiment was also well disciplined, having had two months of training under the watchful eyes of professional officers at Strathbogie Castle. The regiment was raised again in 1644 to take part on the Royalist side. In an apparent effort at standardization with other government forces, the Regiment's pikemen were not issued with armour at this time. The Regiment was heavily engaged during the battles of 1645–1646.

countermarch fire. However, it is clear that as the enemy drew near, the musketeers received the order to 'double the files'. At this command the three rearmost musketeers moved into the interval between their file and the one next to them, thus changing in a single movement from a six- to a three-rank formation. While in this formation the front rank would kneel, the second would crouch and the third would stand. At the command, all would fire at once, as would the attached three-pounder cannon, delivering a devastating salvo into the enemy. If the enemy faltered, the entire squadron would charge forwards in an effort to break the enemy. If the enemy stood firm, the musketeers would reload, behind the safety of their pikemen if necessary, and then deliver another salvo. This would be repeated until the enemy was broken.

The Swedes relied on firepower from their infantry in support of the cavalry as well. While the cavalry undertook offensive operations through the charge (rather than using the caracole tactic relying on pistols), they were often deployed with units of detached musketeers in between the cavalry units. These musketeers provided the defensive support to keep enemy forces at bay until the cavalry were ready to launch their charge.

Under Gustavus Adolphus the combination of pike-and-shot tactics reached their apogee. Gustavus Adolphus had developed an organization and tactics that allowed a greater emphasis on offensive tactics than had been possible up to this point. There were still, however, limitations since musketeers were still vulnerable, especially to cavalry, if caught without being loaded and ready or without the support of pikemen. That would begin to change with some technological innovations later in the century.

> *'The necessity of light troops in war is completely understood; one knows that they are necessary for the safety of the armies, that an army without them cannot survive against an army which is well equipped with light troops...'*
>
> – *JOHAN EWALD,*
> TREATISE ON PARTISAN WARFARE

Breitenfeld, 1631:
Firepower and Flexibility

Gustavus Adolphus entered the Thirty Years' War in June of 1628 in order to reverse the tide of Protestant failures in north Germany. His initial efforts were limited to helping the Danes relieve the Imperialist siege of the Pomeranian town of Stralsund. There were several factors that constrained Gustavus Adolphus' participation. He had only limited resources for building up and maintaining an army in Germany. While he had a solid base with his Swedish national army, a serious effort in north Germany would require that he both mobilize more troops from home, recruit enough mercenaries and allies and then prepare them for battle. Moreover, his limited forces were already engaged. He had been at war with Poland for nearly two years and was maintaining forces there. But his intervention at Stralsund attracted Imperial attention and Imperialist troops were sent to the aid of the Poles. Gustavus recognized that he did not possess anywhere near the resources necessary to fight both wars and quickly made a favourable peace with Poland.

Two years later, in June of 1630, Gustavus landed a small force of 14,000 men in Pomerania. Although there was a sizeable Imperialist army in north Germany, it was scattered in numerous garrisons and the Swedes were left unmolested. Over the next six months he raised additional men and brought his forces to perhaps 50,000. But even this was not enough to both garrison Pomerania and launch an attack against the Imperialists. Although Gustavus Adolphus had hoped to have an additional 80,000 men for operations at the beginning of the campaign season of 1631, he found little support among the north Germans, many of whom were suspicious of

THIS ILLUSTRATION *shows an artillery piece being prepared to fire. First, the crew swabs the barrel with a wet sponge so that no smouldering paper or powder from the previous round ignites the charge*

prematurely. Next, the crew loads the powder and ball into the barrel and uses the ramrod firmly to seat the charge at the base of the barrel.

NEXT, MEMBERS OF THE CREW *lay the gun or target, using a handspike to move the piece back into position as the recoil of gun from the previous round could be*

considerable. Finally, the piece is ready to be fired with the application of a slow match attached to the forked staff, known as a linstock.

his motives or simply unable to provide forces. His plans to invade Silesia and Saxony and drive on the Imperial capital at Vienna were far out of reach. In fact, he had not even been able to prevent the Imperialists from sacking Magdeburg and massacring its population in May. But he soon received support in the form of cash subsidies from both France and Brandenburg and was finally able to recruit additional forces and attract much–needed allies. He was given the command of some 10,000 troops from Hesse-Kassel and was approached by John George, the elector of Saxony. John George had just lost the city of Leipzig. An Imperialist army under John Tserclaes von Tilly captured it by threatening the same fate as Magdeburg should the city resist. The elector of Saxony had remained carefully neutral up to this point and Gustavus only agreed to aid him if he agreed to a formal alliance. In so doing, he openly forced the elector into the anti-Imperial camp.

Having secured this alliance Gustavus Adolphus marched to join forces with John George and his Saxons. The two armies linked up some 32 kilometres (20 miles) north of Leipzig on 5 September 1631. Gustavus had brought a force of 24,000 men. He was joined by the 18,000-strong Saxon contingent. With this combined force he was confident that he could fight and defeat Tilly's army of 35,000 Imperialists. Tilly commanded a veteran army and it is clear that he thought he had little to fear from the Swedes. Moreover, since Saxony had maintained its neutrality up to this point, the land had not been despoiled and so Leipzig and its surrounding countryside provided much needed supplies for his army.

Deployment

As Gustavus Adolphus and John George moved their armies towards Leipzig, Tilly moved his army out to meet them and occupied a ridgeline some eight kilometres (five miles) north of the city. On the morning of 7 September, the armies engaged. Tilly had occupied the ridgeline with his infantry, some 18 *tercios*, occupying the centre and formed in a single line. His cavalry were formed in a single line on both flanks. The left flank, some 5000 horsemen, was under the command of Tilly's lieutenant, Gottfried Heinrich Graf von Pappenheim. The cavalry on the right flank were under Tilly's personal command. The plan was to launch coordinated cavalry attacks against the enemy's flanks, driving them back and then turning back on the Swedish centre in a double envelopment.

Gustavus Adolphus had deployed his forces in two main battle lines, each of which was backed by a reserve. The reserve of the first line was substantial while that of the second consisted of two small cavalry units. Deployed in front of the Swedish centre were 12 heavy artillery pieces with another 43 light field pieces and three-pounder battalion guns interspersed with the infantry units. The majority of the Swedish cavalry were formed on the right facing Pappenheim's troopers, although several units protected the left of the Swedish infantry. The Swedish cavalry had detachments of musketeers, each about 200 strong placed between individual units. The left flank of the allied army was held by the Saxons. They were formed in large regiments like those of the Imperialists and had their own cavalry. Gustavus Adolphus seems to have been content to lead off with his artillery and see how the battle developed.

The ensuing artillery duel favoured the Swedes. Not only did they have a greater number of cannon, but, because of their cased ammunition, they delivered a greater volume of fire than the Imperialist artillery. The fire of the Swedish artillery clearly had an effect. The pounding inflicted on Pappenheim's cavalry provoked him to move forwards to avoid the Swedish cannon fire by coming to grips with the enemy cavalry. Because this move was unexpected Tilly did not order his troops to advance at the same time, and Pappenheim's cavalry therefore advanced without support.

THE TOOLS OF THE ARTILLERY CREW: *(from top to bottom) the ramrod used to seat the round in the barrel; a sponge used to make sure the barrel is cleared of any smouldering embers; a device used to remove any residual paper from a previous charge; a powder scoop; and the linstock with slow match applied to the touch hole to ignite the charge.*

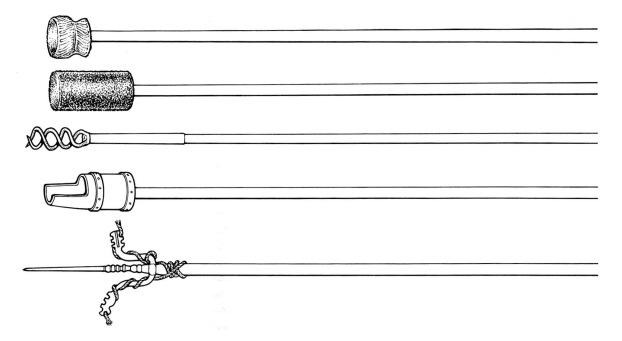

PRÆLII.
INTER
SERENISS: SUECOR:
REGEM ET SAXONIÆ
ELECTOREM NEC NON
CATHOLICÆ LIGÆ GENE
RALEM COM: Á TILI VII.
SEPTEMBER ANNI MDCXXXI
PROPE LIPSIAM COMMISSI,

Pappenheim's cavalry attacked the Swedish cavalry, not by charging in and engaging in hand-to-hand combat, but by using the caracole formation. This involved riding up to within pistol range, firing and wheeling to reload and repeat the process. This was a similar concept to countermarch fire for infantry. But this tactic was not effective against the Swedish cavalry because of their intermingling of detachments of musketeers among the cavalry units. These inflicted significant casualties on the Imperialist horse because their salvo fire was more densely concentrated and their weapons had both greater range and power of penetration. Pappenheim responded by extending his line in an effort to get around the Swedish flank, but the Swedish cavalry extended their own line to match his movements.

On the right flank, things were going better for

THE CONFUSED NATURE *of a 17th-century battle once the infantry became engaged in close combat is evident in this illustration of the Battle of Breitenfeld. The large quantities of smoke generated by black-powder weapons are clearly shown drifting over the battlefield.*

turn the Swedish left with their infantry advancing in support, the Swedish army might have been destroyed.

Fortunately for Gustavus Adolphus, his deployment and the discipline of his men did not allow the Imperialist cavalry to roll up his left flank. The commander of the troops on the now exposed Swedish left was Gustav Horn, one of Gustavus Adolphus' most competent officers. He was able to use the excellent discipline of his troops and the flexibility of the smaller squadron formations to meet the enemy threat. Horn was also able to bring up a reserve since the Swedish formation had more than a single line. Moreover, the speed with which he was able to perform this manoeuvre meant that he was in a position to attack before the Imperialists could effectively redeploy after their quick rout of the Saxons. As fresh Swedes from the reserve and other parts of the battle line arrived, they began pushing the Imperialist forces back with their disciplined volleys.

By this point the battle had raged for some five hours. On the Swedish right Gustavus Adolphus himself had assumed command and Pappenheim and his cavalry had finally been driven off. Exhibiting the *coup d'oeil* of a great captain, Gustavus Adolphus recognized that now was the time to attack. At the head of several troops of horsemen, he led the now unengaged Swedish right against the Imperialist centre. Many of the troops here had moved off in support of actions on other parts of the field.

Gustavus Adolphus and his troops broke through the enemy centre, capturing Tilly's cannon, which he turned on their former owners. The breaking of their centre and the additional artillery pounding was too much for the Imperialists who finally broke. The Swedish cavalry pursued leaving some 7600 Imperialist troops dead and another 6000 as prisoners. The Swedes lost 2000 men.

the Imperialists. Tilly's cavalry, having seen Pappenheim's troopers galloping off to the attack, began to move as well. The brunt of their attack fell upon the Saxon contingent. The green Saxon troops fled before the veteran Imperialist cavalry. With a single blow 40 per cent of Gustavus Adolphus' forces had been driven from the field. Upon seeing this Tilly's troops began chanting 'Victory!' If the Imperialist cavalry had begun to

Musketeer, Colonel Charles Essex's Regiment of Foot 1642

This figure represents a typical musketeer from the period of the Great Civil Wars. He is equipped with a large, heavy, matchlock musket. This weapon was unwieldy enough to require aid in aiming and so the soldier carries a forked rest in his left hand that would support the musket. The musketeer wears a bandolier from which hang a number of wooden vials that contained powder and shot. There were traditionally 12 such vials on the bandolier which led to them be referred to as the 'Twelve Apostles.' On the end of his bandolier, the soldier carries a length of slow match that would be used to fire his weapon. He wears no helmet or armour. These were reserved for pikemen and even pikemen began to forego armour as the century progressed.

R. SCOLLINS

THIS 18TH-CENTURY ARTILLERY *piece has been limbered for movement. By this period artillery pieces had become lighter and more mobile when compared to cannon of the previous century. Also depicted are the major types of munitions (left to right): canister shot, grapeshot, and round shot. The first two were used at close range, scattering a large number of musket balls at the enemy. Round shot was used at longer range.*

The Battle of Breitenfeld showed the superiority of the 'Swedish synthesis' of the combination of firepower and shock coupled with superior discipline and organizational flexibility, especially when led by commanders with experience and initiative. As the Thirty Years' War progressed, many armies, including the Imperialists, would begin to copy the smaller and more flexible units like the Dutch battalion or Swedish squadron.

The Emergence of Linear Tactics: 1660–1715
The Dutch system of tactics and the experience of the Thirty Years' War had moved military thinking on towards the development of what would become the linear tactics of the eighteenth century. The introduction of smaller battalions, the deployment of those battalions in mutually supporting lines and the Swedish introduction of salvo fire, with multiple ranks firing together, all became characteristics of warfare in the eighteenth century.

However, although all of these developments foreshadowed later tactics, there would be a number of changes in the second half of the

seventeenth century that would be crucial. Some of these changes would be technological, though nonetheless slow to take effect rather than revolutionary. Other changes would be more institutional and reflected the growth in the authority of the state in early modern Europe. Taken together, however, these technological and institutional changes set the stage not only for the great dynastic conflicts in Europe but also permitted Europeans to project their military might in other parts of the world.

One of the lessons that armies learned in the course of the seventeenth century was the devastating effect of firepower on the battlefield. The lightening of the musket, thinner formations that brought more muskets to bear, and salvo fire with several ranks firing simultaneously all encouraged the trend towards greater numbers of musketeers in units. In the fifteenth century, Spanish *tercios* deployed three or four pikemen for each musketeer but by the middle of the seventeenth century ratios were close to one pikeman for each musketeer. In the Swedish squadron the ratio was four musketeers for every

Battle of Breitenfeld

1631

Leading his army to attack the Imperialists occupying Leipzig, Gustavus Adolphus was met en route by an Imperial army under Count Tilly. The Imperialist forces were deployed along a ridgeline with large cavalry forces on both wings. Gustavus arrayed his Swedish forces in two lines, each of which maintained a small reserve. The left of the Swedish line was held by their Saxon allies. The battle began with an artillery duel in which the quick-firing and more numerous Swedish guns held the advantage. The battle began as the Imperial cavalry, first on the left and then the right, surged forwards. On the left, they were held by the Swedish horse supported by musketeers, but on the right they routed the Saxons. Fortunately, the discipline and manoeuvrability of the smaller Swedish units allowed them to fill the gap on the left and to attack the Imperialist centre on the right, ultimately defeating the Imperial army.

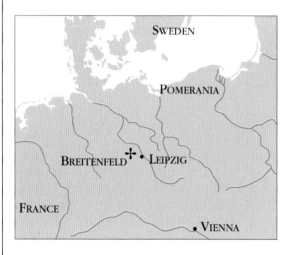

Having secured an alliance with the elector of Saxony, King Gustavus Adolphus of Swedenled a Swedish and Saxon army to liberate Leipzig from the Imperialists. The Imperial army under Tilly marched out to meet him at Breitenfeld.

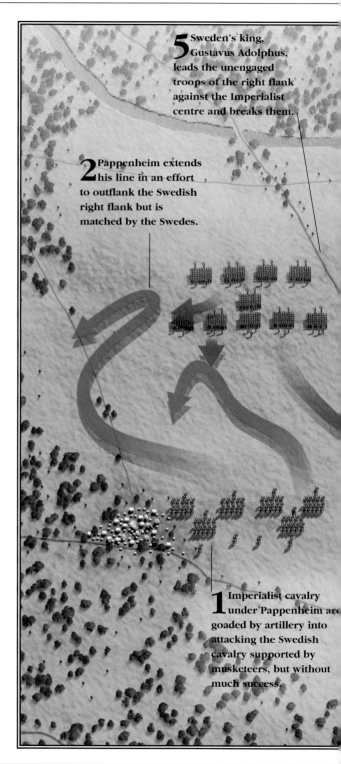

5 Sweden's king, Gustavus Adolphus, leads the unengaged troops of the right flank against the Imperialist centre and breaks them.

2 Pappenheim extends his line in an effort to outflank the Swedish right flank but is matched by the Swedes.

1 Imperialist cavalry under Pappenheim are goaded by artillery into attacking the Swedish cavalry supported by musketeers, but without much success.

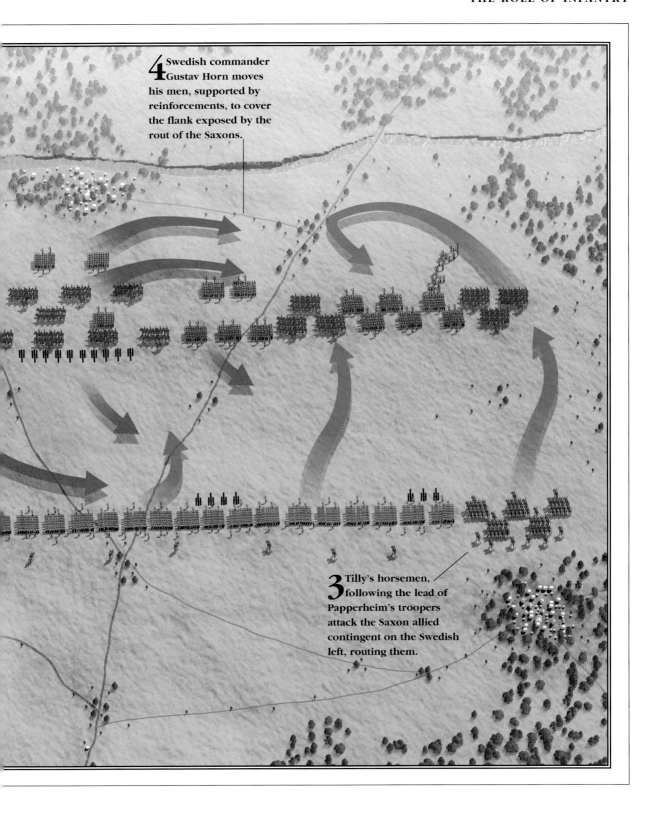

4 Swedish commander Gustav Horn moves his men, supported by reinforcements, to cover the flank exposed by the rout of the Saxons.

3 Tilly's horsemen, following the lead of Papperheim's troopers attack the Saxon allied contingent on the Swedish left, routing them.

AN EARLY 18TH-
CENTURY *infantry
formation with
five musketeers
for each pikeman.
This illustration
shows the
difficulty of
placing the
pikemen in such
a unit. Here, they
are placed in the
rear rank. This
allows a
maximum
number of
muskets being
brought to bear,
but the pikes
can no longer
protect any of
the musketeers.*

three pikemen, although some of these were detached to form separate units.

By the last quarter of the seventeenth century, the ratio of musket to pike had shifted dramatically. In most battalions of most nations of the period the number of pikemen had dropped to between one-fifth and one-sixth of the unit. While this gave much more potential firepower, there were still problems to be overcome, and not everyone agreed that the future lay in gunpowder weapons. Some argued for the return of the pike. Raimondo Montecucculi still referred to the pike in 1674 as the 'queen of foot arms'.

One of the major problems associated with the increase in the number of musketeers was how to protect them when they were reloading, or from attacks by enemy cavalry. How could the small number of pikemen be deployed to protect the larger number of musketeers? For example, a French battalion of the late seventeenth century contained 650 men and was normally drawn up

five ranks deep. Of this number 120 were pikemen, 480 were musketeers and 50 were grenadiers (elite infantry armed with hand grenades as well as muskets and often used in storming fortifications). The standard formation saw the pikemen forming 24 files in the centre of the battalion with 48 files of musketeers on either wing and the ten files of grenadiers on the far right. It is obvious that the musketeers of the outer files and grenadiers were exposed to enemy cavalry charges and were too far away to shelter behind the pikes. The large number of musketeers compared to pikemen also made it difficult for the former to find shelter in between the pikes, as had been common since the fifteenth century.

One alternative that the French employed was known as 'fraising the battalion'. When fraised, the battalion was formed in five ranks. The first two ranks consisted of musketeers, the third rank was made of up pikemen and the fourth and fifth ranks were formed from musketeers. A fraised battalion

allowed the first two ranks of musketeers to fire under the protection of the pikemen. The problem with this formation was twofold. First, fully half of the battalion's firepower was behind the pikemen and so were unable to bring their muskets to bear.

Second, placing the pikes in the middle of formation with their unwieldy weapons tended to disorder the unit when it tried to move. Another solution, instead of putting all of the pikes in the centre, was to spread them out: 60 pikemen were placed in the centre and 30 on each flank of the battalion. Although the intent was to provide pikes along the length, the net result was no different since there simply were not enough pikes to protect all of those armed with firearms.

Another problem was making effective use of infantry musketeers drawn up in more than three ranks. The standard depth of infantry formations by the late seventeenth century was five ranks. The reason for this once again stemmed from the concern for depth in case of enemy cavalry. There was no way for all five men to fire at once and so alternative firing systems developed at this time. One method was firing by rank. With this method, the first rank advanced three paces, fired and moved back towards the battalion to reload, at

THIS ILLUSTRATION SHOWS *the same unit, but with the pikemen to the fore, which allows them to protect the musketeers. However, fully half of the musketeers are not able to fire. Such formations were also unwieldy as it was difficult to bring the pike to the front without temporarily disrupting the unit.*

which point the second rank would advance three paces, fire and return to reload, followed by the third, fourth and then the fifth. This meant that at a given moment one rank was firing, one rank was loading and three were loaded and ready to fire.

This was really a variation on the old countermarch system. Another method was firing by files or divisions. In firing by files, two files, ten men, advanced in front of the main body, formed a line, fired and returned to be replaced by two more files. In firing by divisions the same basic procedure was followed except four or six files, 20 or 30 men would form the firing line. Neither system was very effective, nor did they allow for offensive action.

Two technological innovations that were phased in during the last quarter of the seventeenth century, the flintlock musket and the bayonet, ended the era of pike and shot and

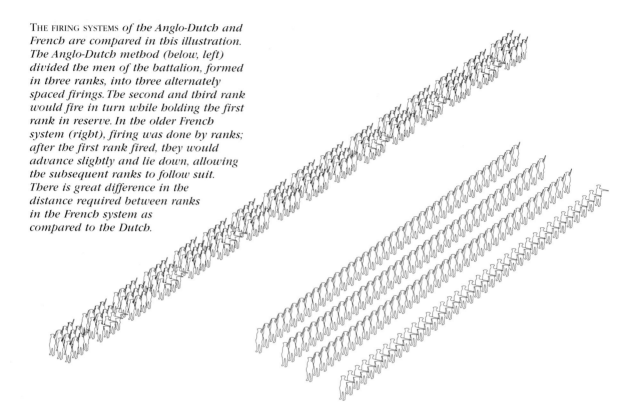

THE FIRING SYSTEMS *of the Anglo-Dutch and French are compared in this illustration. The Anglo-Dutch method (below, left) divided the men of the battalion, formed in three ranks, into three alternately spaced firings. The second and third rank would fire in turn while holding the first rank in reserve. In the older French system (right), firing was done by ranks; after the first rank fired, they would advance slightly and lie down, allowing the subsequent ranks to follow suit. There is great difference in the distance required between ranks in the French system as compared to the Dutch.*

ushered in the age of linear tactics. The flintlock musket had appeared in the middle of the century or earlier, but had long been considered too expensive for use en masse. It was a substantial improvement over its cousin the matchlock. The most obvious advantage was that the powder was ignited by a flint striking a steel frizzen rather than by applying a slow-burning match directly to the powder. This made the flintlock far more reliable with fewer misfires. It also made the flintlock much safer to use in certain circumstances, such as in the presence of large quantities of black powder. There is little wonder that the weapon was first issued to those units whose duty was to guard the artillery train and its large quantities of powder. Such men were often called fusiliers. Another advantage of the flintlock was that it tended to be lighter and easier to handle.

All of these factors combined to reduce the number of movements necessary to load the musket from 44 to 26, making it possible to increase the rate of fire substantially. This was

increased further by the introduction of the paper cartridge. By the late 1690s, the flintlock was being distributed widely in many European armies and became the standard infantry weapon over the next two decades.

The bayonet first appeared in 1647 and by the 1670s was being issued to units like fusiliers, elite units and dragoons. By the middle of the 1680s the bayonet had become almost standard issue. The first type of bayonet was the plug bayonet. The plug bayonet was basically a double-edged dagger blade about 30 centimetres (one foot) long attached to a handle that was the same diameter as the bore of the musket. The bayonet was fixed slowly working the handle into the barrel of the musket. This had both advantages and disadvantages. The advantage was obviously that the musketeer was now capable of defending himself without the presence of pikemen. The disadvantages were that fixing the bayonet was neither a quick nor easy process and during the process the musketeer was vulnerable. In addition,

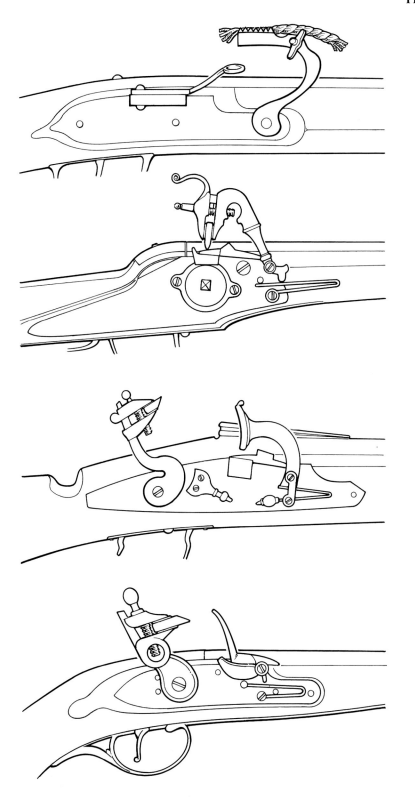

MATCHLOCK MECHANISMS *were the earliest and least expensive firing mechanisms. When the trigger was pulled, the burning match was bought into contact with the priming powder in the pan, in turn causing a spark which ignited the charge.*

WHEELOCK MECHANISMS *were introduced quite early in the history of European firearms. When the trigger was pulled, the spring-loaded metal wheel spun and the hammer holding iron pyrite dropped. The resulting spark ignited the priming powder and in turn fired the weapon. It was too complex and expensive for general issue.*

SNAPHANCE MECHANISMS *were an early form of flintlock firing mechanism. When the trigger was pulled, the flint held in its jaws was bought into contact with a steel plate above the pan, in turn causing a spark which ignited the charge.*

FIRELOCK MECHANISMS *were the most efficient form of flintlock firing mechanism. When the trigger was pulled, the flint held in its jaws was brought into contact with the frizzen plate covering the pan, in turn both pushing the frizzen back to expose the pan and causing a spark which ignited the charge.*

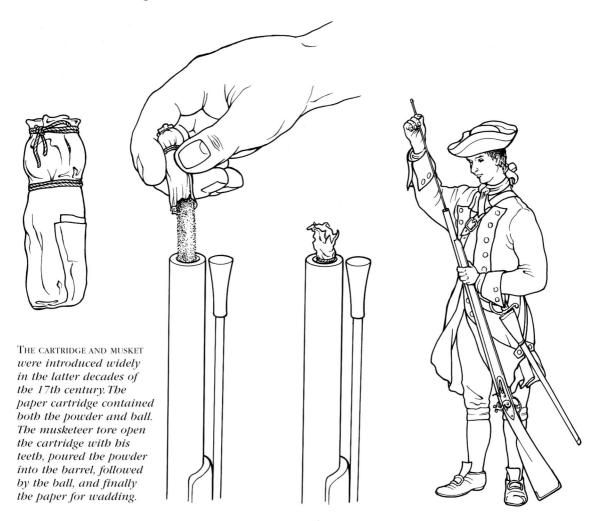

THE CARTRIDGE AND MUSKET *were introduced widely in the latter decades of the 17th century. The paper cartridge contained both the powder and ball. The musketeer tore open the cartridge with his teeth, poured the powder into the barrel, followed by the ball, and finally the paper for wadding.*

once the musketeer had fixed his bayonet he could no longer fire his weapon, becoming, in effect, a pikeman.

In the hands of ill-trained or relatively inexperienced troops the plug bayonet was a liability. For example, at the Battle of Killikrankie (27 July, 1689) during the Jacobite rebellion, some inexperienced Government troops fired a volley at charging Scottish highlanders, which failed to halt them, and were not proficient enough to fix their bayonets in time. In the ensuing rout the Government forces lost 1000 killed and 500 prisoners while inflicting only 200 casualties on the highlanders. By 1697, a more satisfactory variant had been developed and adopted by several German armies and the British, the socket

bayonet. The socket bayonet was a significant breakthrough because it allowed the musketeer to both defend himself in hand-to-hand combat and to fire his musket. By 1703 the combination of flintlock and socket bayonet had made the role of the pikeman redundant and they all but disappeared.

The gradual introduction of the flintlock and the socket bayonet represent improvements to existing technology that had a significant effect and which would fundamentally change tactics. One important change was the thinning of formations down to three ranks and an attendant change in the infantry firing system. One method that received wide acceptance was the Dutch System. Initially used by the Dutch, the English and

THE ROLE OF INFANTRY

their German allies, this system was adopted by most European armies by the end of the War of the Spanish Succession in 1715 (with the exception of the very conservative French).

Under the Dutch system a battalion's centre companies (i.e., all of the companies with the exception of the grenadiers) were divided into four divisions, each of which was in turn divided into four firing platoons. Each platoon was assigned to one of three 'firings.' Each platoon was formed in three ranks with the front rank kneeling. When all of the platoons of the first firing received the order, their second and third ranks presented their weapons and fired, holding the first rank in reserve. The second firing would then do the same and finally the third. By the time the platoons of the third firing had given a volley, the platoons of the first firing would be reloaded and the whole progression would begin again. Volleys would thus roll continually along the entire front of the battalion. Only the French still used a five-rank formation and a form of firing by rank. The

front rank would advance slightly, fire, and then lie down. The second rank would do the same and then the third, fourth and fifth ranks did the same. After the entire battalion had fired, they would all rise and begin to reload.

On the grand tactical level, the intervals between units that had been employed in both the Dutch and Swedish systems disappeared. In their place groups of battalions formed an unbroken line, although keeping a second line in reserve was still considered important. Soldiers did not march in cadence yet and so maintained sizeable distances between ranks and files. Once they reached the battlefield, the battalions would take their allotted position one beside another.

The last major set of changes that helped transform warfare in this period were the institutional changes to the early modern state. Most European nations had centralized their administrations, both civilian and military. This led to the creation of larger armies during this period than had been seen since the days of the Roman Empire.

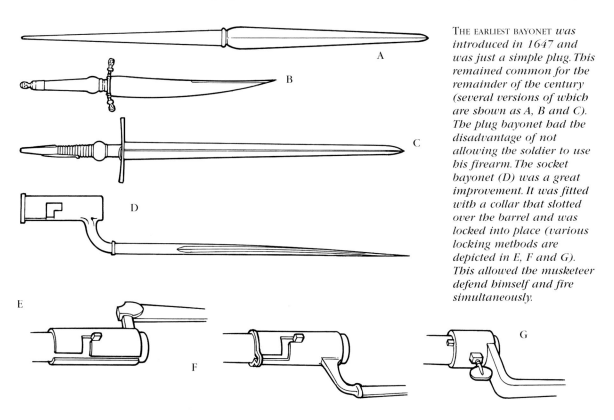

THE EARLIEST BAYONET *was introduced in 1647 and was just a simple plug. This remained common for the remainder of the century (several versions of which are shown as A, B and C). The plug bayonet had the disadvantage of not allowing the soldier to use his firearm. The socket bayonet (D) was a great improvement. It was fitted with a collar that slotted over the barrel and was locked into place (various locking methods are depicted in E, F and G). This allowed the musketeer defend himself and fire simultaneously.*

THE TYPICAL THREE-RANK *infantry formation in use during the 18th century was made possible because of the use of the bayonet. Shown here are infantry prepared to receive cavalry. The front rank kneels to ward off the horsemen with the bayonet while the second and third ranks fire.*

In the War of the Spanish Succession, for example, the French army, including militia forces, numbered nearly 400,000 men. These administrative structures also allowed states to impose a greater degree of uniformity in discipline and drill. Regiments became more permanent structures than ever before. In many armies, regiments would expand the number of battalions during war and contract them in peace-time, but the regiment continued to serve. This led to the creation or regimental identities, traditions and rivalries.

By 1715 most European states were maintaining large standing forces, both for national defence and as instruments of authority at home. The incremental improvements in technology and technique had allowed for the transition to linear tactics and formation and these were in place throughout western and central Europe.

Oudenarde, 1708:
Confusion and Divided Command

The War of the Spanish Succession originated with the death of Charles II, the Hapsburg monarch of Spain. Charles died without an heir, exciting the dynastic ambitions of several European rulers and disrupting the balance of power between them. Despite efforts to resolve the situation before Charles died in November 1700, the major powers discovered at that point that Charles had named Philip of Anjou as his heir; a Bourbon like Louis XIV of France. The implications of this for the balance of power manifested themselves in February of the following year when French troops occupied key fortresses in the Spanish Netherlands, with the full cooperation of their Spanish garrisons. William III of England took the lead in blocking Louis XIV's ambitions. He appointed John Churchill, the duke of Marlborough, as his commander in chief and sent him to the continent to seek out allies for a war against France. An alliance was formed between Austria, Bavaria (which would soon change sides), Denmark, England, Holland, Portugal, Prussia and various other German states. France was joined by Spain, Savoy, Mantua and Cologne. With virtually all of Europe involved the war was fought in numerous theatres including the Low Countries, the Iberian Peninsula, Italy and along both the Rhine and the Danube.

There were numerous sieges and not a few battles including major ones at Schellenberg (1704), Blenheim (1704) and Ramillies (1706), but the war dragged on. In 1707 the war in the Low Countries had reached stalemate. But in 1708 the tempo of the war increased again. Louis XIV sent a large army under the joint command of the seasoned old soldier, the duke of Vendôme and his grandson and heir, the duke of Burgundy. Louis' intention was no doubt to give his grandson military experience and to show him off to the armies of France. But the effect on command of the army proved disastrous. The old soldier Vendôme and the young duke of Burgundy did not get along. For parts of the campaign they rarely communicated and virtually never agreed on anything.

At the end of May the French army of 100,000 men consisting of 197 squadrons of horse and 124 battalions of infantry concentrated at Mons in preparation for an invasion of Flanders. Marlborough was outnumbered, having 90,000 troops composed of 180 squadrons of cavalry and 112 battalions of foot. But Marlborough had already made plans for Prince Eugene of Savoy, who was operating on the Upper Rhine, to bring his Imperial army from the Moselle valley and join him near Brussels. Unfortunately various complications delayed Eugene and greatly reduced (from 40,000 to 15,000) the number of men he was able to move to support Marlborough. Moreover, Eugene's movements were discovered and he was pursued by the duke of Berwick with 27,000 French troops.

Meanwhile, Vendôme and Burgundy made some preliminary manoeuvres but did not commit their army to battle, instead remaining at

A SOLDIER DEPLOYS THE BAYONET *in the position known as 'push' in this illustration depicting bayonet drill, 1730. The musket is supported by the left forearm held at the horizontal with the right hand pressed against the butt. The bayonet shown is the plug type and so probably came from an earlier manual.*

Gembloux. But on 4 July the French army sprang into action, sending columns to Ghent and Bruges in northern Flanders. The French had been in secret negotiations with both cities and the citizens agreed to turn themselves over to the French. By doing so, the French army had cut Marlborough's lines of supply home. Moreover, the French forces were soon in a position to threaten Brussels and the allied garrison at Oudenarde on the River Scheldt. On 5 July Marlborough learned of the French army's movements and turned his forces west, only to learn of the fall of Ghent and Bruges. But he added some 700 troops to the garrison at Oudenarde.

Fortunately for Marlborough, there were more disagreements between Vendôme and Burgundy. The French did not make any major moves, waiting instead for judgment from Versailles. On 8 July Eugene arrived at Marlborough's head-quarters with a small escort. It was obvious to the two allied commanders that they could not wait for the rest of Eugene's troops to arrive, so they decided to attack with Marlborough's troops alone and seek an open battle with the French army. This meant they had to move quickly and place themselves so close to the French that the latter were no longer able to refuse combat.

Marlborough sent out his advanced guard that evening and undertook a series of forced night marches towards Lessines in order to deprive the French of a defensive line along the River Dender. While Marlborough's troops forced marched towards Lessines and the Dender, Vendôme had determined to move there as well to protect his operations at Oudenarde from interference. But the French troops moved at a more leisurely pace and the allied advanced guard under William Cadogan secured the town first. Vendôme learned

'The enemy also made several attacks to come upon us: but as they were necessarily thrown into confusion in getting over their trenches, so before they could form into any order…we mowed them down with our platoons in such numbers, that they were obliged to retire…'

— CAPTAIN ROBERT PARKER AT BLENHEIM

from his cavalry that allied forces occupied Lessines and seems to have wished to attack the advanced guard before the main body arrived, but Burgundy refused to support him, instead arguing for a defensive line along the Scheldt. Vendôme was furious, but withdrew at a leisurely pace across the Scheldt at Gavre, five kilometres (three miles) north of Oudenarde. In the meantime Cadogan pushed forward from Lessines at 1 AM with his advanced guard of 10,000 men and with hard marching reached the hamlet of Eename on the Scheldt. From the high ground he could see that the majority of Vendôme's forces had not completed their crossing at Gavre. He sent messengers back to Marlborough with a report and following his commander's instructions, began laying pontoon bridges across the Scheldt. Marlborough rode ahead of the main army with 20 squadrons of Prussian dragoons as an escort. As he moved, the soldiers of his main body redoubled their efforts, moving at the run to make the best time to the battlefield.

Cadogan's arrival had not been detected by the French and by noon he had secured a bridgehead with 16 battalions and eight squadrons of dragoons. At about 1 PM. Cadogan's dragoons met some pickets from the Swiss Brigade of the Marquis de Biron. De Biron was moving troops to support his brigade but was ordered to halt by the French chief of staff, the Marquis de Puységur. This allowed Marlborough and Eugene to send additional British and German infantry across the pontoons to support Cadogan's infantry and dragoons and shortly after 3 PM they had routed de Biron's Swiss, killing or capturing nearly half his force. By 4 PM some 20 battalions of Hanoverian, Hessian and British foot had crossed and moved towards the Diepenbeek Stream. The audacious

Musketeer, Lord Robart's Regiment of Foot 1643

This musketeer is from Lord Robart's Regiment of Foot, one of the regiments that fought on the Parliamentary side during the Civil War. The regiment was one of 20 raised to fight under the Earl of Essex from 1642–1644 and it served valiantly at the Battle of Edgehill, standing its ground while several other units fled. The unit was to have numbered 800 men, probably two-thirds pikes and one-third muskets, and was uniformed in red coats lined with yellow. By the end of 1644, the regiment mustered only 333 other ranks. This soldier is armed with one of the shorter and lighter muskets that became more common as the war continued. It was capable of being fired without the use of the unwieldy forked rest that was common with the longer and heavier muskets. In addition to his firearm, this veteran soldier carries an infantry sword on his hip.

Battle of Oudenarde

1708

The French invaded Flanders while the Allied forces of the duke of Marlborough and Prince Eugene were separated. The Allies reacted quickly, with Eugene moving to join his forces with those of Marlborough. Marlborough's forces moved to support the garrison at Oudenarde and protect their supply line to Brussels. Joined by Eugene of Savoy who rushed ahead of his troops, the Allies took the initiative by crossing the Scheldt on pontoon bridges. The French commanders, the dukes of Burgundy and Vendôme, who were constantly quarreling, did not launch a coordinated attack against the Allies. Instead, they allowed the Allied forces to consolidate across the Scheldt while sending in their troops bit by bit. The Allies received much-needed reinforcements who were sent on a flanking manoeuvre, crossing the Scheldt via the Oudenarde bridges. The superiority of the Allied infantry fire discipline and coordination in the face of the disunity of the French high command, coupled with the arrival of the flanking force, led to the defeat of the French army.

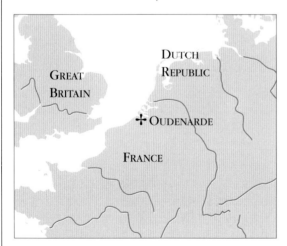

While the Allied forces of Marlborough and Prince Eugene were separated, French forces captured Ghent and Bruges, thus threatening Oudenarde and Marlborough's communications.

4 In order to gain time for the slowly developing flanking manoeuvre, Allied cavalry attack on the right but suffer heavy losses.

3 Danish and Dutch troops under Overkirk slowly cross the Scheldt at Oudenarde in an effort to outflank the French right flank.

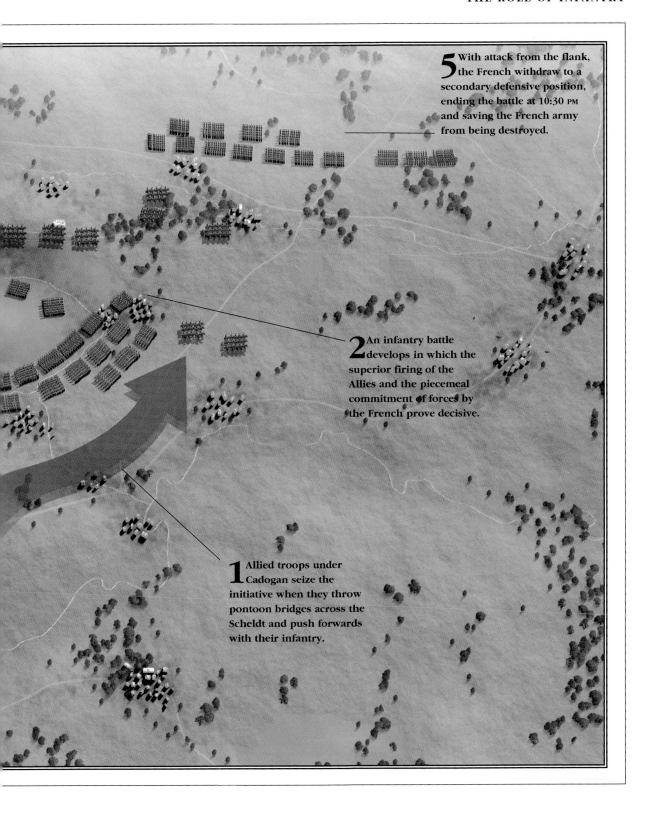

5 With attack from the flank, the French withdraw to a secondary defensive position, ending the battle at 10:30 PM and saving the French army from being destroyed.

2 An infantry battle develops in which the superior firing of the Allies and the piecemeal commitment of forces by the French prove decisive.

1 Allied troops under Cadogan seize the initiative when they throw pontoon bridges across the Scheldt and push forwards with their infantry.

crossing by allied troops had given them the initiative, and although the French had a considerable numerical advantage on the north side of the Scheldt, Vendôme and Burgundy continued to lack any coordination. Burgundy ordered six battalions of French infantry towards the village of Groenewald, but the attack bogged down. Seeing this, Vendôme ordered another six battalions in support and finally led an additional 12 battalions himself. By 5:30 PM, Vendôme had committed 50 battalions to the attack but was unable to exercise effective command since he was personally engaged in the infantry battle. Unfortunately, Burgundy seemed unaware of what was happening and did little to support the attack. He sent 16 cavalry squadrons, but their advance was halted by the marshy ground. The battle raged on and the superior platoon fire of the allies took its toll. But the presence of Vendôme and some of the better French regiments kept the battle close.

On the allied side of the field, the coordination between Marlborough, who was now commanding the allied left, and Eugene commanding the right, was exemplary. At 6 PM Marlborough put 18 fresh battalions of Hessians, Saxons and Hanoverians into his battle line, at the same time pulling back 20 battalions of Prussians and Hanoverians under Lottum. These superbly disciplined troops, who had been involved in the fierce infantry battle, quickly reformed and, replenishing their ammunition, marched off to support Cadogan's forces on the right.

At 7 PM Marlborough received some critical reinforcements in the form of Count Overkirk and his 24 battalions and 12 squadrons of Dutch and Danish troops, who had finally arrived from Lessines. Marlborough intended to use this force to envelop the French right and sent them to cross the Scheldt via the bridges at Oudenarde. But there was a bottleneck that caused a lengthy delay in getting these troops across the Scheldt. In the meantime the fierce infantry battle raged on. Marlborough sent to Overkirk for some immediate relief. Eight battalions detached from Overkirk's column and moved directly towards the hard-

pressed Hessians and Hanoverians on the allied left. To buy time for Overkirk's flanking manoeuvre, Marlborough sent 16 squadrons to support Eugene. Eugene in turn unleashed 20 squadrons of Prussian cavalry who broke through some French cavalry and overran two battalions and a battery of artillery. Unfortunately, these troopers pursued too far and were driven back with heavy losses by the cavalry of the French Guard, the *Maison du Roi.*

Although the battle lasted until nearly 10:30 PM, the arrival of the Dutch and Danes under Overkirk convinced Burgundy that it was over. At 8:30 he and his entourage left the field. Vendôme held on a bit longer, but was eventually forced to withdraw, joining Burgundy on the Ghent road at 10 PM. Had Overkirk arrived earlier, the entire French army might have been destroyed. As it was 5500 French were killed or wounded and another 9000 captured, including some 800 officers. The allies also took more than 100 standards and colours and 4500 horses and mules, losing just under 3000 killed and wounded from their own strength. The

battle had lasted for eight hours and demonstrated the endurance necessary in an infantry battle in this period. The battle had taken place in difficult terrain and at very close range and lacked the neat battle lines associated with warfare in this period, battalions and squadrons coming up to the fight ad hoc and without grand design.

Frontier Warfare and *Der kleine Krieg*

Although the eighteenth century saw armies become more disciplined and sophisticated there were other influences that led to developments in a very different direction. These influences tended to come from either the periphery of Europe, especially the Balkans, or from the extra-European world, notably North America. In these regions linear tactics were not readily applicable either due to the nature of the terrain or the type of enemy or both. Whereas linear tactics favoured the new large armies and large battles, and the drive for decisive victory, *Der kleine Krieg*, the little war, reflected a state of warfare that continued and might have little pretence to decisiveness. This was the kind of warfare along frontiers between hostile powers like the military border that separated the Hapsburg and Ottoman empires or the frontier that separated Britain's North American colonies from the many tribes of Native American people or even the border between the Lowland and Highland Scots. The type of warfare

TURKISH JANISSARIES, C. 1700 were the elite of the Turkish army. They were well equipped with firearms and throughout much of the early modern period were considered one of the best disciplined forces of musketeers in Europe and the Middle East. By the end of the 18th century, however, they were eclipsed by the large, disciplined standing armies of the European powers.

along these frontiers was constant and even in peacetime, there was always the possibility of raids, whether for plunder or just disruption.

The techniques used in *Der kleine Krieg* were very different from those that were developing in western Europe. Battalion-sized units fighting in formation and using a rigid firing system were inappropriate for this type of warfare. Instead, this irregular warfare required troops who could act more independently, fighting in small groups as skirmishers. In the Balkans and in Hungary, this led to the recruitment of Croatian and Hungarian irregulars, usually serving under their own local leaders who had been co-opted to support the Hapsburgs.

The most famous were the Croatian *pandours,* who excelled as light infantry. In Britain, independent companies of Highlanders were organized to keep the peace from government forts. These were later amalgamated into the Royal Highland Regiment, the Black Watch. In North America, the British employed colonial rangers and Native American warriors.

In most cases, these irregulars did not take part in the big wars that were fought during this period in Europe. The major exception was the Austrian mobilization of the manpower that was available from their military border during both the War of the Austrian Succession and the Seven Years' War. At times, they could field as many as 40,000 or more Croats for a campaign. This represented a sizeable portion of the Austrian army's manpower. It also proved, at least initially, to be problematic for the Prussians. These Croats were formed into *Grenzer* Regiments with battalion and company organization. But their style of fighting meant they were deployed as skirmishers rather than in regular formations. They were used to scout, perform picket duty and to harass small bodies of enemy soldiers. Often this harassment was

Prussian Grenadier

This man is representative of the grenadiers of the Prussian army during the reign of Frederick the Great. He wears the mitre cap, typically worn by these elite soldiers. In fact, most nations' grenadiers wore mitre or other tall caps. Originally this was because the cap's lack of a brim did not interfere with the throwing of grenades. Later they wore them simply because they added height to the grenadiers (who were usually chosen from the tallest men to begin with) and served as a mark of distinction. The front plate of the mitre cap was usually made of brass while the back was made of coloured cloth. This grenadier is equipped with a sword as well as his musket and bayonet. In some armies grenadiers carried hatchets in place of or in addition to swords. These small axes were considered useful for the grenadier's role as the leader of a storming party in a siege.

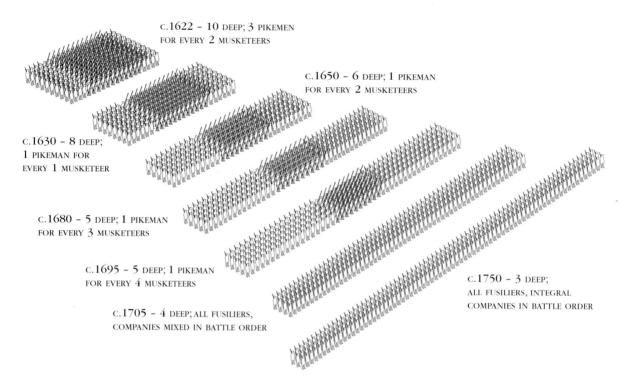

C.1622 - 10 DEEP; 3 PIKEMEN FOR EVERY 2 MUSKETEERS

C.1650 - 6 DEEP; 1 PIKEMAN FOR EVERY 2 MUSKETEERS

C.1630 - 8 DEEP; 1 PIKEMAN FOR EVERY 1 MUSKETEER

C.1680 - 5 DEEP; 1 PIKEMAN FOR EVERY 3 MUSKETEERS

C.1695 - 5 DEEP; 1 PIKEMAN FOR EVERY 4 MUSKETEERS

C.1705 - 4 DEEP; ALL FUSILIERS, COMPANIES MIXED IN BATTLE ORDER

C.1750 - 3 DEEP; ALL FUSILIERS, INTEGRAL COMPANIES IN BATTLE ORDER

extended to the local civilian population as well. But their open order form of fighting could sometimes defeat even the best regular units. For example, on April 23-24, 1757, two Prussian grenadier battalions were virtually trapped on a hill, surrounded by a large number of Croatian irregulars. The Croats caused a significant number of casualties, especially among the officers.

The Croats' success came from the fact that the Prussians initially had few troops who could fight in open order to oppose them. While the Prussians did have a few companies of *Jägers,* these were primarily used as military police and were only later used as light infantry. The Prussians responded by ordering the formation of units of *Freikorps,* often made up from deserters, foreigners and other undesirables. Frederick himself had a low opinion of these troops and seems to have thought them always to be at a disadvantage when facing the Croats. After the Seven Years' War, there was a movement towards *Der kleine Krieg,* (irregular warfare), not with irregulars themselves, but with regular troops under the most capable of officers. This shows the

THIS DIAGRAM DEPICTS *the increasing reliance on musketry from the early 17th century through the middle of the 18th century. As the ratio of muskets to pikes increases, the formations become narrower. Between 1675 and 1705 the number of pikemen became so small as to be virtually ineffective. During this period, the introduction of the bayonet allowed for the elimination of the pike altogether.*

impact that *Der kleine Krieg* had on the military intelligentsia of the time, who saw the possibilities for disrupting communication and gathering information in support of the big wars of the time.

Linear Warfare Comes of Age: 1715–1763

The decades following the War of the Spanish Succession saw a number of changes that allowed linear warfare to develop to its highest point. There were, for example, changes in tactics and methods of firing that further increased the firepower, and the lethality, of infantry on the battlefield. There were also incremental changes in the technology of the smoothbore musket that advanced that weapon to nearly its fullest potential. The centralization of authority in the hands of the state also continued, which in turn allowed for the imposition of ever greater levels of uniformity on the armies of the period including the imposition of strict standards of drill and discipline. Finally, the period was fraught with major wars including the War of the Polish Succession (1733–1735) and the War of the Austrian Succession (1740–1748) as well as the Seven Years' War (1756–1763), which was fought on three continents. One of the consequences was increased writing on and study of the 'science of war' during this period. Writers ranged from those seeking to discern the universal principles of warfare to more didactic works designed to educate officers in the conduct of war.

In the wake of the War of the Spanish Succession, most armies had adopted some form of platoon fire, like the Dutch System, which had been introduced during that conflict. The normal formation for an infantry battalion from the 1720s onward was to be deployed four or three ranks deep, with the latter more prevalent as time went on. Variations of the division of the unit into three 'firings', were adopted by most countries by the middle of the century. The British kept a method of delivering volleys based upon the division of the battalion into the three firings, according to the earlier Dutch System.

The Prussian infantry, developed under the tutelage of Prince Leopold of Anhalt-Dessau, the famous 'old Dessauer', employed a system that had each of the battalion's eight platoons firing separately, one after another. This began with the platoon on one flank of the battalion (probably the senior platoon on the right), followed immediately by the platoon on the other flank of the battalion. The platoon next to that, which had fired first, then delivered a volley to be followed by the corresponding platoon on the other side of the unit. This continued on towards the centre of the unit until each of the eight platoons had fired. The entire process could be accomplished in 15–20 seconds, at least on the parade ground, and by the time the eighth platoon had fired, the first was reloaded and ready to give another volley. Of all of the major armies, only the French retained the method of firing by ranks (though now formed only four deep) until the middle of the century, when they finally adopted platoon fire as well.

Captain Robert Parker, a witness to many of Marlborough's campaigns, provides one of the most interesting accounts of this type of fighting in his account of the battle of Malplaquet in 1709:

'Upon this Colonel Kane, who was then at the head of the Regiment, having drawn us up, and formed our platoons, advanced gently towards them, with six platoons of our first fire made ready. When we had advanced within a hundred paces of them, they gave us a fire of one of their ranks: whereupon we halted, and returned them the fire of our six platoons at once; and immediately made ready the platoons of our second fire, and advanced upon them again. They gave us the fire of another rank, and we returned them a second fire, which made them shrink; however, they gave us the fire of a third rank after a scattering manner and then retired into the wood in great disorder: on which we sent our third fire after them, and saw them no more.'

New Technology

Another development of the earlier period that was universally adopted by the middle of the century was the use of paper cartridges for the smoothbore musket. The powder, ball and wadding were included in a single package. By 1738 every nation had issued their infantry with

> *'Infantry relies upon firepower for the defensive and the bayonet in the attack.... The entire strength of our troops resides in the attack, and we would be unwise to renounce the offensive without cause.'*
>
> — FREDERICK THE GREAT, INSTRUCTION MILITAIRE

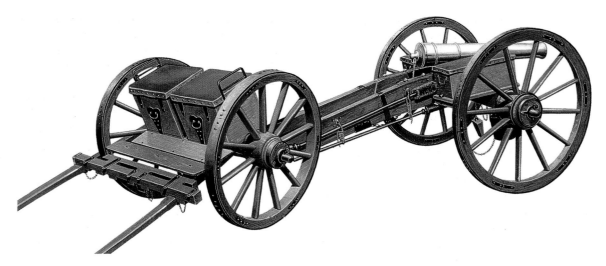

cartridges. This not only increased the speed of reloading and the rate of fire, but also allowed the infantryman to carry more ammunition into battle. Most soldiers in this period carried 60 rounds into battle.

Another important technological innovation in this period was the introduction of the iron ramrod by Leopold of Anhalt-Dessau in 1718. Up until this point, ramrods had been made of wood. While serviceable, the wooden variety of ramrod suffered from some serious faults, especially their tendency to break in the heat of battle. Although the iron ramrod was ultimately a substantial improvement over its wooden cousin, it too was not without its initial difficulties. The main problem was finding the proper composition for the metal used. If the metal were too soft, the ramrod might bend and become difficult to insert and remove from the barrel. On the other hand if the ramrod were made too hard, it might become brittle and subject to snapping just like a wooden one. But once the proper temper was found the iron ramrod allowed musketeers to fire much more quickly. Moreover, states during this period became centralized enough to create standardized muskets and ammunition. The most famous example was the English 'Brown Bess'. By 1730 the barrel was set at 1067 mm (42 inches) with a calibre of .75 (19 mm) and was provided with ammunition of .71 (18 mm) calibre. The smaller diameter for ammunition meant that there was a degree of 'windage' as the ball moved along the

THIS 18TH-CENTURY ARTILLERY piece has been limbered for movement on the battlefield. This also allows some of the crew to ride on the limber. Some of the gun's ammunition would have been carried under the drivers' seat.

barrel when fired, reducing the accuracy. This was considered to be more than compensated for by the ease with which the ball could be put down the barrel and hence the additional speed with which the weapon could be loaded. The Brown Bess was so successful that it continued to be manufactured for more than 125 years, by which time some 7,800,000 had been made.

The new firing methods and technological advancements in firearms allowed well-trained musketeers to fire as many as five rounds per minute. This was, however, in the perfect conditions of the parade field. In battle, things could turn out quite differently, often reducing the rate of fire by more than half. Various factors contributed to the reduction in the rate of fire. First, solders carried many more accoutrements into battle, such as their knapsacks, canteens and so on, than were present during drill. Second, the complex nature of the platoon firing systems tended to break down in the smoke and din of the eighteenth-century battlefield. Both noise and smoke made it difficult to hear the commands used in platoon firing systems. This left soldiers to their own devices and so they continued to fire as individuals. In the confusion of battle soldiers might even give up the use of the ramrod, instead pouring the contents of the cartridge down the barrel, and then banging the butt of the musket on the ground to complete the loading process. This individual fire was common enough that by 1756 the French drill manual included independent fire alongside platoon fire and fire by ranks as an acceptable firing method.

Leopold, the old Dessauer, was also responsible for another innovation of drill that had grander tactical implications. Some time in the 1730s Leopold introduced cadenced marching in Prussian units. With the introduction of marching in cadence, Prussian troops advanced in unison, with each soldier marching in time with his comrades. Troops kept in time with the beat of the drum. This type of marching could only be used by troops who were very well disciplined and of all the armies in Europe, the Prussian was most renowned for its high standards of discipline. This discipline, however, was maintained by harsh corporal punishments.

The use of cadenced marching allowed the Prussians to increase significantly their ability to manoeuvre both to the field of battle and across it. For example, armies that did not use cadenced marching used an open column as their basic formation for advancing to the battlefield. The formation was called an open column since the intervals between the files were quite large, sometimes as much as three metres (ten feet) between them. This was necessary to avoid the unit from losing cohesion, because the troops advanced without a regulated pace. This meant that as open columns advanced on to the battlefield, the evolution of the battalion into line was a cumbersome process as the companies of the column had to not only form line, but also had to close their ranks and files.

The Prussians, using the cadenced system of marching, could form more closely-packed columns and use a variety of different manoeuvres to form line more quickly and more efficiently. Another advantage of cadenced marching was the speed with which it allowed lines to move across the battlefield. Those armies that did not march in cadenced step had to halt frequently to dress their ranks, with officers and

NCOs moving along the front and rear of the unit pushing men back into their proper positions. A Prussian battalion in a line that advanced by cadenced marching could keep its men closer together, often with elbows touching, and kept its linear formation better, which in turn meant fewer halts to dress the ranks.

The Prussian army forged by the Old Dessauer and bequeathed to Frederick the Great was an

A MUSKETEER OF THE STRATHBOGIE REGIMENT OF 1644, *like his comrade armed with the pike (p. 30), wears no armour. He is armed with a matchlock musket, bandolier and dirk. While many musketeers may have carried swords, the heavy musket was equally effective as a club in hand-to-hand combat.*

impressive institution. It was highly disciplined, well equipped, capable of delivering tremendous volumes of firepower against its foes and was highly manoeuvrable on the battlefield. Despite the emphasis placed on firepower by Leopold of Anhalt-Dessau, who actually argued that the firepower of the Prussian infantry would allow them to be deployed in two ranks rather than three or four, Frederick the Great initially chose to use the infantry's manoeuvrability and discipline to bring his battalions into hand–to–hand combat with the enemy. This followed current trends in military thinking, which emphasized the virtues of the bayonet and close combat. But it soon became clear that with improved weapons and firing systems, to march into contact with the enemy without the use of one's own musketry was not prudent. Frederick later allowed his troops to deliver volleys at close range before resorting to the push of the bayonet. By the time of the Battle of Leuthen (December, 1757), Prussian troops relied so heavily on firepower that units required replenishment of their ammunition, having expended the 60 rounds they carried into battle.

By the end of the Seven Years' War it was clear that the Prussian army was the epitome of what could be achieved with the weapons and formations of the age of linear warfare. It was also clear that Frederick the Great was perhaps the practitioner who best understood the possibilities and limits of warfare at the time.

Leuthen, 1757: Victory for Quality

The summer and autumn of 1757 were not kind to Frederick. He had been forced to abandon his invasion of Bohemia after lifting his siege of Prague and had suffered a sharp defeat at Köln, before retiring to Saxony. Moreover, he found himself with more enemies when France, Sweden and Russia all declared war against him, and without his key ally, as Britain withdrew from the war in order to preserve her territorial interests in Hanover. Frederick was, however, able to stabilize the situation in Saxony with a decisive victory over a large force of French and Imperial troops at Rossbach on 4 November. The victory had tremendous implications internationally, bringing Britain back into the war and with her the cash subsidies to support Prussia, and the help of her troops in northern Germany.

But Frederick still had problems on his eastern flank. His forces in Silesia, the *casus belli* back in 1740, under the command of the duke of Bevern, were on the run. They had been defeated by an

Austrian army under Charles of Lorraine and the veteran commander Field Marshal Leopold Daun outside of Breslau on 22 November and were driven back across the River Oder. Shortly thereafter Bevern himself was captured. Frederick had already begun moving to re-inforce his army in Silesia with 18 battalions of infantry and 23 squadrons of cavalry. He sent Hans von Ziethen, the commander of Prussia's hussar regiments, to keep Bevern's force together until he arrived. On 2 December, Frederick joined Ziethen and his troops. His original plan was to get Bevern's forces ready for combat and attack the Austrians at Breslau, but the overall strategic situation forced Frederick to move almost immediately.

The stage was set for the Battle of Leuthen, which was fought just three days later. In this battle Frederick demonstrated the effectiveness of the Prussian army when led by a commander who understood its capabilities. In the course of this battle Frederick used the great manoeuvrability of his infantry to execute his oblique order of attack and to concentrate his outnumbered troops against one wing of the enemy. It also demonstrated the firepower that the well-disciplined Prussian

infantry could deliver in the attack. Frederick's first task was to restore confidence to the officers and men of Bevern's command. The king strolled through the Prussian camp, talking to the troops, offering encouragement, and giving promises of rewards for merit in the action that was ahead of them. He likewise told the officers that they could redeem themselves in the battle they were about to fight. Frederick also encouraged interaction between the forces that had been defeated in Silesia and those returning from Saxony, flushed with the victory of Rossbach the previous month. Frederick hoped that the veterans of Rossbach would help raise the morale of the rest. He also took particular care to look after the comforts of his men, distributing additional rations and spirits to the troops to fortify their strength and courage. He furthermore called his generals and senior field grade officers to his tent where he delivered a rousing speech, calling on them to do their duty and uphold their honour, explaining his basic plan to attack the Austrians at Breslau. But he also promised punishments for failure, noting that cavalry regiments that failed to charge would be dismounted and downgraded to garrison service, and infantry regiments that did not press the attack would be disgraced, losing their colours, swords and having the facings cut from their uniforms.

Frederick allowed his troops to rest on 3 December but the next day advanced on Breslau. While on the march Frederick learnt that the Austrians had left the city and had deployed their army around the village of Leuthen. Frederick had looked for a decisive battle to restore the situation in Silesia and was grateful to Charles and Daun for this move. The Austrians certainly had reason to be confident since they outnumbered the Prussians by nearly two to one, with great advantages in both infantry and artillery. The Austrians had some 66,000 men and more than 200 artillery pieces, compared to the Prussian's

Battle of Leuthen
1757

Frederick the Great and his Prussian army met the Austrians at Leuthen under the command of Charles of Lorraine and Field Marchal Leopold Daun while marching on the city of Breslau. Frederick took advantage of the excellent discipline and mobility of his troops, as well as the terrain, to undertake a daring and complex manoeuvre. Using speed and the cover of some low ridges, Frederick marched his army across the front of the Austrian forces and appeared on the Austrian left flank. A small body of infantry and cavalry were left in sight of the Austrians to keep their attention and give the impression he had deployed his army to their front. Frederick quickly attacked the enemy's exposed flank and routed the *Reichsarmee* units on the far left. The Austrians made an effort to create a new defensive line based on the village of Leuthen, but their slow manoeuvering forced units to attack piecemeal and so the Austrians were driven out of the town and pushed back. Frederick pursued them, but the arrival of night precluded an utter rout.

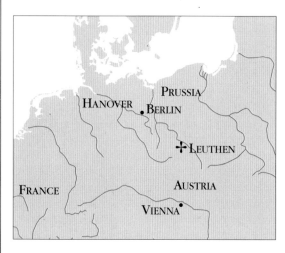

After his victory in Rossbach in Saxony, Frederick the Great quickly moved to Silesia to restore the situation there. He then moved on Breslau. On the way he encountered the Austrians at Leuthen.

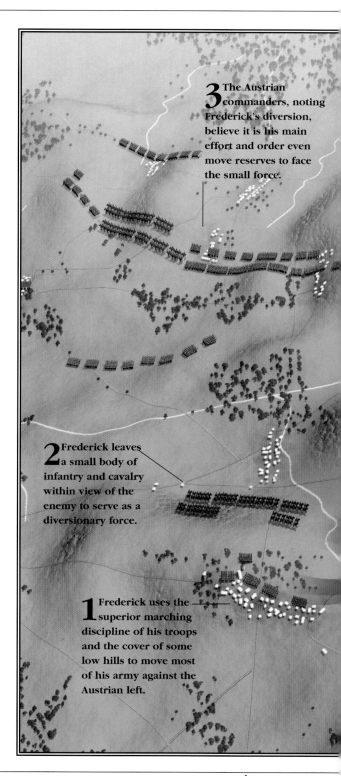

3 The Austrian commanders, noting Frederick's diversion, believe it is his main effort and order even move reserves to face the small force.

2 Frederick leaves a small body of infantry and cavalry within view of the enemy to serve as a diversionary force.

1 Frederick uses the superior marching discipline of his troops and the cover of some low hills to move most of his army against the Austrian left.

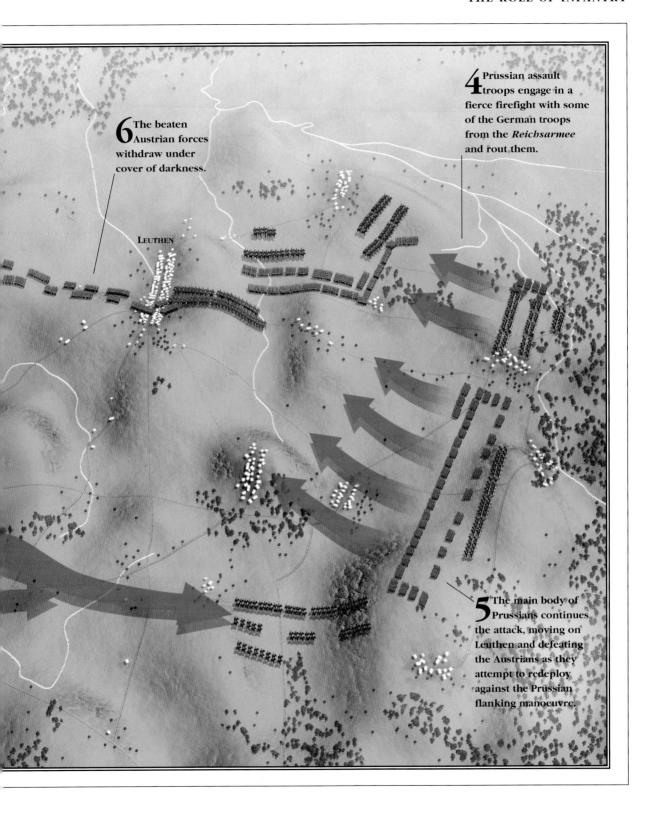

4 Prussian assault troops engage in a fierce firefight with some of the German troops from the *Reichsarmee* and rout them.

6 The beaten Austrian forces withdraw under cover of darkness.

LEUTHEN

5 The main body of Prussians continues the attack, moving on Leuthen and defeating the Austrians as they attempt to redeploy against the Prussian flanking manoeuvre.

39,000 men and 170 guns. Moreover, about two-thirds of the Prussians had been part of Bevern's force, which they had already defeated. Frederick seems mistakenly to have believed the Austrians were comparable in strength to his own forces.

The Austrians were encamped along a front about five kilometres (four and a half miles) long between the small hamlets of Nippern and Sagschütz, with the village of Leuthen behind their lines. Charles and Daun seemed ready to give Frederick an open battle, relying on their numbers to give them the victory. The Prussians made their advance to the battlefield beginning about 4 AM, and were deployed in two large infantry columns each flanked by a column of

cavalry. There was also a sizeable advance guard of light infantry, including some rifle-armed *Jäger*, and hussars led by the king himself.

Battle is Joined

The action began with the Prussian advanced guard easily brushing aside a small force of Saxon dragoons and Austrian light horse, taking 200 captive. Frederick ordered these men to be paraded past the army as it advanced, to raise the morale of his troops. As Frederick viewed the long white lines of Austrian troops deployed in front of Leuthen the great size of the enemy's army became clear to him and it was plain that they had the numerical edge. But, using the *coup d'oeil* for which he was famous, he noted two key features of the battlefield's topography. The first was that the Austrian left had not taken advantage of some marshy ground to anchor their left flank, which was consequently left exposed, although they had hastily constructed some barricades and redoubts for their batteries there. Moreover, there was a small ridgeline that ran in front of the Austrian left, which could be used to conceal his movements in front of the Austrian left flank.

Frederick quickly determined to take advantage of the vulnerable Austrian flank and to use the low ridges to mask his manoeuvre. To keep the enemy occupied, the Prussian cavalry of the left wing supported by some of the Prussian foot would feign an attack to keep the Austrian centre and right wing distracted. The idea of splitting an inferior force and marching a large part of it across the length of the enemy's line, all the while presenting the flank of advancing columns to musket and artillery fire, might have seemed suicidal, but because of the nature of the terrain and the speed and manoeuvrability of the Prussian infantry Frederick was willing to take the risk. By 11 AM Frederick had made his deployments, with his

THE BANDOLIER HAD BEEN *replaced by a cartridge box by the 18th century. This soldier, a British Guardsman of the Coldstream Regiment of 1742, carries both a bayonet and an infantry sword. By the end of the century, many armies will have abandoned the sword as redundant except for certain special or elite units.*

left-flank cavalry, supported by a small force of infantry, slowly advancing against the right flank of the Austrian line. The Austrian commander there immediately called for assistance, assuming that his flank was the object of Frederick's main assault. Charles and Daun responded by shifting their reserves to support the right, and galloped over to the right wing to oversee the engagement in person. In the meantime, the bulk of the Prussian infantry and their right-wing cavalry had begun their movement across the front of the Austrian line. The infantry, formed in two columns, moved with amazing speed due to their disciplined cadenced marching. In less than two hours they had started to form a line of battle at right-angles to the Austrian left flank, with the right-hand units extended slightly behind the Austrian line. The assault troops consisted of three excellent line infantry battalions, supported by a column of four additional battalions, three of gre-nadiers and one more from a crack line regiment. There were also 20 heavy twelve-pounder guns in support. The majority of the remaining Prussian infantry were deploying *en echelon* behind the assault force and spreading out to its left. Frederick retained 53 squadrons and six battalions in reserve. What made this manoeuvre possible was the low ridgeline that obscured the Prussians' movements. The position was strengthened by the fact that the Austrian commanders had moved over to their left flank, and so were even less likely to discern Frederick's intent. Indeed, although they noticed the Prussians moving behind the hill, they could not determine numbers or directions and assumed them to be in retreat. By 1 PM Frederick's forces were in position and ready to begin the assault.

Where the Prussian attack hit the Austrian left the troops were composed mostly of soldiers of varied quality from those minor German states whose contingents were combined to form the *Reichsarmee*. They were under the command of General Franz Nadasdy, a bold Hungarian hussar general. The Prussians advanced on the troops of the *Reichsarmee* and engaged them in a fierce firefight, routing the Württembergers and pushing them back into the Bavarians, who joined in the rout. The firepower delivered by the assault troops must have been crushing – they were running out of ammunition by the time the supporting units arrived. Fortunately Frederick had brought ammunitions wagons with him. These units drew more cartridges and remained in the battle line. Nadasdy tried to restore the situation by attacking the Prussian foot with his dragoons and hussars, but he was countered by the 53 squadrons of Prussians from Frederick's reserve under the command of Ziethen. The Prussian cavalry overthrew the Austrians. Rather than pursuing the cavalry, they turned to complete the destruction of Nadasdy's broken infantry, taking over 2000 Württembergers and Bavarians prisoner.

> 'It is necessary to impress upon the men that they are not to fire until ordered....
> The regimental commanders must see to it that such platoon firing is done in an orderly fashion.'
>
> – FREDERICK THE GREAT,
> INSTRUCTION MILITAIRE

Having realized that the attack on the right was a diversion, Charles and Daun tried to turn their centre 90 degrees to face the advancing Prussians. The Austrian line was to be anchored on the village of Leuthen itself. But there was little time to plan the redeployment and units were sent in piecemeal, not properly deployed into firing lines. The manoeuvre was much more difficult for the Austrians, who did not manoeuvre in the closed columns of the Prussians. As they performed it they were subjected to intense Prussian musketry and the fire of 40 twelve-pounders now moved up to the high ground overlooking Leuthen. At about 3:30 the Prussian infantry began their assault against the new Austrian position. After a sharp struggle they cleared Leuthen, which had been admirably defended by a few Austrian units and a

PRUSSIAN GUARD GRENADIERS *storm the graveyard at Leuthen. Frederick the Great believed in the importance of the bayonet in the attack and here crack Prussian Guardsmen storm a breach at the point of the bayonet.*

Würzburg regiment of *Reichsarmee* troops. Another Austrian cavalry charge was made but was driven back by the Prussian cavalry. At this point, the Austrian army broke. Frederick attempted a pursuit but the weather, time of day and exhaustion of his troops prevented this being very effective.

Leuthen was a great victory for Frederick but it was also a costly one. Frederick lost 6000 men, nearly one-fifth of his forces. He in turn inflicted 10,000 killed and wounded, took more than 12,000 prisoners, and captured more than 100 cannon. A further 17,000 Austrians surrendered when Breslau capitulated later in the month. Leuthen demonstrated just what could be accomplished in the age of linear warfare with an army as disciplined as that of Prussia, especially when commanded by one of the 'Great Captains' of the period.

Conclusion: Integration and Formation

By 1763 the infantry had become the dominant force on the European battlefield, both in terms of numbers and decisiveness. Battles were fought and won by clashes of infantry manoeuvring in linear formations. While cavalry and artillery played important roles, they were usually in support of infantry units. Neither could win battles by themselves. Moreover, the great varieties in the type of infantryman and the different styles of fighting that had prevailed in the early sixteenth century – pikeman, *arquebusier*, halberdier and sword-and-buckler man fighting as skirmishers or in blocks, *tercios* or battalions – had given way to a single integrated type of foot solder fighting in a single type of unit and formation. Although armies contained soldiers who bore a variety of names such as musketeer, fusilier or grenadier, these were for the most part terms that related to tradition or status rather than function.

At the end of the Seven Years' War virtually every army had adopted the same mode of

operation: a battalion drawn up in a three-rank formation and firing by platoons. Although light infantry forces had appeared on the battlefield, they had not yet become a permanent feature of most European armies. Mostly, except in the Austrian service, they remained relegated to the

little wars that were fought along the frontiers. The model for this system was the rigidly disciplined and magnificently trained army of Prussia under Frederick the Great. His army represented the epitome of the techniques for infantry combat for another quarter of a century. At the end of that period another great change in warfare would take place, but it would be based on dramatic social and political changes, that would expand the size of armies yet further, creating the concept of a nation-in-arms and new motivations, necessitating new tactics and new command structures.

CHAPTER 2

MOUNTED WARFARE

The history of the cavalry in the early
modern period is a continuation of the story
of the duel for supremacy on the battlefield
between shock troops armed for hand-to-
hand combat, and missile-armed, firepower
troops. In this struggle each arm varied their
tactical and fighting techniques to try and
outwit and outfight the other.

Medieval warfare in Europe had been
somewhat limited in that well-armoured,
heavy cavalry usually decided the day in
melee – the balance was tipped in favour of attack
because of the impetus and valour of these battle-
winning troops. Indeed the social structure
revolved around the mounted knight whose
prowess in arms often dictated his success in life and
society. The perception of the mounted warrior
charging into his foes with his couched lance
reigned supreme, and battles could be interpreted
as a great charge followed by innumerable

*THIS 17TH-CENTURY PAINTING shows cavalry engaged in
combat during the Thirty Years' War. It illustrates all
the confused savagery of a cavalry melee and its
mixture of weapons and fighting styles designed
simply to kill as many of the enemy as possible.*

individual combats in which command and control or tactical evolutions played only a minor part. Advances in weapon technology were mostly limited to those which influenced hand-to-hand combat, although the shadow of the archer loomed in the background. Bowmen, javelinmen and slingers were inferior classes of fighting men and their weapons were not those of the warrior elite who dominated military thinking.

For about 1000 years, warfare followed a familiar pattern. The supremacy of the armoured, mounted warrior and his brutally simple technique of the charge into melee had been maintained by the armourer's skill. First these expert artisans made mail and then plate defences to make man and horse impervious to crude war arrows, which could bring down the lightly armoured.

Then, when the mounted charge met an inglorious hiatus in the mud of Crécy (and again at Agincourt) and this supremacy seemed threatened by the longbow and the bodkin point, the knights paid for lighter, ridged and fluted defences to deflect the deadly shafts.

'Would to heaven this accursed engine had never been invented… so many valiant men have been slain for the most part by pitiful fellows and the greatest cowards; poltroons that had not dared to look those men in the face at hand, which at distance they laid dead with their confounded bullets.'

— BLAISE DE MONLUC

The Sixteenth Century: Pike and Shot

It was the arrival of firearms that brought Medieval warfare to an end. Although the armourers responded with a better quality metal and the mounted knight sacrificed speed and impetus for heavier and thicker plate to resist bullets, the battle of Pavia in 1525 probably marked the end of the dominance of noble, heavy cavalry, as the flower of French aristocracy was brought crashing down by massed shot. The longbow and then the *arquebus* made the battlefield the province of the foot soldier, as the serried ranks of steady missile-armed men proved concentrated firepower could stop a mounted charge in its tracks. Added to this commoners could kill nobles. Despite pikemen being needed for defence if the cavalry got through the shooting, this marked both a technological and philisophical revolution, begining the swing from impact melee to firefight.

The rate of change was a slow one. This was not due to the inherent conservatism of the mounted elite but the slow emergence of Swiss pikemen as a battlefield phenomenon. The Swiss had used some pikes as early as 1339 at the Battle of Laupen, but the real impact of the pike, which had helped Alexander conquer his known world, came late in the fifteenth century when the Swiss defeated Charles the Bold of Burgundy in three battles whose impact echoed across Europe. The huge Swiss pike block, protected at first by crossbows and handguns and then by *arquebuses*, became the dominant instrument for waging war, and was widely copied. It was an offensive weapon, which steamrolled its way over its enemies on foot and brushed aside those on horseback, and it could defend itself against cavalry from any direction.

The Swiss met their match in prepared battlefield works at Marignano in 1515 and Bicocca in 1522, when their crushing advance faltered in the face of artillery and massed firearm infantry. They suffered high casualties and realized that they, like their mounted adversaries, had failed properly to adapt to the rapid expansion in the use of gunpowder weapons.

It was the Spaniards who successfully blended the pike and firearms in the creation of their famous *tercios*, which were the next to dominate the battlefield. But the adoption of the musket made the *tercio* more defensive through its increase in firepower range: the formation was slow, cumbersome and was prone to interference by cavalry. Cavalry could stop the *tercio* by surrounding it, but if it was to to be destroyed the massive square had to be broken into. If enemy cavalry could get into it then they could impose the hand-to-hand melee in which they were so effective: the cavalry needed to breach the *tercio*.

Breaching a formed *tercio* could be done by a massed charge with the lance, especially if the cavalry formation was dense enough to prevent horses from shying away from the points of the pikes, and if the speed of the advance into contact was sufficient to carry it into the packed ranks despite the casualties. But cavalry commanders were reluctant to try it. Instead they decided to do it with shot themselves. Early attempts to equip mounted troops with firearms proved impractical and inefficient. The handgun or petronel braced against the flat of the chest, or sometimes with its barrel lodged in a cradle incorporated into the armour on a horse's neck, seemed to do little for the rider's ability to aim and hit his mark, or for the horse's willingness to be controlled when the gun went off.

There were many experiments with *arquebus*, hackbut and dragon, but the handling of the lighted match and the complicated processes of firing and reloading were two-handed operations necessitating mounted troops to be both proficient musketeers and experienced horsemen capable of controlling their mounts with only their knees and heels. Another technique of firing was required.

The answer was the invention of the wheel-lock, which did away with match as the means of ignition. It depended upon winding up a clockwork, serrated-steel disc or wheel. A short length of chain connected the wheel's spindle to a powerful mainspring, so when the spindle was wound by use of a spanner, this chain, under tension from the mainspring, wrapped around it. The action was then locked by a standard trigger mechanism. When he wished to fire the rider clicked the dogshead, which held a piece of pyrites in a set of screw-up jaws, down onto the wheel. On squeezing the trigger the spring was unlocked, the chain whipped back, unwrapped

A PISTOLEER PRACTISES *firing techniques in this depiction of early period pistol combat. He practises firing at the enemy rider and his horse, while below two heavy horse lancers continue their fight with pistols after their lances have been broken.*

and caused the spindle to revolve. The rapidly rotating serrated wheel grated against the pyrites and produced sparks. These ignited the priming charge in the pistol's pan, firing the main charge in turn through a touchhole in the barrel. Wheel-locks were highly robust but they did have certain drawbacks. For example, if they malfunctioned, a gunsmith with special tools had to repair them. Also the pyrites, a soft mineral, broke, chipped or wore away and needed frequent replacement. Small fragments often worked their way into the mechanism. Wheel-locks worked well and could usually be relied upon to fire first time, but reloading in action was difficult, hence the tendency to carry a carbine on a sling and a pair of pistols slotted into holsters strapped over the pommel of the saddle, perhaps with another tucked into a boot. The rider could load and span all his weapons while awaiting the order to advance, and go into action with carbine and pistols ready to fire. He had only to point and pull the trigger.

Reiters to the Fore

Contemporary tests with wheel-locks recorded an 85 per cent success rate for hitting a man-sized target at 27 m (30 yards) and reasonable rates of penetration of 2-mm (.07-inch) steel plate, although we are not told what a 'reasonable rate'

was, nor whether these were pistols or petronels. Tests performed by the author with an accurate reproduction wheel-lock petronel showed accurate shooting was possible at 9 metres (10 yards), and even up to 18 metres (20 yards) it was 'reasonable', averaging about 80 per cent. Beyond that accuracy was haphazard, with a dramatic drop to around ten per cent.

A flintlock pistol fared somewhat better but was more prone to misfires. Perhaps it was a case of better marksmanship but the period advice about touching your enemy with the muzzle before pulling the trigger says more about the general efficiency of the weapon than any test. Even if the range was short, pistol-armed horsemen were instructed to close the distance with the *tercio* and deliver enough shot to make a breach in it, into which their supporting lance-armed colleagues could charge and cut up the enemy at close quarters.

IN THE MOUNTED CARACOLE *formation, each rank of a troop of horse goes forwards in turn to fire its pistols at the enemy then retires to the rear of the formation to reload, preferably stationary. This was a complicated action that demanded steadiness of both horse and rider under fire. It was not helped by contradictory advice in drill books on how to perform the manoeuvre.*

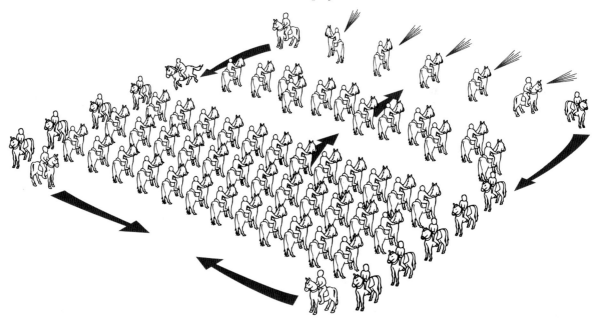

Wheel-lock and Caracole

Pistol-armed horse became the new innovation, fashionable and practical. The desire to charge was subsumed in the interest of winning back tactical supremacy, and by extending the use of these new weapons to the heavily armoured horse as well as the light cavalry, the dual function of shooting and close combat was achieved. Fully-armoured, *cuirassier* horse equipped with a brace of pistols who could shoot their way into a formation and then fall upon it with the sword became a common battlefield sight and these mounted pistoleers, called *reiters*, soon became feared throughout Europe.

But this new technique of fighting on horseback had serious implications for cavalry tactics and formations. At St Quentin the cavalry adopted a deep formation rather than their usual deployment in lines. Unlike the Swiss pikes or the later infantry column this was not done to increase the mass of a moving block in order to maximize the impact of a charge. It was based on a drill-manual based idea of increasing the rate of fire the *reiters* could deliver. The best-known advocate of mounted firepower was probably Cruso, whose *Militarie Instructions for the Cavallrie* was reprinted many times in different languages across Europe. His theories were put into practice by many of the great captains of his age. Military manuals for the cavalry of this period are full of complex techniques for performing tactical manoeuvres to bring maximum firepower to bear on various enemy formations and arms. The most favoured system was called the caracole.

The caracole was performed by first drawing up the riders in a column at least six ranks deep and anything from six to 20 files wide. This cumbersome formation would slowly trot towards the enemy. They would get to within 28 metres (30 yards) and fire first one pistol and then the second. Exactly how this was done depended on which drill book was being followed. Some advocated firing by ranks, others en masse, which would seem dangerous for those at the front. Some argued fire should be discharged forwards, either one pistol at a time or even both together; others advised turning the horse first right and firing the left-hand pistol sideways, and then turning left to shoot the right-hand pistol. Having fired, the cavalry retired to reload, and there were different opinions about how best to do this. Some preferred wheeling by ranks, some by facing to the side and riding Indian file to the rear of the block, while others argued that counter-marching each file was better. We have the advice, but unfortunately there is insufficient evidence as yet to say which method was most widely employed, though there is a reference to some rear ranks firing into the air when ordered to shoot en masse.

> *'The most pernicious habit of the pistoleers was the 'caracole'...this was a cause of disorder and confusion, unless the men were extraordinarily well trained and all of good morale.'*
>
> – SIR CHARLES OMAN

Although cumbersome and slow moving, seldom being performed faster than the trot, the major problem with the caracole was that although it delivered shot it could never deliver enough to do much harm. Cavalry battles became slow and noisy affairs and although they could, in theory, disrupt an enemy formation they apparently did not cause many casualties, unless the cavalry commander was able to bring overwhelming numbers of units into action.

Even with enough numbers it was difficult for cavalry to defeat foot. The *arquebus* and the musket could outrange their pistols and deliver heavier balls with greater force, and as foot could also bring to bear a better density of fire, the chance of the cavalry winning such a duel, even though they could ride off and reload in relative safety, was minimal. The attempt to turn the cavalry into mounted firepower succeeded only in rendering them tactically useless. Despite the outstanding performances of heavy lancers at Mook in 1574 and Gembloux in 1578, the majority

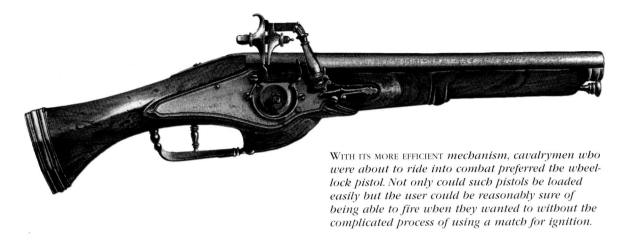

WITH ITS MORE EFFICIENT *mechanism, cavalrymen who were about to ride into combat preferred the wheel-lock pistol. Not only could such pistols be loaded easily but the user could be reasonably sure of being able to fire when they wanted to without the complicated process of using a match for ignition.*

of troopers were now armed with pistols and the lance began to disappear. The Dutch formally banished it 1597. The long thrusting cavalry sword, the medieval *estoc* and its descendants, also vanished, and riders relied upon shorter swords in the close quarter melee; or even their pistol butts. In the drive to increase firing efficiency, hand-to-hand combat skills went unpractised by individuals and commanders. Even if breaches had been made in enemy formations few units were any longer proficient in charging into contact, and heavy lancers were more or less 'troops of show', fit more for parades rather than the bloody business of the battlefield. Horsemanship went into decline. With the cavalry unable or unwilling to close for combat and 'reduced to the pointless popping of petit pistols', this great experiment is sometimes referred to as 'the debilitation of the horse'.

Pistol-armed cavalry were so widely adopted that they even made a significant appearance in the Polish Army, which had always been fiercely proud of its cavalry-charging tradition. Unlike many of their European counterparts they did not wholly relinquish the lance and could and would still charge into action. At the Battle of Klusino in

POLISH HEAVY CAVALRY *of the 17th century continued to wear both mail and plate armour long after it had fallen out of fashion in western Europe. The photograph, left, shows the vambraces and couters of the lower arms have been replaced by mail to give greater flexibility in handling the lance.*

1610 there was a telling incident when the Swedish and Russian *reiters* tried to retire after performing a grand caracole. The Poles went in with swords, at the gallop. They bowled over many in the huge block and broke it to pieces, scattering them and driving large numbers from the field. At least in one corner of Europe the cavalry had not been entirely debilitated, but in general the end of the sixteenth century saw fewer great battles. The slow movement of both the *tercio* and the *reiters*, and their reliance upon firepower, coupled with the rising popularity of artillery and fieldworks, put the emphasis firmly upon defence. The close-quarter melee became a last-resort gamble.

Lützen 1632: Swedish Reforms
So reduced was the cavalry's contribution to the winning of battles that Maurice of Nassau, a notable military innovator of the age, failed to devote much attention to the arm, preferring to focus his reforms upon the foot. He reduced the depth of the cavalry formation to four or five but he remained fixated upon the classical Roman practice of using cavalry as missile rather than as close-combat troops.

The signal for change was to come from an unexpected direction – Sweden. In the early 1600s Karl IX of Sweden inherited a cavalry corps almost entirely comprised of lightly-armoured pistoleers – poorly equipped, ill-trained and mounted on small, weak horses. They could fend off Russian Cossacks but could not protect the foot in open country

ONE OF THE MORE FANCIFUL *ideas for defeating a charging enemy is shown in this 17th-century illustration. Seemingly inspired by classical references to Alexander's phalanxes opening to allow chariots to pass through, this drill manual forgets that horses are not good at moving sideways, and, once turned, would expose their own flanks to attack by any supporting troops.*

from other cavalry forces, especially not from the Polish heavy horse. At the Battle of Kirkholm in 1605 the Poles lured the Swedes forwards with a feigned retreat and then turned on them. The Polish cavalry drove into and then dispersed the Swedes, despite their attempts to pistol them down. Lacking cavalry protection their foot, not

having adopted the pike in great numbers, then fell prey to a combined assault, in which the Polish cavalry played a major part. Kirkholm inspired a reaction against cavalry as semi-mobile fire platforms, and the effects of this were seen in the Thirty Years' War. The innovations of the king of Sweden, Gustavus Adolphus, in the organization and fighting techniques of his army saw a return of the horse to the offensive. Gustavus also placed an emphasis upon shock action.

Conceding the superiority of foot in a firefight with horse, due to weaponry and formation, the Swedes held that the contest was doubly unequal when one considered the size of the opposing targets. The horseman had to hit something

Imperialist *Cuirassier* (c.1630)

Cuirassiers *of the Thirty Years' War continued to wear plate armour for maximum defence but had discarded the lance in favour of pistols. Often poorly trained, they were required to perform the complicated caracole and only when they had caused enough firepower casualties and disrupted their enemy's formation did they risk going into action with their swords. Their armour was usually of a good quality and could stop both sword cuts and pistol balls. It was also articulated, which means the many layers could slide over each other, allowing a lot of movement. However, it also earned them the nickname of 'lobsters'.*

approximately 1.7 metres (five foot six inches) high and .6 metres (two foot) wide while the musketeer's target could be 2.4 or 2.7 m (eight or nine feet) by about 1 metre (three foot six inches). But they also argued that the musketeer was only able to fire twice per minute 'on a good day'.

So a horse moving at speed could in theory cover the intervening ground in time to limit the number of volleys they had to endure. With all these things taken into account, the Swedes believed that cavalry had a chance of returning to the old-fashioned style of shock-impact and melee. Although experience with the Poles may have inspired the Swedes to change, they never seriously considered taking up the lance. Instead they became

THE BATTLE OF LÜTZEN, *shown in a copper engraving by Matthaus Merian (1593-1650), was fought on 16 November 1632 between the Protestant army under Gustavus Adolphus and the Roman Catholic Imperialist forces under General Wallenstein. It resulted in a victory for the Swedes but at a considerable cost that included the life of their monarch.*

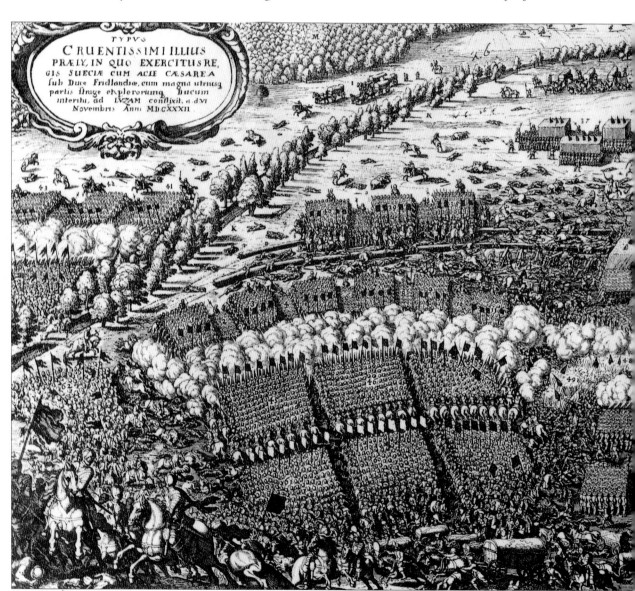

adept in the training and battlefield practice of the charge to contact, preceded by close-range pistol fire. The proportion of horse in the composition of the Swedish army increased and the king spent a lot of money on equipment and better-bred mounts. He also paid well and gave land and tax exemptions. The quality of men and horses improved dramatically but they would not have been considered 'heavies' by their contemporaries. They did not wear the full *cuirassier* suit, often restricting their armour to breastplates and helmets. Nor did they ride big horses, for although stocky and well bred, their mounts were seldom over twelve hands. By the mid-1620s Gustavus Adolphus' reforms had reorganized the cavalry into squadrons and by the 1630s into regiments. Theoretically the regiment comprised two squadrons with each squadron being four companies of 125 men, meaning that on paper the regiment was 1000 strong.

There are no sources yet to prove that these cavalrymen were issued with uniforms although the Swedish foot were slowly adopting something

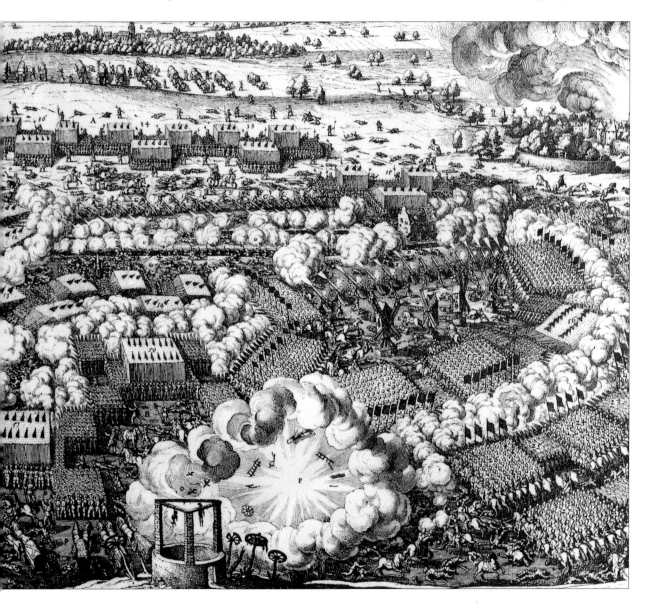

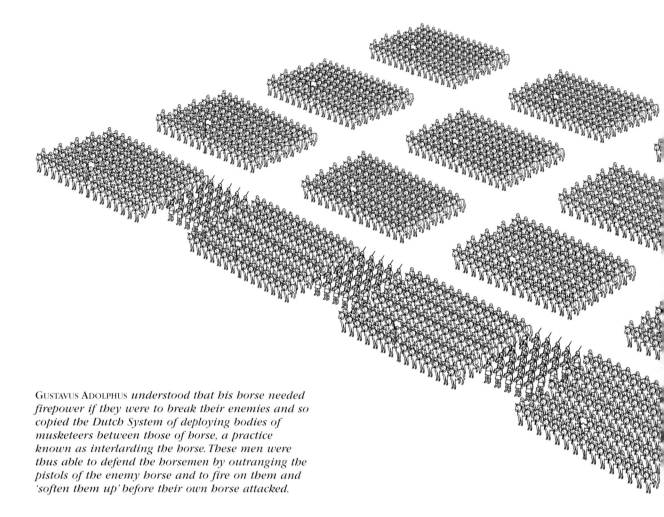

GUSTAVUS ADOLPHUS understood that his horse needed firepower if they were to break their enemies and so copied the Dutch System of deploying bodies of musketeers between those of horse, a practice known as interlarding the horse. These men were thus able to defend the horsemen by outranging the pistols of the enemy horse and to fire on them and 'soften them up' before their own horse attacked.

along those lines through a central clothing establishment. The lack of armour also meant many wore a thick leather buffcoat for protection. Some may have worn a steel vambrace on the bridle-arm, but for most, deep-cuffed riding gauntlets sufficed.

Before the Swedish System was created, European battles were governed by two tactical methodologies: the Dutch and the Spanish. These revolved around the deployment and fighting techniques of the foot, and the placing of the artillery. The horse were relegated to the flanks to perform their complicated but useless caracoles until called upon to chase after a broken enemy. Both systems relied upon firepower. The Swedish experience of fighting the Poles had taught them

lessons and Gustavus Adolphus put them to practical use. He realized he needed three essential improvements across his army: to increase its firepower; to use horse, foot and guns together; and to return his cavalry to shock action. He believed the cavalry could once again be a battle winner, if the impact could be delivered at speed by trained men on good horses. He gradually evolved his system and used the battles of Wallhof, Mewe and Dirschau in the mid-1620s virtually as experiments in the field.

At Dirschau in 1627, the Swedish horse with accompanying musketeers held their own against their Polish adversaries. At Burgstall they drove off Tilly's Horse, who tried to caracole. Then at Breitenfeld Gustavus interspaced bodies of

fast becoming outdated and the caracole with it. Although the Swedish horse still carried a pair of pistols they were under instructions that only the front rank was to use them in the charge, and then only one of them and only at close range. The rest were only to draw theirs in emergencies.

The Swedish System's tactics became well established and was used by several of the great captains of the Thirty Years' War. Even the great Imperialist commander Wallenstein adopted it in part, mixing bodies of musketeers into his cavalry wings. At the Battle of Lützen, Gustavus Adophus oversaw the deployment of the whole Protestant Swedish-Saxon army, which he had marched to attack the Imperialist army of Wallenstein. The Protestants wanted to take advantage of the absence of Pappenheim's command, which had been observed marching to Halle. In fact Wallenstein had decided to go into winter quarters, and having chosen Lützen as his HQ had dispersed his regiments across the district. As the Swedes approached he ordered their immediate return and re-assembly.

This chapter focuses on mounted warfare and so the descriptions of the battles within it are made without telling the stories of the infantry, except where they play a role in the cavalry action. Obviously these are not full accounts, but Lützen, like the other actions covered, was a great battle spread over a lot of ground and involved many units; we cannot tell all their stories.

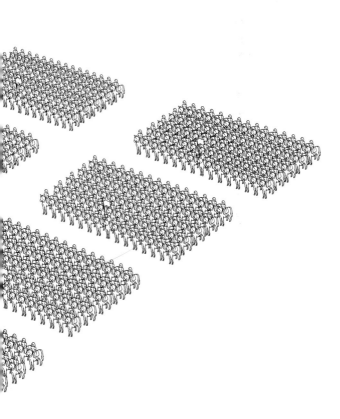

Wallenstein

Lützen was a small market town, around which Wallenstein had ordered his men to dig entrenchments. On the morning of 6 November 1632, as his dispersed army began to arrive, he drew it out into the surrounding fields. Knowing he might have trouble until Pappenheim could return he created a defensive line, with his right protected by the town and its castle. Against this barrier he formed his anchor, a large battery of 14 heavy guns among some windmills and outbuildings in the suburbs. He spread the remaining ten guns along his front. He deployed his main line behind a substantial ditch that ran alongside the roughly east-west axis of the Lützen to Leipzig road. Other than this obstacle the

musketeers among his cavalry and left gaps in the infantry line to allow the reserve horse to pass through them, all covered by guns along the front; the three arms working together. Gustavus Adolphus also made sure that each of his lines also had a cavalry reserve. This deployment and tactical innovation surprised both friendly Saxons and the Imperialist foe, especially the defensive firepower afforded to the horse, and their offensive tactic of charging into contact once their enemy had been disrupted. Even the great Pappenheim and his *cuirassiers* could not defeat them. Such was the impact of these new fighting techniques that drill masters and military theorists began serious analysis of what happened and published manuals on the Swedish System. The Spanish System was

WEIGHTY HORSE ARMOUR *was worn by heavy cavalry of the 16th and 17th centuries. The unarticulated wrist of the gauntlet on his right arm would suggest that his principle weapon was the lance as the rigidity helped resist the shock of impact. The lack of armour on the fingers further suggests his hand was covered by a guard attached to the shaft of the lance.*

battlefield was good cavalry country, being generally open and flat. He could have covered his left with the small Flossgraben stream, but unfortunately Wallenstein did not have enough men to reach that far.

Wallenstein had about 8000 foot and 8000 horse if all his regiments managed to assemble. He drew them up in the tried-and-tested manner, with his infantry in the centre flanked by two wings of cavalry. He also threw forwards detachments of musketeers to occupy the ditch and shoot the Swedes' horses in the belly as they tried to clear it. Historians have disputed the number of lines in Wallenstein's deployment, whether two or three,

but there is a tradition that he gathered his camp followers together at the back and, putting a few infantry standards among them, hoped the morning mist would help convince the Protestants that they were facing a much larger force. This might have been his third line. As well as having horse on his flanks he deployed a small cavalry reserve in the centre behind the first line, which the Imperialists had not done before. Emulating the successful Swedes he also reduced the depths of his formations, with the infantry now arrayed ten deep, and the horse in files of six.

To fight this deployment the Swedish king, having got his force over the Flossgraben without difficulty, arrayed them, nearly 13,000 foot and just over 6000 horse, in the same manner as he had at Breitenfeld, with smaller, more flexible units drawn out in thinner blocks to occupy more frontage, bringing more men into action and not wasting them at the back of a formation doing relatively little. He too anchored his right, on a small plantation of trees and then formed in two lines with 20 field guns spread along their front. Both lines had six brigades of foot in the centre and both were flanked by six squadrons of cavalry on each wing. Five bodies of 200 musketeers were placed at intervals among the cavalry of the first line on each wing; 1000 muskets per wing were far more than Wallenstein had allocated. It was to prove a sound investment in manpower.

The Swedish method of alternating charges with volleys is best explained by eyewitness Robert Monro: '...at a neere distance our Musketiers meeting them with a Salve; then our horsemen discharged their Pistolls, and then charged through them with swords; and at their returne the Musketiers were ready again to give the second Salve of Muskets...'

Each of these interlarded musket bodies was accompanied by two small pieces of artillery – regimental pieces sometimes called the Swedish leather guns. That meant each wing had 1000 muskets and ten guns to provide its firepower.

ALTHOUGH A 16TH-CENTURY reiter *combat formation created plenty of noise and smoke, the only way pistol-armed cavalry could defeat each other was through having far superior numbers.*

5   *Spann your Pistoll.*

6.   *Prime your Pistoll.*

7.   *Shutt your Pann.*

8   *Cast about your Pistoll*

Gustavus Adolphus had also reduced the depth of his cavalry formations from files of six to files of three. He was short of men and the winter campaign had killed many horses, but it also meant he could extend his line, cover more ground, overlap flanks and speed up the advance as it did not have to wait for rear ranks to keep up with the charge. He had two reserves: one of foot behind

DEMONSTRATING A REITER'S POSTURES, a heavy pistoleer goes through the various movements of spanning and cocking. These movements were necessary to prepare his pistol to fire while on the move.

the first line; and one of horse behind the second. He also opted for dispersing his 20 pieces of artillery and created four five-gun batteries across his front. Again, as he had at Breitenfeld, Gustavus Adolphus took command of the right but this time he faced Holk, while Bernard of Saxe-Weimar had the left, opposite Wallenstein.

Deployment for Battle

After prayers, a thick mist arose, halting the Protestant attack and buying time for Pappenheim. He abandoned his infantry to come up as fast as he could, pressing on towards Lützen with his horse. A sporadic two-hour phase of bombardment, with both sides shooting through the fog occupied most of the morning and although the Swedes tried unsuccessfully to feign a general withdrawal in the hope of luring the Imperialists out of position, Wallenstein did not fall for it. Holk on the left had trouble restraining his men and his horse edged forwards up to the line of the ditch. This feigned retreat was a movement that could only be performed by horsemen accustomed to manoeuvring in smaller, more flexible formations, but even then it must have been a complicated thing to do and almost impossible to co-ordinate, especially in poor visibility. Then, at 11 AM, just as

'Nowadays one fights more like a fox than a lion, and war consists more in sieges than in battles.'

– HENRI DE ROHAN

the mist seemed to be lifting, the action commenced in earnest. Perceiving that Holk's men had advanced to the ditch and had reduced the ground to their front over which they could build up speed, Gustavus Adolphus ordered a cavalry charge by the Swedish right wing. This is where the Swedish System had the advantage. The cavalry wings were mobile and trained to attack, but their advance was preceded by fire from the supporting muskets and light artillery, and they could rally back behind the defensive bodies of shot. It was a fine example of combined-arms technique, but it did restrict the early stages of the advance to the slow trot; the speed of the accompanying foot and gunners. When they got to within musket range the small arms and guns fired and blew holes in the ranks opposite.

The Swedes continued their advance, led by their king. They cantered forwards under orders not to fire their pistols until after they had received the shot from their foes. They did so and then put spurs to their mounts and tried to gallop. They crashed into Holk's cavalry and a furious melee ensued in and around the ditch. The Imperialist musketeers did indeed

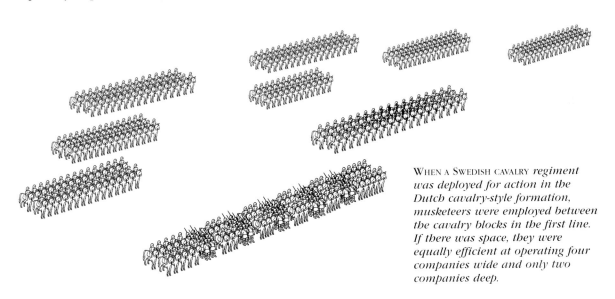

WHEN A SWEDISH CAVALRY *regiment was deployed for action in the Dutch cavalry-style formation, musketeers were employed between the cavalry blocks in the first line. If there was space, they were equally efficient at operating four companies wide and only two companies deep.*

Battle of Lützen

1632

Wallenstein's Imperialist army went into winter
quarters at Lützen, dispersing Pappenheim to Halle.
Taking advantage of this situation the Protestant
army of Gustavus Adolphus attacked. Wallenstein
formed a defensive position behind a deep ditch
alongside the Lützen–Leipzig road. On the right the
Swedish horse had some success, but on the left
they were pinned back by Croatian light cavalry.
In the centre, the infantry locked together, but
superior Protestant firepower drove the Imperialists
from their ditch. Meanwhile Pappenheim's force
returned, attacked and pushed back the Swedish
right; however, even though supported by
Piccolomini's reserve horse they could not break
the Swedish flank. The battle raged until pressure on
Wallenstein's right caused it to retreat. The
Protestants tried to roll up the Imperialist line but
the troops would not run, and – under the cover of
nightfall – Wallenstein withdrew to Leipzig,
abandoning his guns. However, with Adolphus'
death, the Swedes lost their dynamic leader and the
'heart' of their army.

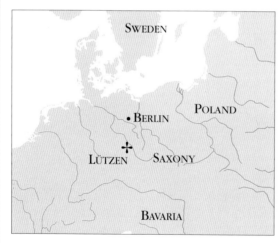

*Lützen is in Germany, nearly 24km (15 miles)
south-west of Leipzig in the direction of Erfurt.
The battle was fought to the east of the town in
the flat fields either side of the main road.*

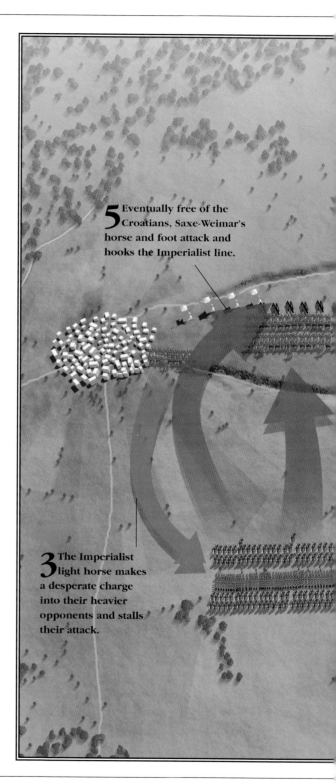

5 Eventually free of the
Croatians, Saxe-Weimar's
horse and foot attack and
hooks the Imperialist line.

3 The Imperialist
light horse makes
a desperate charge
into their heavier
opponents and stalls
their attack.

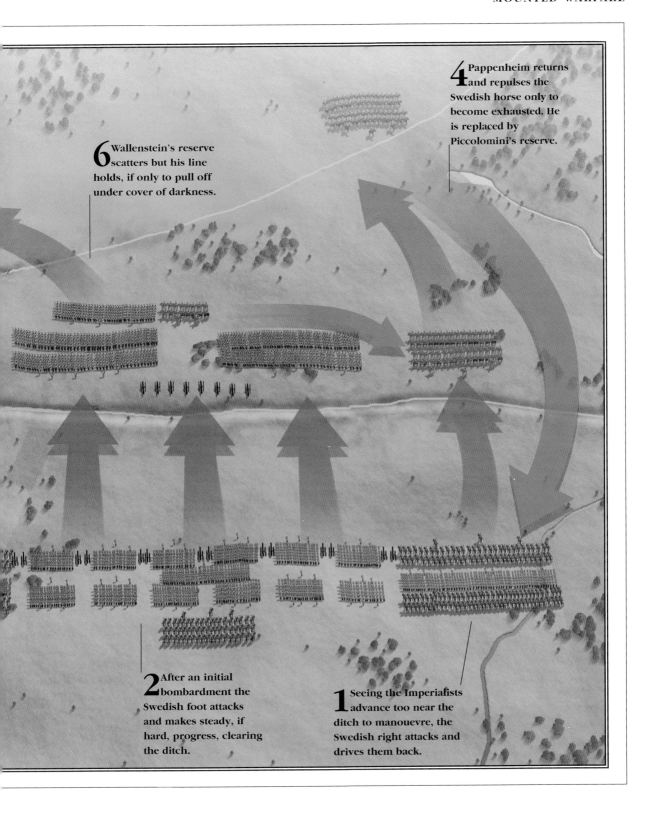

4 Pappenheim returns and repulses the Swedish horse only to become exhausted. He is replaced by Piccolomini's reserve.

6 Wallenstein's reserve scatters but his line holds, if only to pull off under cover of darkness.

2 After an initial bombardment the Swedish foot attacks and makes steady, if hard, progress, clearing the ditch.

1 Seeing the Imperialists advance too near the ditch to manouevre, the Swedish right attacks and drives them back.

fire into the bellies of the Swedish horses but they were soon engulfed in the general scrimmage and many were cut down. The initial impetus and the ability to overlap gained an initial advantage but after driving the Imperialists back onto their second line the forwards momentum was absorbed by the depth of the men they had to fight. By adding their second line to the melee another wave of impetus was applied to the swaying mass and gradually the Swedes regained the momentum.

They forced their way forwards over the ditch, expelling the musketeers and sending the cavalry reeling back to re-form. Although Wallenstein had placed shot among his horse they were too few in number to stop the retreat. Again led by their king, the Swedes followed up, driving Holk's unformed cavalry back, overwhelming their musket support. The Imperialist left was collapsing before the onslaught of the Swedish right-wing horse, who began wheeling inwards to strike at the already engaged foot.

In the centre the Swedish foot were also gaining the upper hand. They too had got over the ditch and on the right centre had taken seven guns, which they turned on their former owners.

But all was not going so well for the Protestants on the other side of the field. Wallenstein had ordered fires to be set in Lützen and it was soon ablaze. Smoke billowed and, caught by the wind, it drifted into the faces of Saxe-Weimar's men who were also receiving cannon-fire from the guns by the windmill. At close range they were causing considerable damage. Adding to the problems, the mist returned. This and the smoke masked the attack of Wallenstein's Croat cavalry who careered into the half-blind Saxon horse.

These were different men to those who had fled at Breitenfeld. The Croats were light horsemen not used to falling upon formed horse, preferring to fight open-order infantry, baggage guards or civilians. Holding their ground the Saxons slugged it out with the Croats, but numbers looked like they would tell, especially as the foot of both sides also fell. Saxe-Weimar steadied the morale of his men, committed the second line to stem the pressure and used the protective interlarded muskets as shelter to rally the first line. The Saxon

left held. Meanwhile Gustavus Adolphus, managing to understand the situation despite the smoke and fog, rode across from the right to add his forceful personality, and the Smaland regiment, to the conflict.

There is another big debate about the timing of this battle, for some sources state that Pappenheim, rapidly returning from his march towards Halle, arrived on the field about noon, others say it was not until early evening. No matter what the hour may have been, Pappenheim's arrival on Wallenstein's left overlapped the Swedes and they could do little to prevent him driving into them. He ordered two attacks. He sent his light cavalry to attack the Swedish baggage train, trying to cause a

distraction, and then personally led his own *cuirassiers* in an all-out assault on the exposed Swedish flank.

This was not Pappenheim's *reiters* popping off with their pistols at long range and then falling back to reload. This was a charge in the style advocated by the Swedish king himself: the steady roll forwards, the gathering of pace, the close-range pistol fire and the final spur into a charge into action with the sword. It was successful. They hit the Swedes hard and sent shock waves rippling through the whole formation. Being mounted on smaller horses and not having the luxury of full *cuirassier* armour the Swedes, still fighting, gave ground. The momentum pushed them backwards

HAVING PLUNGED INTO THE MÊLÉE *to shore up a faltering brigade, the Swedish king's wounded horse carried him into the enemy ranks where, deprived of his escort, he was surrounded by Imperialist troopers and shot in the back despite efforts to capture him.*

in an arc and soon they were retreating over the same ditch that they had fought so diligently to clear. It would appear that two things stopped this retreat being turned into a rout.

These were, firstly, the defensive firepower of the Swedish interlarded foot and their supporting leather guns and, secondly, the small cavalry reserve from from behind the second line, which was able to plug the gaps. The Swedish System for cavalry had shown both its offensive and its defensive qualities. The Imperialist's success in pushing back their enemies came at a price. The Swedish regimental guns and musketeers made devastating salvoes into the advancing Imperialists at close range and Pappenheim was shot through the chest. A cannon ball penetrated his lung and, choking on his own blood, he was carried from the field in a cart to his coach, where he later died. But another great captain was also to fall leading a cavalry charge at Lützen.

Smoke, Fire and Fog

As Gustavus Adolphus rode to the left to restore the situation on that flank, he saw through the now-enveloping fog that one of his brigades of foot was being hard pressed, and immediately ordered his Smalanders to their assistance. He charged into the melee with his small escort about him. Out in front he was a prime target and a musket ball struck him in the left arm, shattering it. Another hit his horse, which panicked, carrying him away from his escort and deep into the melee. He was stabbed in the side and an Imperialist horseman pistoled him in the back. He toppled from the saddle but his foot caught in a stirrup and he was dragged until he managed to free himself. As he lay face down, critically wounded and exhausted another pistol shot was put into the side of his head between the right eye and the ear.

The Smaland regiment also met with a reverse and several of the Swedish cavalry fled. Not being able to see clearly, they believed they were being hotly pursued. In the midst of this crisis the king's horse reappeared out of the smoke and the press, thrashing and leaping about wildly in its pain from the wound in its neck. There was blood on its

'...the horsemen on both wings charged furiously, abiding unloosing a pistol, till the enemy had discharged first, ...our Musketiers meeting them with a salve: then our horsemen discharged their pistols, and then charged through them with swords; and at their return the Musketiers were ready again to give the second Salve...'

— ROBERT MONRO

empty saddle. The Imperialists heralded the news with jubilation and the Swedish officers tried to play it down, but to no avail. Word of the death pf Gustavus Adolphus spread throughout both armies. There was a waver but instead of causing panic, the news of their king's fall appears to have put a spirit of vengeance into the hearts of the Swedes in the centre. No doubt encouraged by the defiant psalm singing led by Gustavus' personal chaplain Fabricius they went forwards once more. It was proving a brutal slogging match.

On the right things had shifted again. Both sides were tired but the Swedish cavalry had gone forwards, retaken the ditch and thrown back Pappenheim's men, who were now aware that their leader was down. Despair set in among Pappenheim's troopers. One colonel refused to charge and took his men off. With their leader dead and their morale badly shaken they began to break.

Wallenstein sent Ottavio Piccolomini to try and rally them, but they routed from the field, pursued by some Swedish horse. The majority of Swedes stayed, posing a threat to Wallenstein's centre. Piccolomini's own large *cuirassier* reserve came up and reinforced the Imperialist left. There followed one of the bitterest of the hard-contested actions of the day. Piccolomini made seven full-scale, combined attacks on the whole of the Swedish right centre. His men eventually retook the seven captured guns and once more drove the Swedish cavalry back.

Piccolomini had been grazed by six or seven bullets and several horses had been shot out from under him. But he had restored the situation and the battle swung in favour of the Imperialists. It was about 2 PM.

Swedish Cavalryman (c. 1650)

Gustavus Adophus reorganized and re-equipped his horse, forming them into regiments about 1000 strong. They were officially Light horse but were to set the pattern for heavy cavalry across Europe for years to come. To increase speed, they reduced the amount of armour worn to a pot helmet and back and breastplates. Instead, they relied upon their thick leather buffcoats for general protection. These coats were sometimes made of several layers of hide stitched together and often dyed yellow. They were capable of absorbing the blow of a sword while preventing penetration. Trained to fire their pistols only at the last minute before contact and then go in with the sword, these men proved especially effective against their more cumbersome, pistol-firing, cavalry enemies.

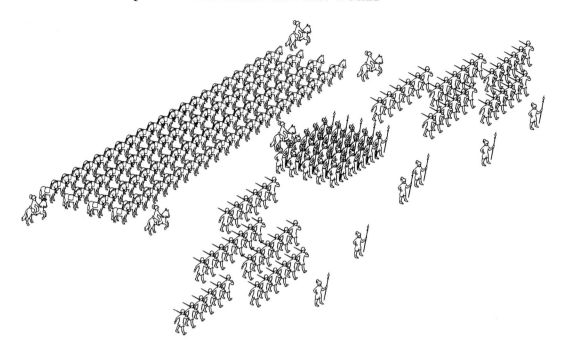

DISMOUNTED DRAGOON formations from the Thirty Years' War emphasized the use of dragoons as mounted infantry in relatively close order. They operated in ranks rather than files. Another interesting facet is the acquisition of a body of men carrying half-pikes, presumably to defend against attack by horse, although the usual tactic was to run for their own mounts and ride away!

All along the line the infantry was locked in a deadly life-and-death struggle surging backwards and forwards across the road and ditch, but on the Swedish left towards Lützen itself, Saxe-Weimar, ignoring advice to retire and now in overall command, ordered the guns to be moved and brought over to his left centre, while the second line of horse, who by now had also retired and re-formed behind their supporting musketeers, were to launch another attack. Between 3 and 4 PM the Saxon cavalry drove forwards yet again and pushed Wallenstein's horse, mixed with some of his infantry, back towards what had become the blazing inferno of Lützen. The Imperialist troops on the far right broke and ran, leaving those Saxon cavalry which did not pursue them to rally and re-form as best they could, before launching yet another attack. This time they turned inwards and went into the flanks of the now-amalgamated

front and second lines of infantry. Their foot assaulted at the same time, and, pinned at the front and attacked in flank, Wallenstein's right centre began to withdraw. Other parties of Protestant cavalry congregated on the flank of the Imperialists' small cavalry reserve and charged it, while others turned into the side of the battery of guns at the windmills. The fortified windmills fell one by one and the battery was overrun. News of the death of Gustavus Adolphus finally reached the Swedish cavalry on the right, and with renewed vigour they too joined the attack and threw themselves against Piccolomini for another bloody encounter. The whole of Wallenstein's line was withdrawing, bending back from its right.

It has been argued that if the Swedish horse had not been so exhausted they might have mounted a pincer from both flanks, which could have utterly destroyed Wallenstein's army. However, Piccolomini's wing was too strong and the Imperialist foot too tenacious. And Pappenheim's foot and guns had finally arrived. When night fell the battered Imperialists were able to draw off under the cover of darkness, back to Leipzig, leaving all Wallenstein's artillery and baggage. The Swedish–Saxon army was too exhausted to pursue.

The corpse of the Swedish king was found that night, naked except for his shirt, under a pile of dead in the famous ditch. The advocate of cavalry combat with the sword had been killed by bullets. But the innovations of Gustavus Adolphus had won the day, especially those he had introduced to render his horse more effective and the fighting techniques in which he had trained them.

Edgehill, 1642: Full Tilt

Gustavus Adolphus' Swedish cavalry technique showed how the horse could once more become a battle-winning, shock-action weapon. By trotting up, firing at close range then spurring forwards, putting the emphasis upon impetus and the sword, they proved they could overcome their foes.

This practice was emulated all over Europe and one of its students, Prince Rupert of the Rhine, brought it to England at the start of the English Civil Wars. The Battle of Edgehill, which took place in

1642, is an interesting battle in the development of mounted warfare. It not only shows the redundancy of firepower cavalry, but illustrates two other emerging techniques: the deliberate avoidance of contact in order to turn the flank of the enemy and the necessity of a retaining a powerful reserve, not just for defence but to exploit offensive opportunities. Edgehill has yet another important lesson. It shows that the superiority of the Swedish technique in horse-versus-horse combat could also be beaten in battle. To understand this we need to look at Rupert himself. A great admirer of Gustavus Adolphus, Rupert was a voracious reader

ONE SIMPLE PIECE *of drill-book advice concerning the accuracy of the pistol is found in the exhortation, 'fire when touching', meaning, 'place the muzzle against the body of the opponent before pulling the trigger'. At Roundway Down, 1643, Sir Arthur Haselrig survived even this close-range shooting.*

Royalist Horse (1640s)

The cavalry that mustered for the king during the early part of the wars came mostly from the landed gentry and their retainers. They rode their own horses and wore their own clothes. The armour they used was from their family's past military service. This man is well equipped with old-fashioned cuirassier *armour, a buffcoat and a new bridle arm. Apart from the king's Lifeguard they had no central purchasing and no supply depot, and so had no uniform appearance. Few had firearms and although the odd pistol might be tucked into the boot, their principal weapon was either a short mortuary sword, the more expensive Pappenheimer rapier or a pollaxe. These were individuals, temporarily woven into ad hoc formations. They were capable and brave, but independent of spirit.*

of military treatises and seems to have shared the Polish scepticism of any cavalry that continued to employ mounted firepower and viewed the Swedish System as 'a timid compromise'.

Parliament's control of the manufacture of weapons meant that most of their horse had been issued with two pistols. Some also had carbines and their dragoons carried muskets. We are told that Royalist troopers would 'pass muster if armed only with a sword'. The majority of Royal cavalry considered themselves to be gentlemen and the pistol was not their weapon of choice. They, and Rupert, preferred cold steel and the full-tilt gallop, as on the hunting field.

The Battle of Edgehill was fought because the king had manoeuvred his army across the earl of Essex's lines of communication with London, and the Parliamentarians had virtually bumped into them. The Royal army had formed on the top of the steep hillside known as the Edge while Essex offered battle deployed partially on 'a little hill in the Valley of the Red Horse' between the Edge and the village of Kineton. The Royalists came off the Edge and deployed on the lower slopes in the Swedish System with five brigades of foot in chequerboard formation, flanked by two large bodies of cavalry, both in two lines. Regiments of dragoons were posted on the wings and while six heavy guns were grouped in a battery to the right rear on Bullet Hill, 12 lighter pieces were spread out along the front. Rupert went past Gustavus Adolphus' 'timid compromise' and had neither accompanying shot nor guns allocated to the horse.

The earl of Essex adhered to the Dutch System with three brigades, the van, the battle and the rear being drawn up from right to left across the field.

'Prince Rupert…giving positive orders to the Horse, to march as close as was possible, keeping their Ranks with Sword in Hand, to receive the Enemy's Shot without firing either Carbin or Pistol, til we broke in amongst the Enemy and then to make use of our Firearms as need should require.'

— SIR RICHARD BULSTRODE

The first two were on 'the little hill' while the third was slightly refused on the left to take advantage of another rise in the ground. Nine field guns were spread along the centre, and cavalry were positioned on both flanks: Sir James Ramsey had command of the left wing of horse, and he had musketeers line a hedge both in front of him and in some others to his left. He also had three guns with him. On the other flank Sir William Balfour had two regiments of dragoons in some bushes on his right and four guns to bolster his firepower.

Although it was a general attack, Rupert, influenced by Gustavus Adolphus' maxim about cavalry impact in the early stages of battle, launched his own cavalry wing first, although it was preceded by a large regiment of dragoons working up the flanks and driving the Parliamentarian-commanded muskets from the hedges. His wing consisted of 21 troops of horse in the front line and seven in the second. The role of the second line was to re-inforce the first, and to counter threats or exploit situations if opportunities presented themselves.

Charge

Unfortunately for the king there was both a strength and weakness in the quality of men who served in the Royalist cavalry. Their arrogance was a positive feature, but it intruded upon clear judgement and receptiveness to orders. Prince Rupert was fortunate that so early in the war he had such men to launch a Swedish-style charge into combat, but they were also men who would prove difficult to restrain.

Sir Richard Bulstrode, who rode in the charge, tells us of Rupert's command 'to march as close as possible, keeping their Ranks with Sword in Hand, to receive the Enemy's Shot without firing…till we broke in amongst the Enemy'. This was different from the Swedish technique. Nobody was to fire until they had engaged in melee. In ranks composed of files of three, the whole of the right wing moved forwards: 'the Royalists march'd up with all the gallantry and resolution imaginable…while they advanced the Enemy's cannon continually played upon them as did the small Divisions of their foot…neither of which did in the least discompose them so much as to mend their pace.' This was the slow march advance under fire of disciplined troops, with the troopers keeping line abreast and filling any gaps in the ranks torn by cannon balls and musket shot. Ramsey had chosen a good position for the firepower tactic and had found his men higher ground on a gentle hill with a small stream at the foot of its forwards slope, and hedges to their front and left. Crossing these obstacles would disrupt and delay the Royalists, during which delay they could be shot. Ramsey's fire-based deployment used the technique of 'interlarded muskets' among the horse. Both horse and foot were six ranks deep, so that by firing by ranks and then retiring to reload they could keep up a steady rate of fire. Early war numbers being small, their frontages were narrow; each 'unit' of men being approximately nine troopers or six musketeers wide. But Ramsey's deep formations caused him deployment problems. Rupert was using the Swedish three-deep line and as it formed so it began to overlap Ramsey's flank. Ramsey was forced to draw out his left 'to a great breadth' but we are not told how. He could have doubled his files to the front and extended each body, or he could have widened the intervals between them, or indeed, opened his order.

He had time to do any of these, but the effect would have been to either decrease his rate of fire by increasing the loading time or to allow gaps in his line and lessen the advantages of mutual support. No matter which option Ramsey chose, the effect of

'A small squadron of cavalry, acting promptly, can wreak havoc amongst large infantry battle lines.'
— RAIMONDO MONTE CUCCOLI

drawing out to his left spread the line and weakened his ability to withstand Rupert's attack.

The Royalists 'were fain to charge them uphill and leap over some five or six hedges and ditches'. That sort of terrain disorders formed cavalry, and despite riding ability honed while hunting, to go into action over this ground would soon destroy the cohesion of an attack. Nor were Rupert's men the trained cavalrymen of the Swedish army; they were unlikely to keep their ranks and files and probably resembled a fast-trundling 'mob', bunching and veering from fire as they came forward.

As Rupert's attack got nearer, the response from the Parliamentarian horse was almost immediate. Observing drill-book training technique they stood their ground, presented their weapons and 'gave fire with their cannon lined amongst their horse, dragoneers, carabines and pistols, but finding they did nothing dismay the King's Horse and that they came more roundly to them'. Coming 'more roundly to them' probably means that a trumpet had unleashed the fall-on and the final phase of the 'charge' now took place.

Despite not keeping their order, Rupert's attack seems to have followed the pattern of a Swedish charge. First the walk, then the slow trot and the 'good round trot', followed by the canter with individuals or packets of men spurring to the gallop. Balls would undoubtedly have brought down some but several may well have just fallen off. The noise of the guns and the men's shouts must have made the unaccustomed horses skittish, to say the least. The direction of the attack also took them obliquely across the little stream,

PRINCE RUPERT VICTORIOUS? *This rather romanticized contemporary illustration shows Prince Rupert and his cavalry charging the Parliamentarians at Naseby, 14 June 1645. Rupert's tactics proved rash and ill-considered on this occasion, and at the hands of Fairfax the Royalists suffered a resounding defeat from which they never recovered.*

Battle of Edgehill

1642

King Charles I manoeuvred his army between the earl of Essex's Parliamentarians and London, forcing them to offer battle near the foot of Edgehill escarpment. With both sides deployed the Royalists chose to attack. On both wings their dragoons cleared the hedges and then launched a general advance. On the Royalist right Rupert's horse broke Ramsey's combined horse and musketeers, and helped rout Parliament's central brigade of foot. On the left Wilmot's horse broke Fielding's regiment and left-hooked the main Parliamentarian line. Flushed with success both wings chased their foes off the field. Meanwhile the remaining Parliamentarian foot managed to close the gap and hold the Royalist infantry. Then, aided by their cavalry reserve, they punched a hole in the Royal line, broke two of their brigades and drove the king's army back to their starting positions. The victorious Royal horse returned too late to prevent a tactical victory for Essex.

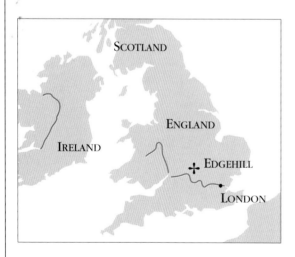

Edgehill is near Kineton in the English Midlands, 32 km (20 miles) south of Coventry, halfway between Stratford-upon-Avon and Banbury. The battle was fought on open, boggy, moorland. Today much of it is covered by a military depot.

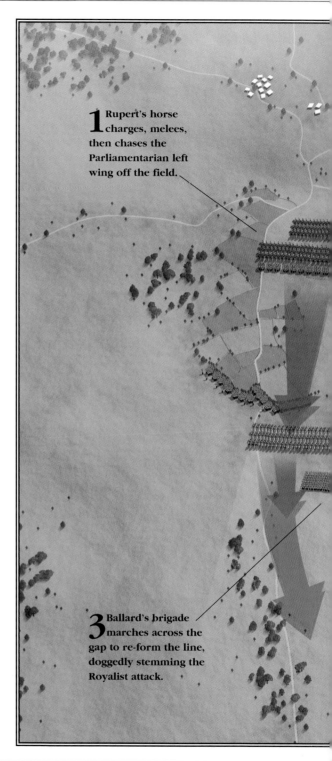

1 Rupert's horse charges, melees, then chases the Parliamentarian left wing off the field.

3 Ballard's brigade marches across the gap to re-form the line, doggedly stemming the Royalist attack.

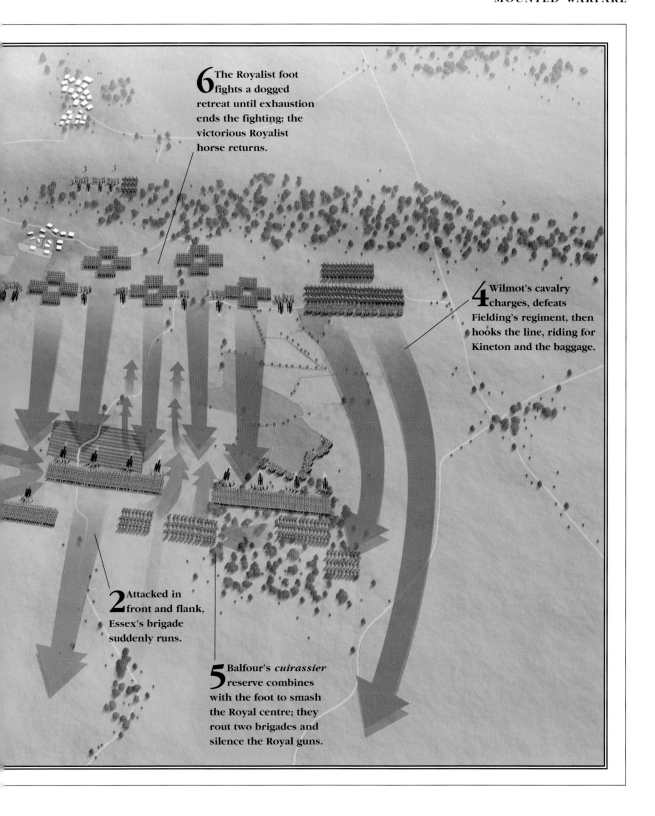

6 The Royalist foot fights a dogged retreat until exhaustion ends the fighting; the victorious Royalist horse returns.

4 Wilmot's cavalry charges, defeats Fielding's regiment, then hooks the line, riding for Kineton and the baggage.

2 Attacked in front and flank, Essex's brigade suddenly runs.

5 Balfour's *cuirassier* reserve combines with the foot to smash the Royal centre; they rout two brigades and silence the Royal guns.

known as Radway Brook, which must have caused further disruption. The whole wing appears to have taken this stream, and then spurred up the slope towards the waiting ranks of musketeers and carbine-armed troopers. The old tactical mounted-fire platform was about to prove futile as Ramsey's men fired their 'long peeces afarre off and without distance', which is to say they fired too soon, beyond the effective range of their carbines. In the firepower defence, fire had to be delivered at a range at which the majority of balls would not only hit a target, but would also penetrate, wound or kill. Ramsey's men did not have the experience or the nerve to hold their fire to the very close range necessary – or it is perhaps possible that some early shots led to a general discharge.

The men emptied their pieces when they could do little damage. After firing carbines, they drew pistols but these too seem to have been fired too soon or had little effect. It was a similar tale with the interlarded muskets, but with so few men in the firing rank their contribution would have been minimal.

Reverend Marshall wrote that 'our left wing, upon the second firing, fled basely'. It seems that only the second ranks had time to fire before the Royal horse was among them. Here was another feature of the so-called English System. By refusing firepower support the speed of the charge is increased and the time it takes to make contact reduced. There were no delays waiting for the foot to keep up, or to rein in to deliver a pistol volley.

The failure to fire at the proper time meant the Parliamentarians threw away their chance to use their firepower, but many of Ramsey's men fought on with their swords. However, the speed of the charge, the inability of the shot to cause significant casualties, as well as the ferocity of the impact, shook the nerve of his brave but inexperienced troops.

Exuberantly Impetuous

Ramsey's men were driven back until a rout spread through them. Once troops begin running it is very difficult to stop them but it was equally difficult to stop the victors pursuing them. Rupert appears to have led this pursuit and Bulstrode lays the error of this battlefield 'technique' at his door,

'the Prince being extreamly eager of this Advantage (which he knew better how to take than to keep) was not content with their Canon and keeping their Ground, but eagerly pursued the enemy, who fled on the other side of Keinton towards Warwick'. Despite Bulstrode's criticism, his own regiment joined in the chase. Nor did the second line resist the temptation, 'seeing none of the enemy's horse left, thought there was nothing more to be done but to pursue those that fled'. They 'could not be contained by their commander, but with spurs and loose reins followed the chase'. The way whole cavalry wings joined pursuits soon became a feature of this faster advance to contact, in which cohesion and control was sacrificed for the sake of impetus and shock.

Yet this was what the cavalry of the period were expected to do. By driving their opposite wing from the field they stopped them taking any further role in the action, and, if they could thoroughly scatter them it might take them out of the campaign. If they could rally themselves after sealing their victory they would have done their job and would seek less arduous tasks, like intercepting enemy reinforcements or seizing the enemy's baggage, horse lines or carriage park.

Contemporary military manuals state that an army whose horse had run would lose their communications, supply lines and war chest, and would surrender. The loss of Rupert's second line to the chase deprived the Royal army of half its cavalry reserve, but for a cavalry wing to defeat the enemy horse and switch attention elsewhere was unusual and it took the lessons of these English Civil Wars to make them understand the value of re-forming and returning. The chase did, however, do some good for the Royalist cause. Some routing cavalrymen made for their foot regiments as bastions of safety. Charles Essex's Brigade was engaged to its front by Royal infantry about to 'fall on', when some friendly horse broke through them, followed by their pursuers. With some of their own men already running to the

THE COMBINED ARMS *of cannon and cavalry look down on a company of Civil War pikemen whose steel-tipped ash pikes were used to protect musketeers from the cavalry.*

rear and the enemy horse coming into their brigade's flank, one by one the four regiments broke and ran, leaving Essex with a big gap and even bigger problem.

Most of the fleeing Parliamentarian horsemen and their pursuers reached the village of Kineton, where the Royalists fell upon the enemy baggage, despoiling coaches, carriages, carts and wagons. This was not the taking of the enemy's material of war as advocated by the military theorists, but plundering and taking booty. This pursuit, like so many of the age, degenerated into a rampage and a complete loss of discipline.

A similar fate awaited the Parliamentarian right wing. The horse on this side of the field were also arrayed to fight in the Dutch fire-based manner. Balfour who commanded this wing had three regiments of horse but they had been weakened by Essex's decision to form a cavalry reserve out of his 'heavies'. Essex compensated by increasing Balfour's

firepower, allocating both his dragoon regiments to skirmish among the gorse and briars on the right flank. He also saw to it that 'the best of our field pieces were planted upon our right wing'. Balfour also had the terrain in his favour. The right flank rested on another small stream, slightly deeper than Radway Brook, but also surrounded by bogs and tussocks. In 1642 this was a wet part of the heath, but the right flank of the little hill had a liberal

ARMOUR CHANGES ACROSS THE YEARS. *A) Shows Turkish and Mogul influences in early 17th-century Eastern European armour, which covers most of the upper body. B) By the middle of the 1600s the horse relied on simple back and breast plates, although the English developed the distinctive tri-bar cavalry pot helmet, with its articulated neck-guard. C) By the 1700s the helmet had been reduced to a steel skull-cap worn under the tricorn and body armour to the more ornate Prussian style, short cuirass; some nations even discarded the back plate altogether.*

A   B   C

scattering of gorse and the scrubland in front of it was crossed with ditches and water-courses. This was not cavalry country; it was difficult for all close-order troops but it was natural dragoon country.

Dragoons rode horses but they were not considered part of the cavalry. Their use was still in its infancy but these men were mounted infantry whose technique was to ride to their position, dismount, tether their horses and fight on foot, often in loose-order groups making what use they could of cover and terrain features. The ground here suited their battlefield role of securing the flanks of armies and breaking up cavalry attacks by enfilading their advance with shot from cover. Fighting as open-order skirmish troops they could also be deployed in advance of the line, and at Edgehill both Royalist cavalry wings were preceded by dragoons to prevent Essex's 'skirmishers' from disrupting them. One dragoon regiment on Balfour's wing suffered less than the other, which might mean they made it to their horses before the Royalist horse hit them. It seems Parliament's dragoons were outfought in the practice of dismounted skirmishing and quickly quit the field.

Hooking the Flank

On the Royalist left flank the Royalist horse Commander, Lord Wilmot, was trying another cavalry technique to overcome his enemy; that of hooking the flank. One deployment theory has Wilmot's brigade coming onto the battlefield down Sun Rising Hill, from where Wilmot would have had an excellent view of Essex's position and could have seen a way round his southern flank. As an experienced cavalry commander who understood mounted warfare he would have seen this tempting opportunity and begun his advance against Essex's right fully aware that he could overlap the outside flank, hook the position and fall upon the enemy's rear.

Their natural target would have been Balfour's two forward regiments, but Balfour seems to have withdrawn his first line behind the right wing brigade of foot, out of the target zone of Wilmot's charge. One argument is that they helped plug the gap left by the rout of Charles Essex's brigade. This apparently happened just as Wilmot's attack

veered south intent upon left-hooking the line, but there must also have been a tendency to shy away both from gorse bushes and cannon fire, and to avoid their own dismounted dragoons. In addition to these factors, riding across a slope usually causes a horse to pull sideways. Even though it goes forwards, it drifts off course. It cannot be certain that it was by design, but a significant part of Wilmot's command went to the left and around Parliament's flank, and did not make contact.

Eyewitness Nathaniel Fiennes wrote, 'I could never speak with any of our Army, that either saw any such number of horse, or could tell what they did, unlesse they went directly to Keynton to plunder the Carriages without charging our Army at all.' Still, part of Wilmot's command swept forwards on an angle and crashed into Fielding's regiment as it stood in Balfour's erstwhile second line. The Parliamentarians tried to fire carbines and pistols before drawing swords, and were hit stationary by double their numbers. Overwhelmed and broken, they fled, and Wilmot's troopers gave chase. The rout seems to have overtaken some dragoons, either trying to reach their horses, or only recently mounted.

Untrained and unprepared for a mounted melee, their retirement also turned to flight. As with the Rupert's wing we get a dramatic picture of swirling horsemen, both vanquished and victors, sweeping from the field as, on the other wing, the triumphant horse wreaked havoc among the foot. Fairfax's regiment, fired once but was then ridden into and broken.

Wilmot's second line, commanded by Lord Digby, joined the chase. This was the second half of the Royalist cavalry reserve, and this too was a waste of man and horsepower. The Parliamentarian right had been scattered, but so too had the Royal left. Wilmot's command broke into piecemeal ad hoc units. Wilmot had got himself involved in a fight around the Little Kineton enclosures while Digby went looting.

Sir Charles Lucas managed to do what the more advanced military theorists advocated. Pre-dating Cromwell's tactical reforms he managed to rally about 200 troopers from three different regiments into a provisional fighting force and resolved to bring them back into action. However, he selected one of those less arduous tasks and all he did was charge into the already running foot. One of his captains, John Smith, did recapture the Banner Royal in one incident, but even Lucas could not see beyond the prescribed maxim of keeping the enemy running. This was to prove a crucial factor in the battle, because with the Royalist horse victoriously leaving the field and the king ordering his Pensioners to escort his sons to safety, the only cavalry remaining on the field were Parliamentarian.

Bring on the Reserves

Essex had formed a cavalry reserve. By withdrawing all his *cuirassier* troops from their parent regiments he created a substantial body of well-armoured shock troops, capable of plugging a gap or making a decisive strike. The concentration of the *cuirassier* troops showed understanding of the essential differences between *cuirassiers* and the usual horse. Many of these men were also veterans of the Thirty Years' War and, like Rupert, they too knew of the speed and impact of a charge that did not have to wait for fire support.

At a crucial moment in the action, when Parliament's foot soldiers were hard pressed, Balfour committed part of this heavy reserve. Putting them into lines of troops he threw them into the very heart of the battle, against the king's foot. These troopers were well armoured gentlemen in complete *cuirassier* suits, mounted mostly on good horses from their own stables. This was a formidable body which, 'observing no horse to encounter withal, charged them with some loss from their pikes, tho very little from

FLAGS CARRIED BY *Civil War cavalry troops were usually painted silk or taffeta about .2 metres (two feet) square, had parti-coloured fringing and were very varied in design, often sporting political or personal references to valour or religion. These cornets were all captured by Essex when he defeated Sir Nicholas Crisp's force at Cirencester in 1643.*
Top left: An unknown captains troop.
Top right: Captain P Cooper's Troop.
Bottom left: Sir John Culpepper's Troop taken at Cirencester 1643.
Bottom right: Lord Henry Spencer's Troop taken at Cirencester 1643.

their shot'. But although they did not take too much damage their impact was insufficient to break into the Royal foot and they retreated to their former station.

Balfour then committed the rest of this reserve, exploiting a tactical error by Fielding's brigade, which had spread itself too thinly, exposing the flanks of one the elements of its brigade formation. Advancing on an angle into the flank and front of this disjointed formation, Balfour's heavy *cuirassiers* 'with great resolution...charged into the enemy's quarters'. One foot regiment was left isolated and Balfour's attack was able to concentrate upon it. He charged 'and breaking into it, cut most of it off; and after by the assistance of some of our foot, he defeated another regiment'.

By keeping a cavalry reserve, Parliament beat and ruined two foot regiments. Soon Fielding's whole brigade gave way and Balfour's troopers drove them from the fighting line. In their flight they swept away the men working the light guns and several Parliamentarian troopers carried out cavalry's most effective technique of silencing artillery; they dismounted and hammered horseshoe nails into the touchholes, rendering them useless. Some others cut down fleeing men, keeping the enemy going, but, unlike Rupert and Wilmot's 'cavaliers' they did not get involved in the traditional undisciplined foxhunt for the baggage. The majority rallied, gathered prisoners of quality, and abandoned colours and personal trophies. They made their way back to their own lines and the safety of the re-forming ranks of the other half of the Reserve.

Among those who did not rally back was Balfour himself. Following their commander, he and a group of companions went on the tactical offensive and headed for the main Royalist six-gun battery on the slopes of Edgehill. They charged into its flank, scattering its guard of firelocks and its gunners. Having no nails to spike the pieces they cut the horse traces and rope traction harnesses, which were used to re-position the heavy guns after firing. Despite other adventures, the lack of any enemy cavalry reserve meant they too got back to their own lines in time to re-form, re-order and rest.

Left on the field with no other horse to oppose them, this *cuirassier* force was able to take part in other dramatic actions. Assisting the foot in a combined-arms attack they smashed into the flank of more weakened Royal pike blocks including those of the two best regiments on the field. Aided by the foot they drove them back, broke them and scattered them. Then again, late in the day they also charged into some Royalist horse struggling back onto the field. Free to roam and throw its powerful mass at any target directed by its commander it made the vital difference, turning Parliament's inconclusive infantry victory into a decisive army victory. Both sides fought each other to a standstill but Essex won the fight and his reserve of heavy horse had won him the day.

Towards nightfall the triumphant Royalist horse began returning to the field, expecting to see a victorious Royal army; they found it beaten and battered, dug in along the Radway Brook. Both Rupert's and Wilmot's horse were too dispersed, too tired and too late to do anything. They may have won fights on their respective wings but their failure to rally afterwards lost the Battle of Edgehill. They had successfully proved the English charge as a fight-winning weapon, but by failing to capitalize upon its superiority in horse-versus-horse combat, they had transformed it into a battle-losing technique.

It was a lesson not wasted on those who witnessed or took part in it. In July 1643, both Byron

> *'When the cavalry charges, one cannot impress on it enough the need to keep closed up together, and not pursue in a scatter....One should set off at a slow trot for a hundred paces; speed it up as the distance narrows...'*
>
> — DE SAXE

JOHN CHURCHILL, DUKE OF MARLBOROUGH (1650–1722), is portrayed wearing full cavalry armour. One of the greatest generals of his era, he delivered victories for the allies at Blenheim (1704), Ramillies (1706) and Oudenaarde (1708). This portrait was painted by Adriaen van der Werff Holland (1659–1722).

go again was elevated to a disciplined art by Oliver Cromwell and his 'Ironsides' and became a battle-winning factor of the later conflicts of the English Civil Wars, notably Marston Moor. The successful use of the unsupported, shock-action mounted arm in the middle of the seventeenth century did not result in a worldwide abandonment of cavalry firearms but it did help implant the belief that the charge could overcome firepower, if undetaken with spirit, determination and discipline.

Ramillies 1706: Cavalry en Masse

In the late 1600s spirit and determination were the hallmarks of the French cavalry, reputedly the finest in Europe. The exemplary bravery and steadfastness under fire of Louis XIV's mounted *Maison Roi* (Household troops) took disciplined horse action to new levels of proficiency, effectively combining firepower and shock action in a well practised and executed drill that was spread to the rest of the French horse. Their technique, honed in long wars with the Dutch, the Imperialists and the English, was a return to the caracole, but performed with better training and more reliable weapons.

The French return to firepower influenced western Europe's cavalry commanders. Most cavalrymen of the early eighteenth century carried two pistols and a sword, while some, including the Dragoons, had carbines as well. Although still outranged and easily shot down by infantry regiments the French horse still preferred

and Wilmot successfully drove their Parliamentarian opposition off the field at Roundway Down, rallied their commands and returned to the fray to pin and then destroy Waller's army. The ability to re-form and

using its firepower to disrupt enemy cavalry before going in with the sword. They would form a column of troops, or if space permitted column of squadrons, and advance towards their foe at a slow trot. At about 50 metres (54 yards) from the enemy they drew their first pistol and fired.

Replacing it in the saddle holster they drew the second and at about 25 metres (27 yards) fired that too. They then wheeled about, usually by ranks, and retreated back to a safe distance to reload before coming forward to repeat the process. Then the other troops performed the same manoeuvre. Despite better manufacture, pistols were still inaccurate and only effective at close range. When the moment to switch to shock impact came the first body would advance and fire as before, but after 20 metres (22 yards) the troopers would replace their second pistol, draw sword and keep going at the same slow trot until they reached the enemy lines. The charge was cohesive with none of its energy dissipated by a loss of order or variation in speed, and being delivered in close order, with riders boot-to-boot, it had the impact of a mobile wall. Once in melee the French would chop and hack their way through the enemy mass. The discipline and courage of the French made them unquestionably formidable in this demanding technique.

The Allied answer to this lay in encouraging the men to get to grips with an enemy and kill him. They rejected the formal delivery of fire, stayed out of effective range until the time for close combat, and left it to the individual to use his pistols in emergencies. They followed the English System and, relying on swords, went forwards, increasing their speed from a walk, through the slow trot and then crashed into the enemy, similarly boot-to-boot, but at the 'fast trot'. Having more impetus than the slow trot they had greater impact, and the second rank arriving shortly after

'My Lord, I never saw better horses, better clothes, finer belts and accoutrements; but money…will buy clothes and fine horses, but it can't buy that lively air I see in every one of these troopers' faces.'

— EUGEN, PRINCE OF SAVOY

the first imparted a secondary surge. Although not the canter of the English Civil Wars or the galloping charge of the Polish, they still hit their foes at speed, often bowling their opposition over. One innovation of the Allies was the breeding of large and powerful warhorses, kept well fed and groomed so as to be in the best condition for battle. Prince Eugene, a great Imperialist comander, was not the only senior military officer to remark upon the excellent condition of the English, Danish and Dutch horses. The impact of this disciplined moving wall of big men on big horses caused disruption and confusion in opponents; yet through training and experience they maintained their own close order. This meant that in the fighting two men could often face one, which was a distinct advantage. Then, when order broke down in the pell-mell, they could reach for their unfired pistols.

Jammed tightly together they did not need their hands on their reins, so with sword in one hand and pistol in the other they now had two weapons to one. This was another distinct advantage, especially as the range was now point-blank and pistols very effective. An empty pistol could be simply be thrown, used as a club or even just used as a threat. One English source recommends thrusting the muzzle into an enemy's face before firing becacuse man with a pistol thrust into his face is not to know that it is empty. This would cause an involuntary flinch or moment of hesitation during which instant the blade could find an opening. The wicked steel swords could be used to cut off slices of flesh or the hilt pommel brought down on the forehead of an opponent's horse, giving a stunning blow.

The gentlemen of the *Maison Roi* were experts in the stylish execution of their opponents. It could be argued that they were not accustomed to the savage butchery of the back street, of the style of the gutter-fighters in the Allied ranks; but that is doubtful. In the middle of the seventeenth century there had been an emphasis upon the melee technique of slashing at the head of the horse, to cut the bridle and cause the bit to fall from the mouth to make control difficult. In the early eighteenth century melee cavalrymen were often jammed so tightly together that horsemanship was less of a factor. The Allies placed more emphasis upon cutting at the man's head and face than that of his steed as a facial wound, although seldom mortal, would be distressing psychologically, both to the victim and his companions, and a man with blood streaming into his eyes from a head gash was effectively disabled.

Another major factor influenced mounted warfare. Contemporary drill books taught cavalry commanders to exercise their units not only in this combination of pistol and sword attacks, but also in techniques for the co-operation of horse and foot acting together. Rupert and then Cromwell in the English System had their cavalry operate independently of the foot, but while it could be highly successful in attack it had little to recommend it defensively. It was also found that when both sides were matched in numbers and quality, this independent technique often resulted in a massive stalemate as neither side had the ability or the tactical advantage to break the other; and in these situations the tenacity and spirit of the French usually prevailed.

This emphasis on combined arms was not a rejection of the English System in favour of the Swedish, but a hybrid technique created by uniting the two. Cavalry operations now involved the sword in offence and the musket in defence; English in attack and Swedish in defence. The French and the Allied styles were to clash in the War of Spanish Succession and the best example

> *'The Duke of Marlborough would allow the Horse but three charges of powder and ball to each man for a campaign, and that only for guarding their horses when at grass, and not to be made use of in action.'*
>
> — GENERAL KANE

is the struggle between Marlborough and Villeroi at Ramillies in 1706. Scouting was not something that regular cavalry of this period did well, and on this occasion the two armies only discovered each other when they converged on the same campsite. They were too close for either to withdraw safely, so both Marlborough and Villeroi deployed for battle. Marlborough had an expansive plain on his left and a river valley on his right. He deployed Overkirk with the majority of the Dutch and Danish horse on his left and Lumley's Dutch and English horse on his far right. His centre, placed upon the eastern high ground of the valley of the Little Gheete, was made up of two lines of brigades of infantry of various nationalities, but his English redcoats were on his extreme right under the Earl of Orkney. Cadogan, his Quartermaster-General, also told Marlborough of a lateral fold in his defensive ridge, in which ran the small stream of the Quivelette. It was to play an important part in the cavalry battle to come.

Also important to the cavalry action was the topography of the southern part of the field. Here the French right was secured by the Mehaine River and the marshes of its tributaries, but it was broad, rolling, open country, almost a natural arena unbroken by obstacles and bounded by the village of Ramilles to the north and Taviers to the south.

Both French and Allied deployments were classical for the day. For the French this arena was allotted to General Guiscard with 82 squadrons of horse, dragoons and the entire French Household Cavalry, including the famous *Gens d'Armes*. Their right appeared to be a mass of horsemen, although they had five units of infantry in support. Their 68 squadrons of horse were drawn up in three lines. The first two had foot deployed alternately with the cavalry for firepower support, while the third, acting as the reserve, comprised only cavalry.

Their right flank was covered by a command of 14 squadrons of dragoons and some Swiss infantry set slightly towards the rear and angled outwards. Opposite them stood 48 squadrons of Dutch horse drawn up in two lines, with two lines of Allied infantry directly behind them. As his reserve Overkirk deployed Württemberg's 21 squadrons of Danish cavalry to their left rear, bringing the combined strength to 69 squadrons facing Guiscard's 82.

A Grand French Plan

French sources say that Villeroi had a grand cavalry plan. His massive cavalry arm was to sweep forwards and, using their pistols, soften up the numerically inferior Allies. They would then fall on with the sword and drive Overkirk's men from the field, using the interspaced infantry to give them firepower and recovery time if it were needed. Having dispersed the Allied horse they would divide. Some were to pursue the retreating horse while others swung left into the Allied line and rolled it up from the south. Lumley's cavalry, on the Allied right, would not have room nor time to deal with the envelopment, while a general advance of the French infantry was to keep the English foot facing front until the time came for their inevitable withdrawal. Then the horse would have their day, cutting them down and turning the retreat into a spectacular rout. A fitting revenge for Blenheim, the plan did not envisage a cavalry defeat. To Marlborough an infantry engagement appeared fraught with problems including wet ground and enemy entrenchments. The cavalry option looked a better chance, if something could be done to equalize the numbers. This meant switching Lumley's cavalry from the right to the left where their numbers and surprise appearance would make a significant difference. This hinged upon the French not knowing that Lumley was coming. The odds could also be shifted in the Allies' favour by taking Taviers and turning the French right.

Shortly before 3 PM the first part of this plan was put into action as the Dutch Guard took Taviers after a savage struggle. Its fall meant guns could be brought up and that the massive French cavalry force could be enfiladed; scything them

STRANGELY, IN THE LATE *17th century both the flag and the officer who carried it were called cornets. This one is shown 'dipping' or saluting on a special occasion that merits rosette ribbons being plaited into the horse's mane. This was limited to important parade duties.*

down where they stood. This caused some panic among the French staff and a large counter-attack was ordered. They sent the nearest troops they had to recover the village. Eight battalions of infantry and 14 squadrons of dragoons that had been posted as firepower support and reserves for the cavalry wing were despatched to the task.

Dragoons were still looked upon as mounted infantry and were paid as such. But although trained to fight on foot they saw themselves cavalrymen and many wore the riding boots of the horse. Sending these men to attack Dutch Foot Guards entrenched in a village was optimistic. They dismounted, sent their horses a considerable distance to the rear and pushed forwards with their carbines across the Mehaigne Marsh in a right-hook counter-attack on Taviers. The ground was very boggy, and wearing big, stiff, cavalry

Battle of Ramillies

1706

Villeroi and Marlborough both intended to camp around the village of Ramillies but the French arrived first and formed a defensive line. The battle opened with the Dutch Guards taking Taviers, which protected Villeroi's right flank; French infantry and dragoons, intended to support the cavalry, then made an unsuccessful attempt to retake it. The Allied line attacked, putting great pressure on the French centre and left, drawing in the remaining infantry meant to support the cavalry. When the cavalry melee began, the Danish cavalry attacked the left of the fighting, turning the French flank, and Marlborough switched his right-wing cavalry down a hidden valley to reinforce his hard-pressed left. After a long struggle the Allies stormed Ramillies, and when the Danes charged the exposed flank of the unsupported cavalry the French right collapsed. Despite Villeroi trying to organize a second position, the Allies rolled forwards, turning the French withdrawal into a rout.

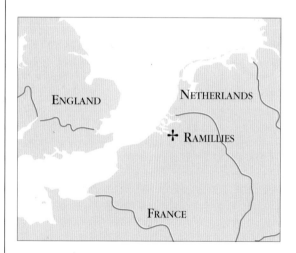

Ramillies is in Belgium, about 24km (15 miles) south-east of Wavre and 19km (12 miles) north of Namur. The battle was fought over rolling countryside. Now farmland with larger villages, it is still easily accessible and has changed little.

5 Marlborough's right wing of horse joins the great melee via a hidden valley. Outnumbered and flank-charged by the re-formed Danes, the French collapse.

7 Villeroi tries to form a second position but it is overrun by an Allied general advance and a rout ensues.

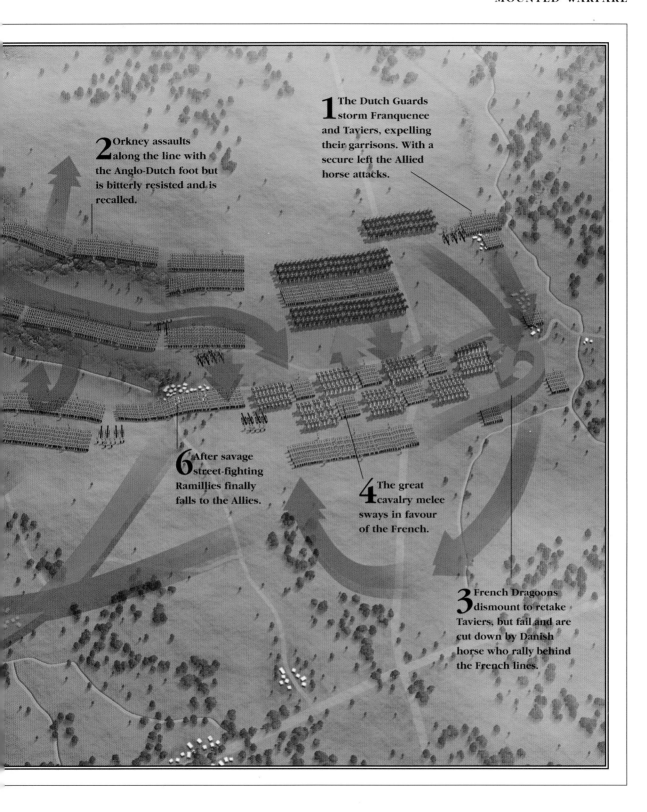

2 Orkney assaults along the line with the Anglo-Dutch foot but is bitterly resisted and is recalled.

1 The Dutch Guards storm Franquenee and Taviers, expelling their garrisons. With a secure left the Allied horse attacks.

6 After savage street-fighting Ramillies finally falls to the Allies.

4 The great cavalry melee sways in favour of the French.

3 French Dragoons dismount to retake Taviers, but fail and are cut down by Danish horse who rally behind the French lines.

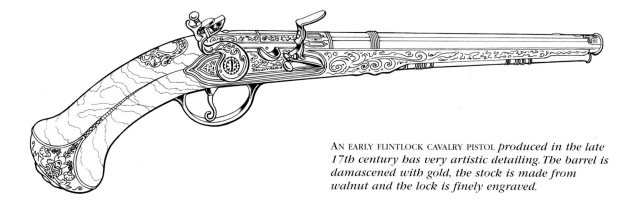

AN EARLY FLINTLOCK CAVALRY PISTOL *produced in the late 17th century has very artistic detailing. The barrel is damascened with gold, the stock is made from walnut and the lock is finely engraved.*

boots rather than the dragoon gaiters of a few years later, they got stuck. They appear to have attacked in two dismounted waves emulating cavalry tactics but those in the first wave who reached the village were shot to pieces by muskets with longer range. The dragoons fled.

Their infantry support fared better and were joined by the dragoons' second wave, led on by their commander d'Aubigni but he was soon killed. Although this combined attack got into Taviers, it was repulsed after a desperate battle. The fleeing dragoons and infantry crashed into and disordered the second infantry attack, which also broke and ran when fired upon. The serried ranks of French cavalry could only watch in dismay as the broken dragoons and their own erstwhile infantry support scrambled out of the marshes in disorder. The use of dragoons on foot had not proved a success.

Concealed Movement
On the right wing an attack by Orkney had caused a northwards shift along the French line. Some French infantry that had begun the battle around Ramillies as support for the horse had been moved northwards to replace battalions drawn into action against Orkney. But no matter how many squadrons Lumley had, they were never going to cross the Little Gheete to support Orkney, and leaving horse where they could not be used was a waste of precious resources. Marlborough sent to Lumley for the majority of his cavalry to wheel sharply to their left and move off unseen down the shallow Quivelette valley towards the centre. It was a

calculated risk and it took some time to effect, but it was done well and in good order. This shift left only four squadrons to support Orkney, but the movement had been well hidden and the French had no reason to suspect they were no longer in position. When the first 18 squadrons of Lumley's command arrived, Marlborough had enough horsemen to risk undertaking a melee en masse with the best cavalry in Europe.

Despite the failure of the French dragoons and their infantry to retake Taviers, the French decided the moment had come for their cavalry to be let loose. Reduced in number from 82 to 68 squadrons by the loss of the Dragoons, the combined French cavalry arm rolled forwards into Overkirk's 69. A cavalry charge on such a scale had seldom been seen before. Literally thousands of horsemen walked and then slow-trotted forwards, boot to boot. This was no furious charge, as beloved of Hollywood, but a steady steamroller of an advance. It seemed set to flatten everything in its path, that is, until it met the Dutch cavalry going in the opposite direction.

They too came on, led by Overkirk, in lines four deep, and the two sides crashed into one another at the recommended good round trot, spilling men from the saddle and knocking horses over and sideways in the crush. A furious melee ensued with both sides' reserves cannoning into the rear of their own formations and sending shock waves of impetus through the densely packed mass. The Dutch gradually got the upper hand, but Guiscard still had some of the infantry Villeroi had placed in between the squadrons, and these were able to fire as their own horse fell back through the gaps to their flanks. Under this musketry cover the French Household cavalry withdrew, re-formed and then went in again. The Dutch also re-formed and trotted forwards to absorb the shock. The huge struggling mass swayed to and fro.

With Taviers in Allied hands the Danish Cavalry was able to swing round the extreme left of this surging melee. Before them they saw the defeated relief force struggling back from Taviers, and led by Württemberg, 21 squadrons of Danish horse charged forwards to ride them down. This was the headlong charge of a pursuit, unlike the ordered advance into contact. They swept on, dispersed the disordered mass easily and even broke the remaining battalion of reserve infantry. They had performed sterling service and had got round the French flank. Here was the perfect left hook as earlier demonstrated by Wilmot at Edgehill, but unlike his force of some 64 years earlier the Danes had the discipline to exploit the feat tactically. The Danes rallied around a landmark, the tomb of Ottomond, and re-formed their line facing north. They had completely turned the French right and were now angled against the right rear of Villeroi's whole line.

The last 48 squadrons of Dutch cavalry held in the centre and refused to be pushed back by the desperate efforts of the 68 squadrons of French, Spanish and Walloon horse. The massive melee was emptying saddles quickly but so were the infantry of both sides falling as they stood in its midst. The whole affair hung in the balance and nearly cracked in favour of the French when, despite being inadequately supported, the *Maison du Roi* broke through two lines of Dutch just south of Ramillies and appeared to be on the point of bursting through the whole Allied line. They ran into four regiments of foot deftly placed by Marlborough himself, who then moved his headquarters to the slope directly opposite Ramillies so he could observe both the northern and southern sections of the field. The cream of the French cavalry was checked by the textbook combination of horse and foot. Every time they gained an advantage and caused their opposite number to fall back, their Dutch foes did so between the gaps in the supporting infantry line, allowing the muskets to go to work on the

French. 'The foot on both sides often stopped the squadrons in their career' but there were not enough French foot to stop them everywhere.

Charge and Counter-Charge

On the French side too many of the horse's supporting infantry units had been drawn off to the north to go to the assistance of their fellows in resisting Orkney's attack. Even the Swiss and the Bavarian reserves had been wasted on Taviers. The absence of foot support began to manifest in other ways. Horse and foot had been deployed alternately in the French lines, not in ranks as in the Allied deployment. Now the infantry had largely departed the line was no longer solid. It had huge intervals, and the Dutch cavalry poured through them.

Face to face the elite French had the better of the Dutch, and their superior numbers meant that relieving units were always on hand to replace a beaten or blown squadron. But the Dutch were able to fall upon their flanks and even on the rear of some squadrons, which redressed the balance. Squadrons charged, fell back, re-formed and went in again and again. Yet again the bravery of the *Maison du Roi* caused the Allied horse problems for they 'repulsed, renversed and then put in great disorder' ten Dutch squadrons. With the Danish Reserve gone, the Allied horse did not have the numbers to counter the quality and they began to give ground on their right. They fell back and the line looked as if it might break. It was a crisis, made worse because as the Dutch horse fell back so they uncovered the left of the whole Allied line. If the French drove them back further then their supports could sweep into the infantry's flank and roll up the line. Marlborough had no choice but to throw in Lumley's troops as they came up.

The valley of the Quivelette opened onto the plain in the right rear of the grand cavalry melee. Placing himself at the head of the 18 newly arrived squadrons, Marlborough personally took them in. Their unexpected arrival caused the backwards-moving mass to halt. He returned to his slope in time to see the second command of 21 squadrons arrive from Lumley on the right. He collected and led them into the melee; into a mass of some 25,000 fighting horsemen. There was wave upon

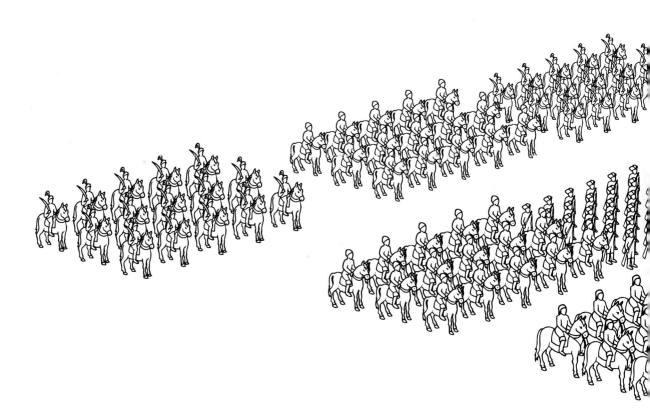

wave of charging and counter-charging cavalrymen all hacking, thrusting and slashing at each other in the passionate grip of bloodlust. Marlborough was caught up in the fighting for at least 20 minutes until he realized the crisis was over. It was now a matter of time and attrition.

The Allies were now winning the cavalry struggle, with a numerical superiority of 87 to 68 squadrons, and a further 21 lining up to deliver a flank charge. The Allied horse drove the French back. They were now aligned some 45 degrees to their original position with Ramillies acting as the pivot on which they hung, but still they would not break. Weary and nearing exhaustion, both sides did their best to re-form and reorder their ranks. Urgent dispatches brought up the remaining reserves from anywhere they could be found and then Overkirk began to wheel the entire mass to its right towards the regrouping French.

Just after 6.00pm, as part of Marlborough's order for a general advance, some of the guns that had battered Ramillies opened up on the French cavalry, obliging them to move. They went forward and were caught up once again in a heaving mass of men with flashing blades and cracking pistols, horses kicking and biting. But numbers began to tell and the French were slowly driven back. The French Household cavalry had done their best and lived up to their fame, but after nearly two hours of charging and counter-charging, hacking it out and then falling back to re-form, they were finally being overwhelmed, and were now fighting with intervals between their squadrons. The Allied horse, whose line was complete, pinned them frontally and surged through the gaps to surround and annihilate them.

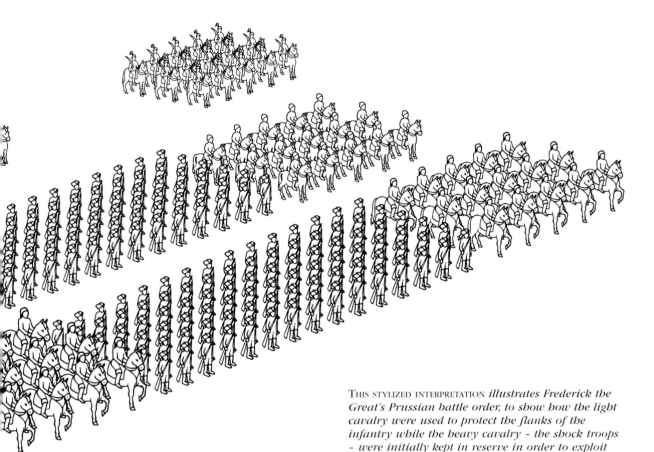

THIS STYLIZED INTERPRETATION *illustrates Frederick the Great's Prussian battle order, to show how the light cavalry were used to protect the flanks of the infantry while the heavy cavalry - the shock troops - were initially kept in reserve in order to exploit any advantage gained.*

Collapse and Flight

Rested and re-formed, the 21 Danish squadrons to the south-west, flanked the struggling French, who needed to re-form their line to face this new menace. Orders to form at ninety degrees to their first position on a slope behind Ramillies were dispatched but could not be completed. The Danes charged and the Allies, sensing victory, unleashed their final effort, driving into them and capturing the kettledrums of the *Maison du Roi*. What infantry was left to hold the backward push was too little to resist the overwhelming weight of numbers and they were soon disordered by their own retreating men. Then they were ridden down by the Allies.

The Danish reserve squadrons launched themselves into the flank as well, and that was the end. The French horse broke and what was left of the great French cavalry streamed to the rear, hotly pursued by the reasonably fresh Danish horse and such of the more intrepid Allied cavalrymen whose mounts were not blown. The mass of broken cavalry became indiscriminately mixed with the infantry fleeing from Ramillies, and the southern region of the plateau of Mont St Andre became a confused crowd of men struggling in an attempt to reach safety somewhere.

On the northern flank meanwhile Orkney assaulted once more, and the brave Frenchmen who had held Autre Eglise all day retreated. The one remaining English cavalry brigade Marlborough had not moved to the centre now appeared behind the French, having somehow got across a more northern portion of the marshy stream. Not bothering to re-form they went forward 'a la hussarde, sword in hand and at a gallop' and slammed into the retreating infantry. Those not cut or ridden down threw down their weapons and surrendered, but as these dragoons moved off, large numbers of resentful French picked up their muskets and opened fire. The troopers turned and charged back into them, chopping down every last man with a weapon in his hands.

There followed a classic cavalry pursuit. Behind Ramillies and facing north-west the huge conglomeration of Allied cavalry rolled forwards. No attempt was made to preserve formations and as they moved forwards sabres flashed and cut down straggling infantry. They rode through the abandoned French encampment, which further disrupted them and added yet more difficulties to any attempt at command and control. This loss of control meant the measured trot advance was abandoned and the whole thing lurched into a fast trot, then a canter and finally into a wild gallop. Behind them the Allied foot formed into columns of battalions in line and set out after their foe.

Villeroi struggled to form a second position on the ridgeline between Offus and St Andre. Amid panic the French and their allies tried to restore their order and their line in order to stop Marlborough's triumphant general assault. With infantry on their flank, their baggage making order impossible, and their own men running through them, the French stood to receive the charge of the jubilant Allied horse.

The Danish were the first to strike. They piled into the Bavarians and brushed them aside, chasing them off in the direction of Thorembais. The rest of the line baulked at the prospect of meeting the Dutch and English horsemen, and the whole 50 squadrons from the left wing 'who had not yet struck a blow, were seized with panic, and

'The enemyes Horse clearly abandoned their Foot, and our Dragoons…made a treble slaughter of the enemy. The French King's own regiment of Foot, called the Regiment du Roy, begged for quarter and delivered on their arms and delivered up their colours…'

– JOHN MARSHALL DEANE

rode in terror through the flying infantry whose retreat they had been drawn up to protect'. General Wood led a disordered charge. This caused the new French centre to collapse in minutes and scattered the new French Headquarters. '…the Elector himself and Marshal de Villeroy were in the crowd and not ten yards from me…they narrowly escaped.' It had been a long hard struggle but the cavalry had won the day. It was hailed in the pamphlets and newspapers as a marvellous victory for the mounted arm and Marlborough's sagacious order to limit the number of pistol balls allocated to each cavalryman was highly praised. His success and the dramatic break through on the flank re-affirmed the reliance upon cold steel. But the euphoria masked the real technique that won Ramillies: the successful combination of firepower, foot and mounted shock.

When working together properly they could not be broken, even by the bravest and most determined horse. The Allies won because the French stripped themselves of this firepower and allowed the Dutch and English to infiltrate their lines through the gaps their absent supports vacated. The Danish horse delivered the coup de grace, but not before 'sword and musket' had already defeated 'sword and pistol'.

Minden, 1757: Glorious Folly
We have already discussed the necessity of keeping warhorses in good condition if they were to fulfil expectations on campaign and in battle. Following sound advice is made a lot simpler once rules have been set down in print, and regulations issued to everyone to follow. The mid-eighteenth century saw an explosion of this mentality and the cavalry were not spared.

FREDERICK'S PRUSSIAN DRAGOONS *disperse some French infantry at the Battle of Minden on 1 August 1759 during the Seven Years' War. This illustration is taken from a 19th-century drawing after Karl Deucker.*

The perception of the cavalry as the elite, glorious arm was encouraged by the media of the day and pamphlets were full of their exploits, often with a certain amount of embroidery. But the press also produced a flurry of material describing and commenting on the cavalry. The numbers of handbooks available to aspiring young cavalry officers in the middle of the eighteenth century were legion. We can learn about almost every aspect of a cavalryman's life from such books and can thus appreciate the techniques used to keep men and mounts healthy and in fighting trim.

A cavalryman's life was very busy, even while off active duty. His most time-consuming activity was referred to as 'stables', which meant looking after his horse. In the 1740s there were two daily sessions in the stables, usually at 8 AM and 4 PM. The

horses were watered and fed according to each regiment's prescribed pattern and most had two waterings in summer. Then the cavalrymen went through whatever grooming method was laid down. This always included combing manes and tails, and NCO-supervised inspections of hooves and rubbing of heels. The horses were taken out to exercise twice daily and twice a week were saddled and ridden. Nobody was permitted to miss stables. Officers were expected to be present and corporal punishment was inflicted on any trooper who dodged his duty to care for his horse.

Similar regulations applied to care of the men. If the cavalry was to be considered an elite then they had to look and behave like one both in public and on the field of battle. Patrols were sent to inns and public houses to round up drunken cavalry and get them back to billets. Barracks were beginning to be built and officers were instructed to make sure fires and candles were extinguished in both the horses' stables and the men's sleeping quarters. 'Airings' of stalls and beds were set up along with kit inspections, which included checks on personal cleanliness and laundry. The trouble with elitism, however, is that it can cause alienation and resentment in partnerships that were once very solid. In the early years of the century Ramillies may have proved the cavalry to be a battle-winning arm, but they did it in co-operation with their foot, something that tended to get forgotten in the mid-eighteenth century.

The Duke of Marlborough's decisive battles and especially the roles played in them by the Allied cavalry at Blenheim, Ramillies and Oudenarde, caught the imagination of public and military men alike. They sent out a signal for the return to shock-melee emphasis, linked to the employment of cavalry 'en masse'. In order to field this amount of cavalry, dragoons were classed as horse and relinquished their mounted-infantry role. Dragoons became horse and the mounted charge and close combat became their prime battlefield technique. All over Europe large cavalry forces were formed, with Fredrick the Great of Prussia encapsulating the philosophy of the aggressive cavalry offensive in his famous instructions:

> *As for the cavalry attack, I have considered it necessary to make it so fast and so close for more than one reason: so that this large movement will carry the coward along with the brave man, so that the cavalryman will not have time to reflect so that the power of our big horses and their speed will certainly overthrow whatever tries to resist them, and to deprive the simple cavalryman of any influence in the decision of such a big affair. So long as the line is contiguous and the squadrons well closed...the enemy, being more open than we are and having more intervals, is unable to resist our shock. The force of our shock is double theirs, because they have many flanks and we have only one which the general protects to the extent possible, and finally because the fury of our attack disconcerts them. If they fire they will take to flight; if they attack at a slow trot they are overthrown; if they wish to come at us with the same speed...they come in confusion and we defeat them in detail.*

Frederick was also keenly aware of important changes happening in eastern Europe that were to influence cavalry tactics and the use of the horse in campaigns. Those of us living off the west coast of the continental land mass tend to forget that much of Russia, Austria, Poland and the Balkans tend to face east and their fighting was influenced by their powerful neighbours, the Ottoman Empire. Although the Turks used considerable numbers of heavy cavalry they were often used in ways other than the massed charge. They pioneered a revolution in the use of speed, dispersal and harassment; indeed what they brought about was the creation of the light cavalry.

Reappearance of the Light Cavalry

The arrival of the hussar was potentially another winning move, but initially their value on the battlefield was to prove limited, especially in the charge-fixated West. Clouds of horsemen may look daunting as they swirl around the flanks or get into the rear and sack the baggage. And on campaign they were invaluable. In eastern Europe

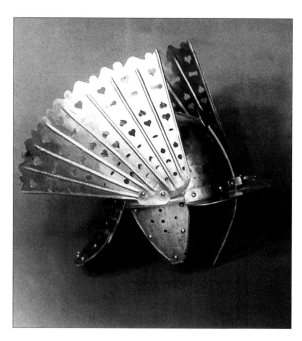

THE POLES WERE RELUCTANT *to give up their distinctive, evocative dress, especially their helmets, as this 18th-century Polish winged helmet shows. The decorative wings make the wearer look more impressive.*

Turkish Soldier (c. 1690)

The Ottoman army contained much light cavalry. Wearing their own clothes, unencumbered by armour and often riding good horses, they proved a swift asset to the campaign. However, they varied in quality and desire to fight. Some were regulars while others were pressed into service. Still others joined simply for booty. They preferred to fight in loose formation rather like a swarm, surrounding and containing their enemies, then picking at their flanks and rear with bows, pistols or light lances. The deadly curved scimitars were drawn to chase broken troops from the field, their slicing arcs cutting down fleeing horsemen and infantry alike. Being so numerous and so fast their attacks were sometimes described as 'Turkish Storms' and mounted soldiers of this type served the sultans for centuries.

the Ottoman light cavalry and the Cossacks led various enemies a tortuous dance and the combination of missile and horse mobility in the horse archer, so devastating during the ancient period, was a serious threat. But the peoples who could have exploited this resented being organized and controlled. Once again it was the Poles who appear to have reached a compromise in their technique and brought large numbers of light horse into their armies, although they too still prized the heavies highly.

Western European armies gradually accepted light cavalry into their ranks. They were cheap and, often treated as mercenaries, could fend for themselves. Looked down upon as not proper cavalry they were often relegated to patrol duties and kept out of the line of battle, unleashed in raids upon civilian populations, or let loose to create mayhem in a pursuit. Light cavalry, hussars and foreign dragoons in particular, soon came to be regarded as little better than bandits who would prey on friend and foe alike. It took the genius of a man like Frederick to bring them into his army properly.

After the initial disaster of his cavalry's poor performance at the Battle of Mollwitz in 1741, Frederick spent time, money and energy restructuring and retraining his mounted arm. Throughout his campaigns and battles he placed great faith in the battle-winning charge. His two famous cavalry generals, Wilhelm von Seydlitz of the heavy cavalry and Hans von Ziethen of the light, showed the success of his reforms. Frederick forbade the use of firearms by the cavalry and these men perfected the galloping charge *en haie* (in line). Whether heavy or light,

> '*Their usual method of fighting is to envelop an enemy squadron, and to scare it by their cries and varied movements…. They have very short stirrups and keep their spurs close to their horses' flanks forcing them to move faster than the heavy cavalry…they are dangerous to fugitives…but cannot hold their own against a squadron in full battle order.*'
>
> — 'PÈRE' R.P. DANIEL

their principal battlefield role was to charge the enemy at full gallop. They relied entirely on speed, discipline, aggression and shock action. This technique was repeatedly imprinted upon the minds of cavalry commanders across Europe throughout the War of Austrian Succession, 1740–1748. The Poles may have been heard to say, 'we told you so', but the Seven Years' War, 1756–63, was to provide the lessons in firepower that well drilled musketeers were able to provide.

Preliminaries

In the preliminaries to the Battle of Minden the Allied army of Prince Ferdinand of Brunswick had been manoeuvring on the line of the Weser trying to deny the French a route into Hanover. The French managed to get across the river, took Minden and concentrated there. Ferdinand needed to force the French Marshal de Contades into a field action before he could break out and put his superior numbers to use. Ferdinand advanced in dramatic style upon the French and deployed, offering battle on the plain of Minden. The opening phases of the battle involved the cavalry in probing and seizing various villages and advantageous tactical features, including high ground and causeways in an area that was notoriously boggy.

The following account of the battle, as before, focuses on the cavalry tactics employed. Both sides made a general deployment forming their lines on a giant right angle conforming to the ground between the Bastau marsh and the River Weser. The French line ran north-east from Hahlen to Maulbeerkamp and turned sharply east across the front of Kutenhausen to rest its right on the Weser. The force facing west was commanded by de Contades and the north-facing force by de Broglie. Opposite them Ferdinand held a line from Hartum to Stemmer while von Wangenheim faced de Broglie. The story involves that western portion of the field where Lord Sackville's cavalry formed the right of Ferdinand's line and the Duc de Fitzjames' cavalry had the centre of de Contades' force.

The battle opened around 5 PM with a clash between von Wangenheim's and de Broglie's corps and they remained embroiled together in firefights and cavalry melees all day. Both sides seemed evenly matched and fought doggedly.

On the western side of the field the battle commenced with an artillery duel around Hahlen, until at about 7 AM a misunderstood order set off the advance of an Allied column of attack commanded by von Sporcken and containing six battalions of British foot and two of Hanoverian guards. As they marched the morning mist lifted to reveal that they were heading directly towards the centre of the French line, where stood the elite French cavalry. The order for this has been blamed upon a confusion arising between German- and English-speaking officers, but it was an extraordinary move, especially as Sackville's cavalry was not supporting them. Ferdinand tried to halt the advance.

Opposite them the French horsemen must have stared in surprise. They watched the line halt

OVER THE EARLY MODERN *period the horse carried a variety of cavalry swords and sabres. Some were decorative, others purely practical. Some were designed for thrusting, some for slicing while others were simply for hacking and smashing.*
A. German Katzbalger *c. 1520.*
B. Two-edged Venetian Shiavona, *c. 1570.*
C. French cavalry sabre, 17th century.
D. German shell pattern, c. 1585.
E. Prussian 18th-century cavalry sabre.
F. Turkish Scimitar c. 1600.

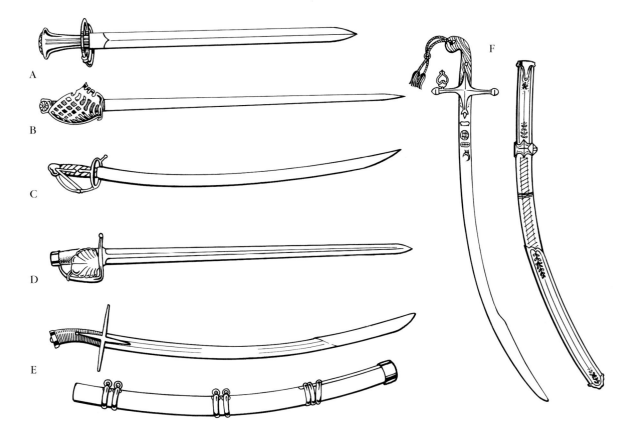

A

B

C

D

E

F

at a depression that ran across the field and presumed they were taking up a defensive position behind this dip, similar to the Imperialists at Lützen. But von Sporcken was only waiting for his second line to come up and redress after emerging from a belt of fir trees. The redcoat line lurched forwards again and came at them, although not directly. It skewed, with its southern end, its left, getting nearer than its right, which also seemed to extend as the two battalions of Hanoverian guards came up almost into the front line.

Against All Odds

Ferdinand ordered support forwards to cover the impending disaster. He sent forwards von Scheele's brigade, the next command in the line. After the initial surprise wore off the situation became clear to Fitzjames: unsupported infantry were advancing on ordered, fresh cavalry who were ready to charge; added to that the redcoats were coming under fire. The days of horse using their pistols were long gone; the fire support was coming from two batteries of French artillery, one near Maulbeerkamp and the other placed by the

brigades under the Marquis de Castries, the second of 22 in three brigades under Lieutenant General de Vogue, and the third of 18 in two brigades under the Marquis de Poyanne. It was a total of 63 squadrons, each numbering around one 120 men – a cavalry force of more than 7500, whose horses were rested and in good condition. Facing them, less than 460 metres (500 yards) away, were eight battalions of infantry: around 5000 men who had been battered by guns and left unsupported. The French squadrons drew swords.

They launched the cavalry attack en masse in the English style. The first wave forwards were 14 squadrons from the brigades of Mestre de Camp and Royal Cravattes. Their trot soon broke into a canter. Shouting began, they put spurs to flanks and surged into the galloping charge. In the front line, Waldegrave's brigade of infantry halted, and presented muskets. The mass thundered nearer and nearer in a desperate, glorious charge until at about 27 metres (30 yards) the order came to fire.

It would appear that rather than the rolling platoon fire of Marlborough's day the line fired by ranks and the first volley crashed into the front rank of the cavalry bringing down men and horses in a sprawling mass. Horsemen in the second rank tried to get their mounts to weave between or jump those who had gone down but the kicking and thrashing of the wounded animals made it almost impossible. They then took a volley from the second rank, which halted most of them; but not all. Such was their courage and élan that some crashed forward, into and through the British line. The two right-hand companies of the 12th foot were ridden down and their battalion gunners cut down. But they regrouped and fell on the blown horsemen, some grasping at bridles and hanging on, hauling the horses' heads down while others dragged the troopers from their saddles and

windmill at Hahlen. It may have been at extreme range but it was the fire from 60 guns, and although the Allied gunners tried counter-battery fire they could not silence them. The cavalry saw their target being 'softened up'. An officer in that march across Minden Heath wrote 'this cannonade would render the Regiments incapable of bearing the shock of unhurt troops drawn up long before on ground of their choosing,' adding, 'but firmness and resolution will surmount any difficulty.'

Fitzjames' cavalry were drawn up in three lines, the first composed of 23 squadrons in three

impaled them on their bayonets. Surrounded and outnumbered, the French cavalrymen had no technique to cope with this type of savage brawl. The mounted warrior elite of the medieval age might have been experienced in this type of individual warfare, but these men were trained to fight in ranks in large numbers and only expected to encounter infantry when chopping them down in a chase pursuit. The survivors of this first attack struggled back to their astounded comrades.

Fitzjames ordered the second line to go; this time, all 22 squadrons of the du Roi, Bourgogne and Royal Etranger brigades. According to past military practice and the drill books, the infantry should break this time before the elite of the battlefield. This wave too gathered pace quickly and flung itself against the red line, but the line did not run and they met the same response of close range fire by salvo. It is recorded by one English soldier that 'almost every ball found its mark' which, although an exaggeration, does give the general impression of the effectiveness of the fire. This second wave was shattered but some of them also broke through the line, emerging from the chaos and the smoke, only to come up against the second line brigade, Kingsley's, whose bayonets kept them at bay, and whose close-range fire shot them down. Cavalry courage and resolution had failed against disciplined firepower.

Von Sporcken's men closed ranks, redressed and began to advance once more, bringing those deadly muskets to Fitzjames' third line. Thankfully for the remaining cavalry, as the Allied formation occupied the ground vacated by the first and second horse lines they exposed their flanks to French foot, who wheeled into them and fired. But such was the level of skill, training and discipline of the redcoats that they too wheeled to meet the threat and, after a ten-minute musket battle, managed to drive this infantry back.

They were assaulted again by more infantry,

> *'The cavalry regiment which does not charge into the enemy the instant the order is given I will unhorse and turn into a garrison unit.'*
>
> — FREDERICK, KING OF PRUSSIA

grenadiers and again caused them to retire. Then eight battalions of Swiss and Saxons were sent from de Contades' left to attack them in flank. Kingsley's second line came up, half wheeled to its right and three battalions defeated eight in another amazing display of steadfastness under fire. During these infantry battles Fitzjames and the third cavalry line commander, de Poyanne, brought up 18 squadrons of the Gendarmerie and Carabiniers de France. These 2000 troopers were the elite of the elite.

Theirs was not to be the same frontal attack as launched by the two previous waves. The intervening infantry combats had not only caused the redcoat line to wheel and angle, but de Poyanne had also marched his cavalry round to the right and drew up aiming his squadrons at von Sporcken's left flank and rear. The heaviest impact of the charge fell on the Hanoverian battalions and the 23rd foot; despite their fire it broke through them. The cavalry rallied and charged again, but the rear ranks of the infantry faced about and again poured fire into them, 'such terrible fire that not even lions could have come on.'

More charges went in and more fire scythed them down: 'such a number of them fell, both horses and men that it made it difficult for those not touched to retire.' The third cavalry attack had been repulsed and the remnants withdrew, but the line, now blackened, battered, tattered and worn wavered. Surely a final charge would dislodge and scatter them.

Fitzjames now had only had one brigade left. The Colonel-General's nine squadrons from the first line who had not gone in the first attack had been kept back to serve as a reserve, but the rest of his command was utterly in pieces. Of those still alive or capable of fighting, the Brigade du Roi had sustained the least damage. It was hastily retired, but for the dispersed rest many of its officers

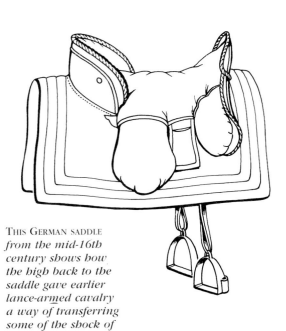

THIS GERMAN SADDLE *from the mid-16th century shows how the high back to the saddle gave earlier lance-armed cavalry a way of transferring some of the shock of impact to the horse.*

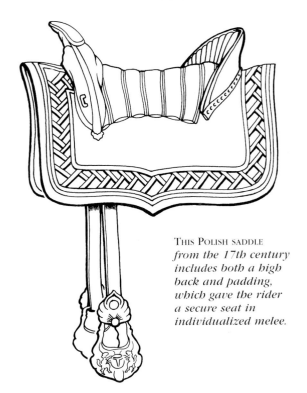

THIS POLISH SADDLE *from the 17th century includes both a high back and padding, which gave the rider a secure seat in individualized melee.*

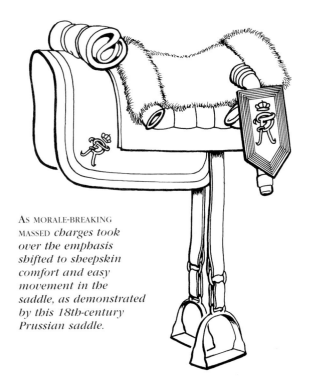

AS MORALE-BREAKING MASSED *charges took over the emphasis shifted to sheepskin comfort and easy movement in the saddle, as demonstrated by this 18th-century Prussian saddle.*

ARAB SADDLES *from the late 16th century were lightweight with short stirrups. Although the rider would sit with legs bent, the short stirrups allowed him to more easily stand to fire a bow.*

125

Battle of Minden

1757

The Allied General Prince Ferdinand of Brunswick
had to prevent Marshal de Contades breaking into
Hanover, and offered battle on Minden Plain. The
clash of arms divided into two sectors, and
although the northern one was bitterly contested,
the decisive action came in the west from an
unintended, unsupported advance in the centre by
eight battalions of British and Hanoverian infantry.
Against all expectations, these units defeated the
opposing French cavalry. Ferdinand seized the
opportunity of this mounted failure and led a
fighting advance, despite the scandalous inactivity
of the supporting British cavalry. The struggle in the
north was a hard pounding match but the French
were forced to retire when their western line
collapsed. The battered remnants of the French
mounted arm managed to cover the retreat of their
army to the safety of Minden, but the breakout had
been prevented.

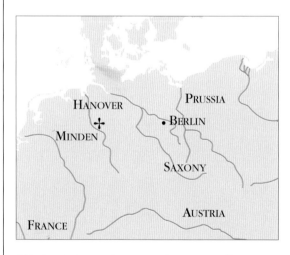

*Minden is in northwestern Germany, 56km
(35 miles) east of Osnabruck towards Hanover.
The battlefield is relatively unaltered and is on
the open moor on the west bank of the River
Weser, northwest of Minden itself.*

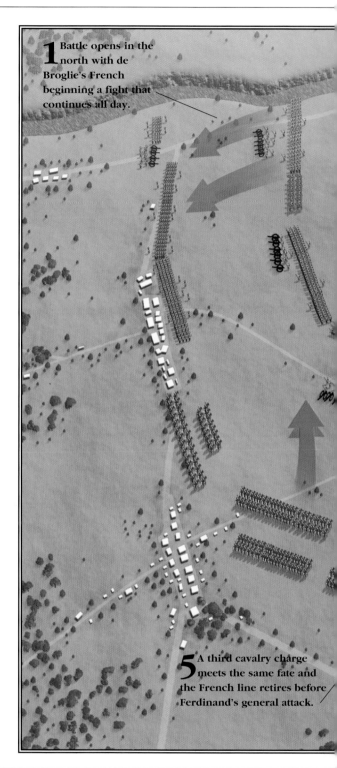

1 Battle opens in the
north with de
Broglie's French
beginning a fight that
continues all day.

5 A third cavalry charge
meets the same fate and
the French line retires before
Ferdinand's general attack.

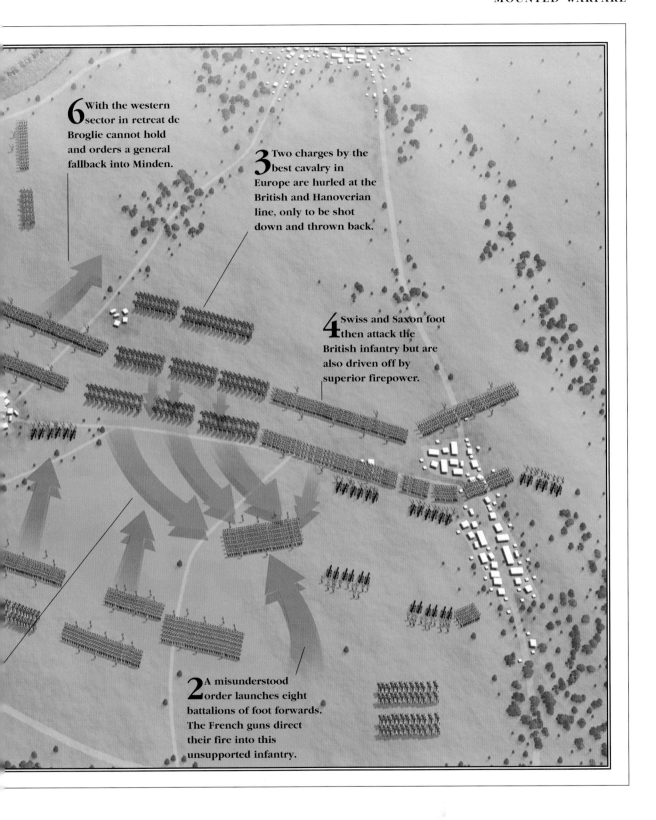

6 With the western sector in retreat de Broglie cannot hold and orders a general fallback into Minden.

3 Two charges by the best cavalry in Europe are hurled at the British and Hanoverian line, only to be shot down and thrown back.

4 Swiss and Saxon foot then attack the British infantry but are also driven off by superior firepower.

2 A misunderstood order launches eight battalions of foot forwards. The French guns direct their fire into this unsupported infantry.

were dead and riderless horses made re-ordering impossible. The finest cavalry in Europe had been wrecked and there was no hope of rallying them. The technique of the unsupported charge of cavalry en masse had been defeated by defensive firepower of unsupported infantry in line who had 'not even paid them the compliment of forming squares to receive them.'

With the French cavalry in ruins and their centre wide open it was time for the Allied cavalry to strike: to charge and pour through de Contades' line, wheel left and right and roll up the line in both directions. But their general, Lord George Sackville, did not charge. His conduct and that of the British and German cavalry was to become a scandal, and his court martial attracted great attention. Their behaviour was contrasted with the bravery of the French, especially as Fitzjames' cavalry made yet another two charges.

> '*I have seen what I never thought to be possible – a single line of infantry break through three lines of cavalry ranked in battle order and tumble them, to ruin.*'
>
> — DE CONTAGES

The first of these charges indicated the cavalry had learnt nothing from the earlier disaster. They did not charge von Sporcken but instead went for a large Allied battery in the centre. Desperate to redeem the reputation of the horse, their commander, the Comte de Cologne, launched the same dramatic technique of a gallop charge straight at the guns. At point-blank range the gunners fired double canister. Hessian and Brunswick infantry added their musketry and Cologne's nine squadrons disappeared into smoke, figuratively and literally. They were chopped to pieces, the survivors riding back to the French lines as best they could.

The Allies pressed forwards all along the line except on their right where Sackville, soon to be dubbed 'The Coward of Minden' still sat with his cavalry. After bitter bayonet work and an advance by the German cavalry the day went to Prince Ferdinand. The rout of the French army in the southern sector was prevented by a charge on the Hanoverian heavy cavalry by Fitzjames' regrouped Brigade du Roi, but de Contades' command streamed back into Minden. In the northern sector the hard-contested stalemate between de von Wangenheim's and de Broglie's Corps was terminated when the French had to fall back and cover their retreating friends.

Minden was a battle won by the musket and the bayonet. The lesson for the cavalry was that if infantry stood and could deliver disciplined firepower at close range they could stop the gallop charge in its tracks.

Conclusion: Dreams of Glory

Whatever the lessons learnt in the middle of the eighteenth century, western European cavalry could not be weaned off of the obsession with the all-out charge. Even the experienced Frederick the Great went on to organize his cavalry into enormous, deep formations where skill and spirit was subordinated to numbers and mass. The huge cavalry charge of von Seydlitz at Zorndorf in 1758 was emulated by Napoleon, whose support for the gallant and romantic Joachim Murat led to the massed cavalry charges at Eylau in 1807 and Wagram in 1809. But the epitome of the cavalry sabre charge for once overcoming musket-armed infantry occurred when Le Marchant's cavalry overwhelmed their opponents at Salamanca in 1812.

This had a lasting effect upon the mind-set of the British cavalryman and his senior officers. One only has to read the papers of the young Winston Churchill to witness his enthusiasm, which verged on the ecstatic, for the charge. Even as late as the early twentieth century cavalry journals were full of debates arguing the varying merits of using the edge or the point of the sabre, and in World War I cavalry generals were still discussing the tactical value of the charge and hoping for a cavalry breakthrough despite knowing full well that the wire and the machine gunners were waiting.

Prussian Hussar
(c. 1750)

Frederick the Great increased his number of hussar regiments from two to ten, forming about ten per cent of the army. They performed the usual light cavalry duties including police work, but slowly became primarily battlefield troops with a reputation for dash and outstanding bravery, enhanced by their colourful and outlandish dress. Although armed with carbines as well as curved sabres, these troopers rarely used them in battle. They took part in Frederick's massed cavalry charges, often galloping into action to outstrip the heavies. So successful and popular were they that many gentlemen served in their ranks and their officers were drawn from the best Prussian families. Known for spirit and élan 'going a la hussarde' became synomynous with the death-or-glory charge.

COMMAND AND CONTROL

The evolving nature of warfare, technological advances, increasing state revenues and larger populations all brought huge changes in the nature of military command during the early modern period. The establishment of military institutions created a bureaucracy to wage war and the evolution of leadership over the period created a military administration to direct it.

I n late 1624 Albrecht von Waldstein, better known as Wallenstein, count of Friedland, approached his emperor and king, Ferdinand II, and offered to raise an army of 50,000 men for employment in Germany. Wallenstein would recruit, equip and supply the army while the emperor would merely provide financial subsidies. This was not the first time Wallenstein had made such impressive promises. Since the beginning of the rebellion in Bohemia in 1618, the wealthy

FREDERICK THE GREAT's *Grenadier Guard battalion epitomized the highly-disciplined, professional army that emerged over the course of two centuries. Led by the colonel – on horseback – Frederick's soldiers met the Austrians at Hohenfriedberg, 4 June 1745, during the War of Austrian Succession.*

nobleman had offered his services to the Habsburg emperor. Wallenstein also lent money to the financially and militarily bereft monarch over the course of seven years. Wallenstein now pledged not only to raise an army much larger than the one paid for by Ferdinand's sometime ally Maximilian, duke of Bavaria, but to lead it as well.

Wallenstein was the epitome of the military entrepreneur or contractor, which had been a phenomenon in Europe since the Renaissance. Although mercenary in spirit, Wallenstein was not strictly speaking a mercenary. His support for the Habsburg cause was sincere, although he used his wealth and position to increase his own power and influence within Bohemia and later the Holy Roman Empire. Many military leaders of the early modern era were cut from similar cloth. Yet, the period also marks the Military Revolution in Europe, where technological innovations and the increasing flow of specie allowed for the expansion of armies and a redefinition of the martial nobility. Along with the contractor, there were soldier–kings, and by the end of the seventeenth century, the general was no amateur but a seasoned professional who spent a lifetime involved in the business of war.

Warfare since the fall of Rome had been the monopoly of the European nobility. Military leaders were drawn exclusively from the nobility. War was not merely an art, but a way of life and a fundamental part of their culture. Monarchs and their military leaders contended with a myriad of issues prior to taking the field. Armies had to be raised, but first the war chest had to be examined. No army marched; no battle was fought without adequate financing. Generalship in the early modern era, perhaps more than ever before, had to

> *'Mercenary captains are excellent men of arms or not: if they are, you cannot trust them because they always aspire to their own greatness, either by oppressing you, who are their patron, or by oppressing others contrary to your intention; but if the captain is not virtuous, he ruins you in the ordinary way.'*
>
> — NICCOLÒ MACHIAVELLI, THE PRINCE

consider the cost of war before waging it. In the medieval period vassalage required a noble to provide a specified number of 'lances' for the king as part of his military obligations. As armies became larger and the nobility no longer formed the core, the cost of war increasingly passed to either the monarch or others to shoulder the burden. When Ferdinand II found himself in the midst of the Bohemian revolt, with a Czech army bearing down on Vienna, the unfortunate reality was that he was devoid of an army or resources with which to resist. He looked to Duke Maximilian of Bavaria, and Philip III, his wealthy Spanish cousin, to provide him with support.

Part of a monarch's dilemma came from the lack of standing armies. It was not until the fifteenth century that the first monarchs considered establishing permanent forces. By the beginning of the sixteenth century the Spanish monarchy introduced the first permanent military formations, which became the vaunted *tercio*. Comprised initially of veterans of the campaigns against the Moors, the *tercio* became the heart of Spanish military power throughout its diverse and far-flung empire. A colonel commanded each *tercio*, with sub-units directed by subordinate officers. The establishment of the *tercios* in Spain, Italy and the Netherlands ensured the Spanish monarchy a ready source of experienced military personnel. This was also the age of great captains like Gonzalo de Córdoba and Hernando Cortez. With the emergence of permanent forces a monarch could look to the nobility to officer and lead them. It also provided a means by which lesser nobles could serve their monarch and achieve wealth and prestige.

The armoured knighthood, the backbone of

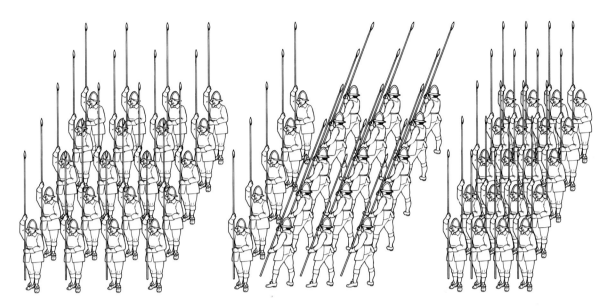

THE DECLINE OF ARMOURED cavalry and the return of the infantryman to the centre-stage of the battlefield was accompanied by a resurrection of military drill. Here a company of pikemen is shown in three distinct formations, as it would have appeared in a military manual of the 17th century.

medieval armies, gradually evolved to become the officer corps of the standing army. This transition took more than two centuries to complete but in the process the upper nobility became servants of the monarch and ceased to be military leaders wielding independent military power. A general of the early modern era served two masters, his monarch and himself. His status among the royal retinue was tied inexorably to his military reputation. Victory brought glory and reward; defeat meant disgrace.

Studying the Art of War

As the changing nature of war led to reorganization of European military systems, military leaders sought guidance in ancient texts. The weight of classical tradition was felt nowhere more heavily than in Italy, at the time of the French invasions and the dynastic contest with the Spanish. Niccolò Macchiavelli wrote at the time of Córdoba's victories over the French in Naples and central Italy. He interpreted what he saw as signifying the decline of the *condottieri*, the mercenaries that had previously dominated warfare in Italy, and the rise of professional armies. Inspired by his observations, war featured prominently in his works *The Art of War*, *The Prince* and *Discourses*. He admired Roman military traditions and recommended that Italian princes rely on similar citizen armies.

Macchiavelli's work was quite influential in the seventeenth century, but while his commentary was noted, Vegetius's influence was perhaps greater.

Vegetius's *De Re Militari* remained a classic work on the Roman military institutions and the art of war. Having survived 1000 years, the book became the standard text on the organization, leadership and conduct of war during the late Roman Empire. Vegetius' discourse was particularly significant because it provided valuable advice for generals. Macchiavelli was not a soldier, and his discussions in *Art of War* were scientific in nature. Although not a soldier, Vegetius was a Roman and his immediate observations held greater weight and influence in the early modern era. *Book III* in particular dealt with the waging of war and the management of an army on campaign. Vegetius advised avoiding battle when odds are not favourable, and recommended outmanoeuvring the foe or relying on alternate strategies to defeat his enemy instead. He stressed the importance of strict military discipline and said the general

133

should know the quality and capabilities of each unit in his army. His writings, along with the resurrection of Aelian's *Tactical Theory*, and Pope Leo's *Tactica*, became most useful in the age of the Spanish *tercio* and influenced a generation of Dutch military leaders in particular.

Around the same time the writings of Justus Lipsius introduced the philosophy of neo-stoicism and linked it to the art of war. Neo-stoicism formed the ideological underpinning of the professional military officer. It demanded an officer go about his duty without regard to conditions or privations; that one must accept the will of God, which determines all things. Lipsius was a Calvinist and the notion of predestination fitted well with the renaissance of this Greek philosophy. By the eighteenth century neo-stoicism absorbed chivalry as the fundamental ideal of the professional officer.

Raimondo Montecuccoli was one of the most influential military writers of the seventeenth century. His distinguished military service with the Habsburg Emperors spanned the Thirty Years' War, the Nordic War, the Turkish Wars and the Dutch War. As president of Austria's *Hofkriegsrat* (War Council) after 1675, he held enormous influence with the Austrian Habsburg court. Montecuccoli's victories included the decisive Battle of St Gotthard Pass in 1664, which ended the Turkish threat to Hungary for 20 years. In 1673 he bested Marshal Turenne, one of the most successful military commanders in Europe. Throughout his illustrious military career Montecuccoli composed four major books, *On Battle*, *Treatise on War*, *On the Art of War* and *On War in Hungary against the Turks*. His subject

A 16TH-CENTURY ARMY *was a polyglot of professionals, mercenaries and entrepreneurs. Beyond martial prowess, a general was required to be a diplomat and a businessman. In this engraving of a 16th-century siege of an Italian city, the artillery and food were provided by private contractors, as was customary at the time.*

matter dealt with everything from command to logistics and although they were read earlier in Vienna, it was not until the eighteenth century that his writings were published and read across Europe.

To ensure the glory and immortality of the author and to provide advice to future generals, such commentaries were an established genre by the eighteenth century. Marshal Maurice de Saxe's *Reveries on the Art of War*, and Frederick the Great's *Instructions, On the Art of War* and *Military Testament* were some of the most significant reflections on the conduct of war and became standard reading for fledgling officers and military commanders when military schools emerged in the eighteenth century.

The Changing Nature of Command

The evolution of generalship in the early modern era was dependent upon two factors, geography and technology. In the first case the character of military leadership was tied to a kingdom or a specific region. The second determinant affected the employment of troops on campaign, as well as the composition and cost of the armies. In the sixteenth century European conflicts involved dynastic interests that extended well beyond a kingdom's borders. Although domestic conflicts continued to appear for another 200 years war became the 'sport of kings' in their attempt to expand their territorial possessions. When Charles VIII invaded Italy in 1494, the French army both faced and employed *condottieri*, along with mercenary Swiss pikemen. Within 30 years on similar ground, Francis I contended with the formidable Spanish *tercios* under Charles V (Carlos I in Spain). As the century progressed, Habsburg military power extended into Italy and the Netherlands. The composition of armies and the nature of military leadership gradually evolved to reflect the dynastic interests involved in these conflicts. *Condottieri* virtually disappeared by the close of the fifteenth century, to be replaced by the generals and the armies of the Valois and Habsburg dynasties.

When Emperor Charles V ascended the Spanish throne in 1516, he was already heir to the Habsburg possessions in Central Europe, Germany and the newly acquired Burgundian territories.

Within three years he came to control a great swathe of Europe under the title of Holy Roman Emperor, king of Bohemia, archduke of Austria and emperor of the Americas. When Francis I pursued French claims in northern Italy he therefore faced the armies of the Holy Roman Emperor and king of Spain, for Charles drew upon his Spanish army to defend his Italian possessions.

In the Spanish army in the early sixteenth century there was a traditional body of noble cavalry and a number of mercenary infantry. This composition changed gradually through the sixteenth century as greater numbers of soldiers were recruited from the mother country. The loyalty of the mercenary to his captain continued to be tenuous at best, so that the wounding or death of the captain could result in the complete dissolution of the unit. Troops raised by noblemen serving their masters tended to have greater cohesion on campaign and on the battlefield. Although desertion plagued all armies these troops tended to desert in fewer numbers. But their loyalty remained with the captain who raised the company rather than with the general or the cause. All of this needed to be seriously considered by the general when raising an army and employing it on campaign.

Gonsalvo de Córdoba's performance in Italy through the course of his military career illustrated his ability to adapt to the changing nature of war, army composition and military technology. When he first arrived in Naples from Spain, his army was composed largely of infantry with the cavalry only one-third of the contingent. This was not uncommon as monarchs went to war providing a cadre of troops paid at royal expense, but the general was expected to augment those forces with mercenaries along the way. Charles VIII of France entered Italy with his *compagnies d'ordonannce*, which together formed a standing army mainly of cavalry: but by then they constituted only a minority of French forces throughout the campaign. Córdoba's army consisted of several 100 *genitors* (light cavalry), 100 heavy cavalry and more than 1000 infantry of various sorts. The mixed nature of the army and the unevenness of its composition and abilities made waging war a rather uncertain affair.

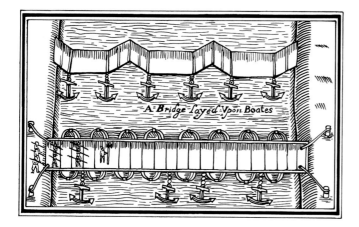

A Bridge layed Vpon Boates

Only the cavalry could be depended upon and they remained the sovereign of the battlefield. Siege was preferred to battle, as the outcome on the field could rarely be guaranteed. Córdoba was the first general in Europe to employ firearms in significant quantities to make a decision on the battlefield. His victory over the French at Cerignola in 1503, was the product of field-works and firearms. In 1525 the Spanish victory over Francis I at Pavia was achieved by *arquebusiers*, backed by artillery and large numbers of pike-armed infantry.

Ferdinand of Aragon, grandfather to Charles V, had introduced permanent infantry formations composed of pikemen, *arquebusiers* and sword-and-buckler men. They were divided into columns of approximately 1000 men and headed by a *capo de colunela*, which evolved into the term 'colonel'. In 1505, there were 20 such columns under 20 colonels, and they served extensively throughout Italy in the first two decades of the sixteenth century. The colonels were chosen from the most prominent and experienced nobles in Spain. The column became the basis for the *tercios*, which were formed 20 years later. They included a much greater number of *arquebusiers* and pikemen, roughly 3000 in all. The *tercios* comprised roughly ten to 12 companies, equally divided between the two arms. To provide effective command and control of the large formations and to coordinate the operations of the shot and pike, the *tercio* included a central staff, along with officers and non-commissioned officers in each company. Each *tercio* also

ENGINEERING GREW IN IMPORTANCE *during the course of the 17th century. As artillery became commonplace, and army numbers grew substantially, it was critical that natural barriers, such as rivers, did not slow an offensive. Pontoons and bridging equipment became standard by the 18th century.*

included soldier-priests among their ranks to provide inspiration during the gruelling wars of religion. The establishment of these permanent bodies gave Charles V (Carlos I in Spain) an early standing army. They were initially formed and employed in Italy, but later fought in Germany and the Netherlands. The availability of veteran formations removed the problem of recruiting thousands of soldiers in advance of a war. Charles and later his son Philip II could rely upon these units to defend their enormous empire. The *tercio* became the core of Spanish armies, supplemented by cavalry and allied auxiliaries. It was not until the seventeenth century that the *tercio* was superseded on the battlefield.

Ferdinand of Aragon, and later Charles V (Carlos I) were more easily able to employ the Spanish nobility as officers in a royal army because the Spanish military experience through the 1400s differed from that of France and Central Europe. Service to the monarch in the *Reconquista* against the Moors created a dynamic between sovereign and the martial class that allowed for an easier transition in the sixteenth century from medieval to a professional army.

The French and German experience was substantially different, as the more independent nature of the nobility made some nobles reluctant to become officers of a royal army. Henry IV relied consistently upon Huguenot nobles to contribute money and men to his cause. Henry IV was one of the few monarchs of the sixteenth century who considered it the duty of a monarch to lead their armies into battle. Philip II of Spain, his contemporary, rarely accompanied armies and never directed operations in the Netherlands. He looked to seasoned officers such as the dukes of Alva and Parma to direct operations against the contentious Dutch. Although the former was related to the monarch Philip ensured that experienced generals advised him.

The Dutch School

The Dutch Revolt (1565-1609) produced what is generally considered by historians to be the first early modern military system. The struggle between the Dutch and their Spanish overlords lasted the better part of half a century and did not officially conclude, as far as the Spanish were concerned, until 1648. The wealth and military might of Habsburg Spain was eventually checked by Dutch forces, but it was in the last decade of the sixteenth century that Maurice of Nassau, son of the slain *Stadtholder* William the Silent, received command of the Dutch war effort. Maurice worked assiduously to reform

the military system in order to take advantage of the increasing availability and effectiveness of firearms. His opponents Alva and Parma, who were vassals of the king of Spain, were often committed by their sovereign to war in France and many early Dutch successes came in the absence of the Spanish Army of Flanders and its experienced generals. When Alva and Parma returned to the Netherlands, the Dutch gains were often reversed.

Justus Lipsius profoundly influenced Maurice. His Calvinism and Lipsius' neo-stoic philosophy provided the prince of Nassau with a model from which to shape the Dutch army. As it emerged the Maurician system of command spread well beyond the Netherlands. Many soldiers and officers in Dutch service were English, German, Scot and Huguenots, coming from other European Protestant countries. Queen Elizabeth too, contributed large sums of money and troops to the Dutch cause. The Dutch military system became the school for Protestant armies in the seventeenth century.

Maurice stressed discipline among the ranks and determined to train a professional officer corps, relying on the teachings of Lipsius and the lessons of the Romans Vegetius and Leo. The senior ranks were drawn from Dutch nobles or appointed by the *Stadtholders*, but the junior

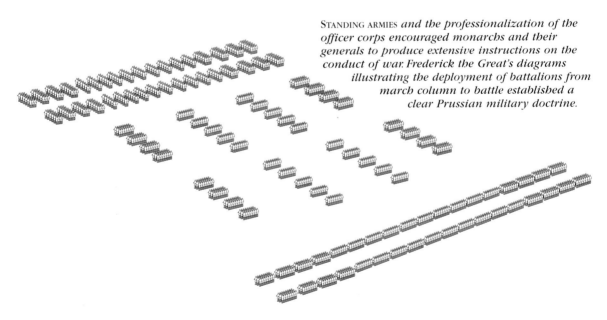

STANDING ARMIES *and the professionalization of the officer corps encouraged monarchs and their generals to produce extensive instructions on the conduct of war. Frederick the Great's diagrams illustrating the deployment of battalions from march column to battle established a clear Prussian military doctrine.*

ranks were filled with members of the middle class whose private wealth allowed them to subsidize the cost of maintaining a company. But all were subject to military discipline and drill, and were required to instil the same into their troops. Each company in Dutch service possessed a captain, lieutenant and ensign along with five non-commissioned officers. The ratio of officers to men was higher in these formations, allowing for better discipline and control in combat. Maurice did not merely apply this system to Dutch regiments but required it of his allies as well. Foreign companies and their captains drilled along Dutch lines and in doing so were able to carry their experience home after their military service.

The Dutch military system was incorporated into the Swedish and English armies in the early seventeenth century. Gustavus II Adolphus, king of Sweden, employed officers formerly in Dutch service to train and lead his regiments, and used the Dutch ideas to develop his own system, using shallower formations and putting greater emphasis on firepower. Gustavus' companies consisted of a similar number of officers, but slightly more non-commissioned officers; and he handled his cavalry quite differently, as explained elsewhere in this volume. Gustavus' system was highly successful, particularly at Breitenfeld when the Swedes smashed the more old-fashioned deployment of the Imperialist Army.

The Dutch military system also influenced Oliver Cromwell's New Model Army. Because a large percentage of Maurice's troops were English, their experience was a powerful influence in the evolution of the English army, and the Puritan captains easily matched the Dutch Calvinists' distaste for Catholics.

Nieuport, 1600: Blood and Sand

Nieuport is important in the history of the Dutch Revolt as it was one of only two major battles fought by Maurice of Nassau. Despite his extensive reform of the Dutch military system, the *Stadtholder* and commander-in-chief of Dutch forces preferred to seize fortified towns and cities held by Spanish garrisons rather than seek pitched battles with the Spaniards. When in 1600 he was directed by the States-General to take the only

field army to the Flemish coast and capture the town of Nieuport, he disputed the logic of the plan. Nonetheless, the great general accepted his orders and personally directed the short-lived campaign. The entire operation lasted less than a month, pitting the Dutch system against a substantial Spanish army.

The Dutch had virtually won their independence by 1599. Upon the death of Philip II in 1598, the Spanish Empire passed to his son Philip III, excepting the Netherlands. The grand monarch willed this possession to his daughter Isabella and her future husband Archduke Albrecht. Since 1595 the archduke had served as governor-general of the Netherlands. Although the new king expected his brother-in-law to aggressively pursue war against the Dutch, Albrecht had other ideas. Spain was bankrupt and there was little money to pay the soldiers of the army of Flanders, let alone launch an offensive to reconquer the Dutch provinces. Albrecht entered negotiations with the States-General shortly after returning to Brussels. The States-General participated in these talks, but secretly hoped to extend their control into Flanders. They were encouraged by news of a mutiny among several *tercios* of the army of Flanders, a victory by Maurice over a small Spanish army at Turnhout in 1597, and the need to put an end to the depredations of Spanish privateers operating out of Dunkirk and Nieuport.

Maurice disliked the idea of an attack on Nieuport, particularly as the plan of the States-General envisaged an amphibious landing. But he was overruled. On 20 June 1600 the Dutch army assembled at Flushing, comprising 12,000 infantry, 2000 cavalry and 38 guns. At least one-third of the Dutch army were from England and Scotland, with more than another one-third consisting of French Huguenots, Walloons and Swiss. Although the fleet was expected to sail on 21 June, weather conditions prohibited an extended journey. Maurice decided to forgo the landing at Ostend in favour of simply crossing the Scheldt and marching down the coast, which had been his preferred strategy all along. The crossing was complete by 22 June and the Dutch army proceeded from Sas van Ghent to Ostend, skirting Spanish-controlled Bruges. Maurice arrived before

UNIFORMS WERE RARE during the 17th century despite the emergence of standing armies. Officers and men dressed according to their financial capacity. French, German and Italian officers could have easily been dressed in a similar fashion as this Irish officer of the English Civil War.

Ostend on 27 June and chased away the meagre Spanish forces observing the Dutch port. He re-inforced the garrison and continued south to Nieuport on 30 June.

Maurice was hoping that the poor condition of the Spanish army in Flanders would prevent them interfering in his offensive. The van of Maurice's army reached Nieuport on 1 July. The limited size of his army and the speed with which it marched prevented him gathering intelligence on the state of Spanish troops throughout Brabant and Flanders. This failure to keep track of the Spaniards in Brabant was the great mistake of the campaign. It created a false sense of operational security. Maurice found all too soon that the rapid advance to Nieuport, and their assumptions about the poor state of the Spanish army were horribly wrong.

For all the glory assigned to Maurice as a general and father of the modern army, Archduke Albrecht deserves credit for acting quickly in the face of the Dutch offensive. Learning of Maurice's crossing of the Scheldt, he assembled what forces he could, and arriving in Brabant appealed to the mutinous garrisons. Relying on their religious zeal and regional loyalties, he promised them whatever they asked if they took up arms. His ability to settle the mutinies within hours allowed him to gather an army of 8000 infantry and 1000 cavalry. When Maurice reached Nieuport Albrecht was only a day behind. The Archduke moved against Maurice's line of communication, cutting him off from Ostend. The manoeuvre trapped the Dutch between Nieuport and Albrecht's army.

Maurice sent his cousin Ernst of Nassau with 3000 men to Leffinghem, hoping to delay the Spanish advance. They were defeated. Taking into account the losses from that engagement and a detachment sent earlier to Ostend, Maurice now faced Albrecht with virtually equal numbers. But Ernst's efforts gave Maurice just enough time to redeploy his army on the morning of 2 July.

Fiasco on the Beach

Maurice deployed on a narrow front, no more than 137m (150 yards) wide. This was the width of the beach, with sandy dunes to the east. Archduke Albrecht preferred the beach as it was firm ground for his *tercios* and cavalry. Maurice favoured a narrow front because it compelled the Spanish to advance head–on against his infantry and their guns. He placed his army in depth, forming three lines. Cavalry covered the sea flank, while the English and Scottish regiments re-inforced by the Dutch Guards were in the vanguard. Maurice's Huguenot regiments supported by cavalry were in the second line, with the Dutch and Swiss regiments in the third. Maurice took post behind the first line, which was under English captain Sir Francis Vere. Maurice's brother Louis commanded the cavalry along the water. Dutch warships from

RECRUITING ARMIES WAS *costly as it included the expense of arming the soldiers with uniform weaponry. Pikes and firearms had to be standardized for production, supply and performance in battle. The conclusion of the 12-year truce in the Netherlands in 1621 led to the arming of Dutch provincial militia in anticipation of the renewed conflict with Spain.*

Ostend were off the coast and moved closer to shore to provide some fire support.

Archduke Albrecht's army was also drawn up in three lines: vanguard, main battle and rearguard. The battle began with light skirmishing around 1 PM. The Spanish cavalry pushed the skirmishers back only to face fire from Dutch artillery. At about the same time the Dutch warships, observing the action, fired upon the flank of the Spanish army. Albrecht was none too pleased. He quickly realized that the flanking fire compromised his position. Worse still, the tide was coming in, further reducing the beachfront. By 2:30 the archduke ordered the army redeployed to the dunes. Only a small contingent of infantry supported by some guns remained on the beach. Maurice followed suit, ordering his army into the dunes.

It was 3 PM before the battle recommenced. The Spanish line extended east with the vanguard nearest the shore, the main battle was next and off to its rear was the rearguard. The preponderance of Spanish cavalry was on Albrecht's far left. Maurice's army was almost oblique to the Spanish line, with Vere's English closest to the sea. A veteran of the Dutch wars, Vere spied two prominent hills among the dunes and placed a picked company of English and Dutch Guards there, while on the other he sited two cannon supported by Dutch infantry. The English and Dutch were forwards of the main battle line, and were meant to break up the Spanish advance. The other hill, 100 m (109 yards) to the rear, became the centre of the new Dutch line. Prince Louis, Maurice's brother, took his cavalry around Vere's position and stood opposite Albrecht's horsemen. Maurice marched his main battle of Huguenot, Walloon and Swiss companies just east of Vere's cannon while English and Dutch cavalry remained along the shore. The rearguard, composed of the remaining Dutch regiments and more English cavalry, was concentrated on a large dune behind the main battle. Maurice took post with the main battle, observing the Spanish attack on Vere's forwards positions. The Spanish mutineer regiments, who had demanded the right to take the vanguard, assaulted Vere's hill with 500 *arquebusiers*. Facing twice their number, the picked Anglo-Dutch troops held their ground. Companies of Spanish pike and shot were fed into the battle for the hill but were unable to dislodge Vere's small force. Shortly thereafter Archduke Albrecht sent four *tercios* against the remainder of Vere's line. Spanish cavalry covered the advance of the Archduke's second line, but was immediately charged by Prince Louis' cavalry. The Spanish horsemen were scattered. Louis pursued, but was eventually forced to retire by the disciplined fire of Albrecht's infantry.

Victory in the Dunes

Maurice watched as two *tercios* advanced against Vere's right. As yet he had not committed any troops from his main battle and rearguard. Fearing that the Dutch companies before him would succumb under pressure from the *tercios*, Maurice ordered up his Huguenot and Walloon regiments to bolster their flank. The Prince's position prevented him observing the movement of the other *tercios* to Vere's left, and he did not send reinforcements to that wing. The combat was heated but Vere was able to hold for some time.

WHEN ARTILLERY *was first introduced in Europe it was extremely cumbersome, requiring teams of oxen, horses and men to draw each piece. Monarchs and their generals were constantly seeking better means of producing stronger, lighter cannon that could be moved with less difficulty and employed on a wider scale for both siege and battle.*

Battle of Nieuport

1600

Maurice of Nassau found himself on 20 June 1600 with his back to the city of Nieuport and a Spanish army across his line of supply and communications. Both armies initially deployed on the beach, eventually moving to a second position on the dunes. Archduke Albrecht began his attack with a concerted effort to dislodge English companies from a forward defensive position on a hill, and eventually committed half his army to overcome this stubbornly defended position. Once Albrecht had committed his *tercios* Maurice sent forward his main battle line. The Anglo-Dutch companies met the Spanish veterans head-on, inflicting heavy casualties. Albrecht finally dispatched his reserves to the fray. This was enough to break Maurice's left, but opened the Spanish oblique advance to Maurice's reserves. Albrecht had no more troops to commit to the battle, and his cumbersome formations collapsed once their forward momentum was spent, and they were assailed from both front and flank.

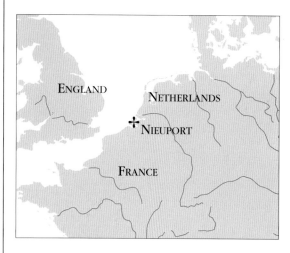

Nieuport is located on the coast of Flanders. It was well fortified and deep in Spanish-controlled territory. Privateers were permitted to use it as a base to prey upon Dutch and English vessels.

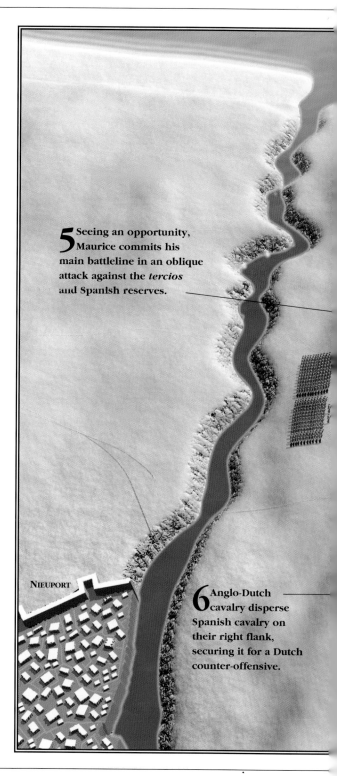

5 Seeing an opportunity, Maurice commits his main battleline in an oblique attack against the *tercios* and Spanish reserves.

6 Anglo-Dutch cavalry disperse Spanish cavalry on their right flank, securing it for a Dutch counter-offensive.

NIEUPORT

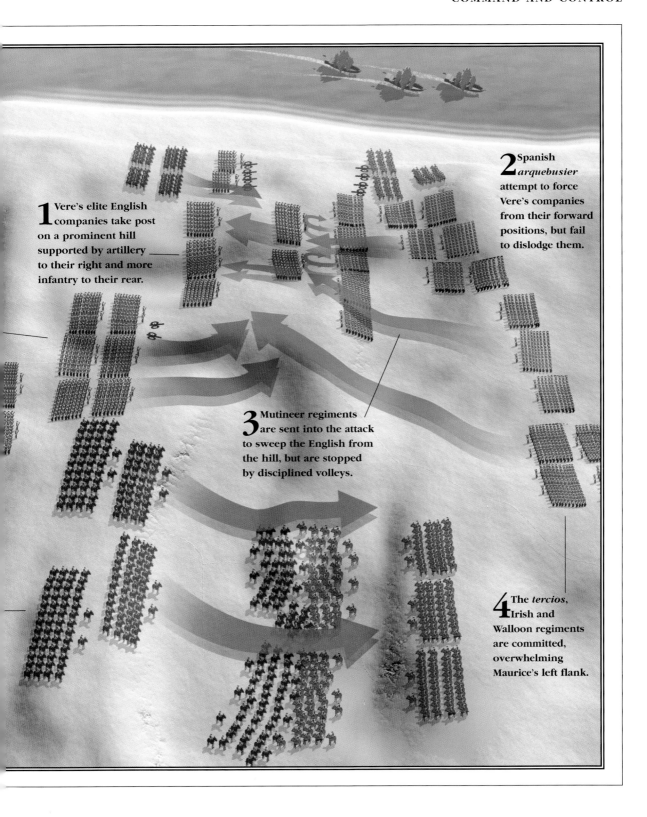

1 Vere's elite English companies take post on a prominent hill supported by artillery to their right and more infantry to their rear.

2 Spanish *arquebusier* attempt to force Vere's companies from their forward positions, but fail to dislodge them.

3 Mutineer regiments are sent into the attack to sweep the English from the hill, but are stopped by disciplined volleys.

4 The *tercios*, Irish and Walloon regiments are committed, overwhelming Maurice's left flank.

The mutineer regiments had little success, and were withdrawn from the attack having suffered grave casualties. To assist the two *tercios* moving against Vere's left and sensing the Englishman could not hold his position against such odds, Albrecht threw in his reserves. His Irish and Walloon regiments finally broke Vere's resistance and his men began to stream back towards the coast. Vere was nearly captured after being thrown from his horse in the retreat.

With Maurice's second line engaged with two of Albrecht's *tercios*, and with the rearguard deployed to the right rear of the Prince's line, there seemed to be few troops to stem the Spanish advance. But their excitement at the sight of Vere's collapse led the Spanish *tercios* and reserves to break ranks as they pursued. The English and Dutch cavalry remaining on the beach in reserve witnessed the flight of Vere's companies and charged the Spaniards. The cavalry fell upon them as they reached the beach, causing utter chaos and panic. What had been the Spanish pursuit became a rout. Seeing Albrecht's left disintegrate, Maurice ordered a general advance, finally committing his rearguard, and told his brother to charge the Spanish horse again. The Dutch counter-attack disheartened the exhausted Spanish soldiers. Albrecht lost control of his regiments who fled the field en masse. Prince Louis' cavalry chased them down, plaguing the demoralized army all the way to Leffinghem bridge.

Maurice's victory was complete. Half the Spanish army were killed, wounded or taken prisoner that day. Archduke Albrecht was wounded in the retreat. All his colonels were killed, wounded or captured, as were more than 50 captains. The Dutch army suffered 2000 casualties, most of them in Vere's English and Dutch companies. Maurice had cracked the *tercios*. Their inability to manoeuvre on the dunes, and the ability of the Dutch army to blunt the weight of their attacks with effective firepower, broke the

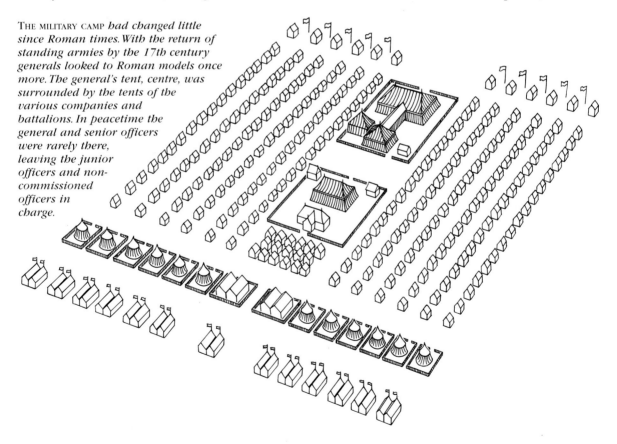

THE MILITARY CAMP *had changed little since Roman times. With the return of standing armies by the 17th century generals looked to Roman models once more. The general's tent, centre, was surrounded by the tents of the various companies and battalions. In peacetime the general and senior officers were rarely there, leaving the junior officers and non-commissioned officers in charge.*

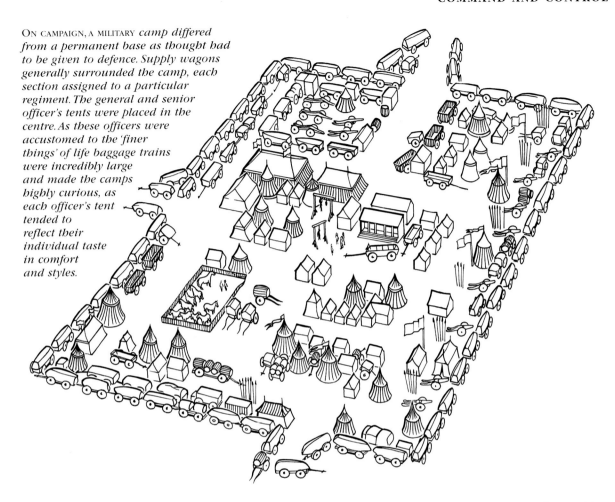

On campaign, a military camp differed from a permanent base as thought had to be given to defence. Supply wagons generally surrounded the camp, each section assigned to a particular regiment. The general and senior officer's tents were placed in the centre. As these officers were accustomed to the 'finer things' of life baggage trains were incredibly large and made the camps highly curious, as each officer's tent tended to reflect their individual taste in comfort and styles.

cohesion of these large units. Worn down and assailed from front and flank, they collapsed. This was the second time the *tercios* had been defeated on the battlefield, and the first time facing Maurice's infantry. The *tercio* had reigned supreme on the battlefield throughout the sixteenth century. It was the formation that other princes copied. But now the Dutch had proved that disciplined fire could wear down the Spanish columns. It was similar to the Roman's success against the Macedonian phalanx at Pydna, a classical parallel that Maurice would have enjoyed.

The victory was short-lived as Spanish reinforcements loomed, and Maurice, whose heart was never in the operation, decided to return to Holland. The Battle of Nieuport not only pit the Maurician system against the Spanish *tercio*, it also illustrates the difficulties that could arise between

a general and his government. Despite his position as *Stadtholder*, and his earlier successes, political opponents in the States-General forced Maurice to lead an expedition of which he did not approve, and fight a battle he never desired to fight.

Standing Armies

Perhaps the most dramatic change to the face of command came in the seventeenth century with the development of standing armies in France. In the later middle ages thousands of noble families were dispossessed of their lands and titles, and many sought glory and reward in the service of the French kings during the Hundred Years' War. Throughout the sixteenth century military service as a means of advancement continued to flourish in the Italian Wars and later in the religious wars, and the phenomenon continued in the seventeenth century. The du Pléssis family was one of hundreds who sought the favour of the king in this way. Their third son, Armand-Jean du Pléssis enrolled in royal military service. Although his career was cut short and redirected towards the Catholic Church, his notions of royal service and its opportunities for others of his status remained keen. When Armand became the Cardinal Richelieu, he transformed the French nobility into royal servants. Nowhere did he see greater room for the nobility to exhibit their martial spirit than by military service in a permanent army raised and paid for by the monarchy.

In the German states, the Holy Roman Emperor had little military authority until the reform of the military constitution and reorganization of the Empire between 1500 and 1512. The empire was divided into *Kreise* (circles) and the princes of these circles were required to contribute men, money and material for the defence of the Empire in the event of a *Reichkrieg* (imperial war). The military contributions of each circle could be doubled, tripled or quadrupled by a decree of the Imperial Diet. Considering the confederated nature and political complexity of the empire, such a declaration of *Reichkrieg* was rare. When desperate for troops, the emperors appealed directly to the circles asking the princes to contribute in the absence of an imperial war. It was an effective means of raising an army in Germany and a significant loophole in the Imperial Constitution. This was the means by which the army of the Catholic League was formed in 1618. Lacking funds, the emperor looked to the Bavarian and Swabian circles.

The empire also contained hundreds of small independent estates and free cities, whose counts, knights and city councils were keenly aware that their independent status in the face of the increasingly voracious appetites of their princely neighbours was only guaranteed by imperial protection. The emperors could call upon them to serve as officers for the *Landsknechte*. German armies of the sixteenth and seventeenth centuries remained a complex mix of mercenaries and *Kreise* contingents. A standing army was impossible.

Change came to Germany after and in reaction to the Thirty Years' War. A number of princes, particularly in northern Germany, established small standing armies. They reasoned that the lack of natural barriers to prevent invasion necessitated the creation of well-disciplined armies to defend their territories. The example of Brandenburg-Prussia is the best known, but the Landgraves of Hesse-Darmstadt and Hesse-Kassel, and the dukes of Hanover acted similarly. In Brandenburg-Prussia the financial and material devastation of the Thirty Years' War substantially reduced the wealth and possessions of the *Junkers* (nobles). Frederick William, the Great Elector and later Frederick I, king in Prussia, struck deals with their nobles gaining their military service in return for sovereignty on their estates. As these German nobles were relatively poor it was dificult for them to oppose their princes.

The quality of these soldiers became evident during the late seventeenth century, and the princes often hired out their regiments. The commanders that took them on could often count on these regiments more than their own hastily raised formations. So valued were they that the Emperor Leopold I agreed to elevate the Elector of Brandenburg to king in Prussia in 1701, in return for 15,000 of his soldiers for his war against Louis XIV.

Kahlenberg, 1683: the Relief of Vienna

The 'Year of the Turk,' 1683, was the high-water mark of the Ottoman Turkish Empire. Never again after this year did the Turkish armies threaten central Europe. The Turks had besieged Vienna once before, in 1529. In 1683 the siege of Vienna began in mid-summer, and their rapid progress made the fate of the Habsburg capital uncertain. Emperor Leopold I's desperate attempts to relieve the city give a vivid example of the problems of coalition warfare in the early modern era. The relief army consisted of Imperial German contingents contributed by numerous princes of the Holy Roman Empire, and a Polish army under King Jan III Sobieski.

Raimondo Montecuccoli's victory over the Turks at St Gotthard in 1664 led to a general settlement between the Habsburgs and Ottomans, and for the next 20 years Turkish expansion was redirected to Poland and the Ukraine. Significant territorial gains were made in southern Poland, but

by the 1670s Jan Sobieski, Marshal of Poland, waged several successful campaigns against the Turks and defeated them at the battle of Chotin in 1673. The following year, upon the death of King Michael of Poland, the Polish nobility elected Sobieski his successor as was their custom.

While Sobieski won his glory and crown in the east, the Habsburg Emperor was distracted by war with Louis XIV of France. Louis XIV encouraged Turkish expansion, seeing it as an effective means of distracting the Austrian emperor.

Since 1526 the borders of the Ottoman Empire extended into Hungary. Their provincial capital of Buda was only a short distance from Vienna. Though peace had been maintained for almost 20 years by 1683, it was broken by Imre Thököly, Prince of Transylvania, who was technically a Habsburg vassal. Thököly's loyalty to Leopold waned, and he sought the support of Kara Mustafa, Grand Vizier of

KARA MUSTAPHA, *Grand Vizier of the Ottoman Empire, had Vienna in his grasp. His tent was prominent among the thousands in the Turkish camp surrounding the Austrian capital. It was captured after he fled with the remnants of his army.*

the Ottoman Empire, to attain a royal title in exchange for becoming a vassal of the Sultan.

Kara Mustafa became Grand Vizier in 1676. He waged war in the Ukraine until 1681 when his attention turned towards Vienna. In 1682 a Turkish army moved into northern Hungary, breaking the general peace with Austria. At its heart was a standing force, the janissary corps, who were professionals trained since youth for military service. The janissaries were feared in Europe and their use of firearms and dedication to siegecraft made them formidable. The corps stood at approximately 20,000 men. The soldiers were

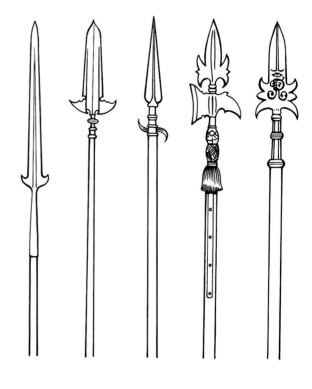

PIKES, BILLS AND HALBERDS *were the weapons of choice for infantry in the 15th century, but by the 17th and 18th centuries they were more commonly carried by sergeants and junior officers, judiciously placed to the front and rear of infantry battalions. Held laterally, they worked well to dress the lines. On the occasion that a soldier would attempt to flee during battle, they were used to dispatch military justice.*

slaves of the Sultan, having been purchased as children from Christians in the Ottoman Empire and raised in the Sultan's palace. Converted to Islam they were trained to serve the Sultan as his elite infantry. The janissaries were the heart of Ottoman armies from the sixteenth to the seventeenth centuries, but by 1683 they lacked the drill and discipline of European armies.

The majority of the Ottoman army was composed of provincial forces, *Sipahis* (noble cavalry) and provincial infantry levies. Tatar horsemen from the Crimea and Caucasus, along with contingents from the Christian princes of the empire accompanied the army. The Ottoman use of artillery and their mastery of siege tactics made their armies formidable, along with their sheer size. The army that marched into Hungary in 1683 exceeded 120,000 men.

Leopold I had no more than 35,000 troops to resist the Turks. As Holy Roman Emperor he turned to the German princes and the Imperial Diet. Pope Innocent XI also took the initiative to broker an

alliance between Leopold and Jan Sobieski, now king of Poland. Papal support included money to raise troops. The Polish monarch agreed to the alliance and pledged 40,000 men for the war.

Tatars in the Vienna Woods
By June Kara Mustafa was in Hungary and on 7 July the emperor and the royal family abandoned Vienna for the safety of Linz, leaving the capital under the protection of Count Ernst von Starhemberg and 16,000 soldiers. Less than a week after Leopold departed Vienna Tatar horsemen swarmed into the suburbs. The city was completely surrounded by 14 July and Turkish cannon opened fire on its outer defences. Kara Mustafa did not waste time. Within two weeks of opening the

siege, trenches were cut, tunnels dug and mines exploded at the two southern bastions. Turkish artillery fire rained down on the city and Count Stahremberg was struggling to hold the outer works. The Grand Vizier sent his Tatars raiding into the Vienna Woods.

It took time to assemble armies in the empire and in Poland to fight the Turks. Leopold appealed to the Imperial Diet at Regensberg and to the individual circles of the empire for military contributions. The Diet approved a tripling of military contingents from the empire, but French military action west of the Rhine prevented some western circles from sending troops. By August the duke of Lorraine commanded approximately 30,000 Imperial troops. John George III of Saxony raised an additional 10,000, and Max Emmanuel of Bavaria raised an equal number.

In Poland Sobieski found it difficult to raise an army in a short time. Sobieski arrived in Cracow by the end of July and remained there until mid-August. Troops were arriving virtually every day, but the Cossacks and Lithuanians were not expected for several more weeks. Sobieski decided not to wait for them. He left Cracow and marched on Vienna.

The various armies converged on the besieged Habsburg capital, and the Poles arrived on 31 August north of the Danube, joining the duke of Lorraine and elector John George with the Imperialist troops. Sobieski had brought only 24,000 of the 40,000 men he had promised, but the combined armies totalled 75,000 men.

Crossing the Danube 20 miles upstream from the city, the duke of Lorraine and Sobieski intended moving into the Vienna Woods, the hilly wooded country north and west of Vienna, and taking the heights where they would launch their attack on the Turkish army. Kara Mustafa was aware of their presence, but discounted the reports of their strength. He was confident that the Tatars and a modest Turkish force in the Vienna Woods would keep his enemy at bay. Vienna was expected to fall any day and he did not want to abandon the siege when he was so close to victory. Ibrahim Bey, the governor of Buda led 23,000 infantry and 5000 cavalry into the hill country to hold back the Imperialists and the Poles.

At a council of war Sobieski and Lorraine agreed to divide the army into three parts. The duke and John George of Saxony would lead the left wing along the course of the Danube to the city. More than 31,000 Imperialists and Saxons took post on the heights of Kahlenberg overlooking Ibrahim Bey's position at Nussdorf. Max Emmanuel of Bavaria, and Prince Waldeck with the Bavaria and Kreise regiments, more than 21,000 strong, was to move on Sievring and Wahring, eventually reaching Vienna. On the right was the duke of Lauenberg with 4500 infantry from Lorraine's army and on the far-right wing was Sobieski and the Polish army, 14,000 armoured cavalry – including the famous winged hussars – and 10,000 infantry.

In the early morning hours of 12 September Ibrahim pushed his troops forwards, probing Lorraine's line. The duke ordered Prince Louis of Baden (later called Türkenlouis) commanding the Austrian regiments to chase them off. To Louis' right the Saxons moved forwards in support. A heated contest between Austrian, Saxon and Turk flared. Initially stubborn resistance was reduced with the aid of Imperial artillery and the ever-increasing weight of Lorraine and John George's numbers. The town of Nussdorf was taken, and Heiligestadt too not long after. In the centre Max Emmanuel found the going more difficult. He and Waldeck encountered troops under the Bey of Damascus who held them in check between Sievring and Grinzing. The Turks had an opportunity to turn Max Emmanuel's flank. Fortunately the Tatars were raiding south of Vienna on the day of the battle and Ibrahim had only a small amount of cavalry available. The Germans formed closed columns to protect themselves.

Winged Hussars

The difficult terrain delayed Sobieski and Lauenberg. The Germans were closer to Max Emmanuel's position and Lauenberg was detached by the Polish king to turn the Turkish centre. Sobieski's cavalry worked their way through the hills and woods and emerged on the far right as planned. Turkish cavalry made determined charges against the Poles as they debouched from the woods. Winged hussars eventually cleared the way between Gersthof and Dornbach and Sobieski was able to deploy all his 14,000 armoured horsemen

Battle of Kahlenberg

1683

The siege of Vienna was in its eighth week when a central European relief army arrived on the north bank of the Danube. The duke of Lorraine assembled an army drawn from the German territories and increased with the timely arrival of a Polish army under King Jan Sobieski. At a council of war, it was decided that the combined armies would cross the Danube 32 km (20 miles) upstream, and advance on the city from the west, through the Vienna Woods. Kara Mustafa was confident Vienna would fall before they could attempt to relieve it. He kept the majority of his army, including the janissaries, in the trenches, while deploying one-third to block the German-Polish advance. From the heights of the Kahlenberg, Lorraine and his allies attacked downslope against the Turkish positions. Heavy fighting through the Vienna Woods slowed the advance but Lorraine broke through along the Danube, and the Poles fought their way through on the right. Sobieski's cavalry poured into the Turkish camp. Lorraine reached the suburbs of Vienna and the Turkish trenches, annihilating the Janissaries still there.

Vienna's strategic position would have given the Turks a foothold in central Europe, threatening future Turkish offensives into Bohemia and southern Germany.

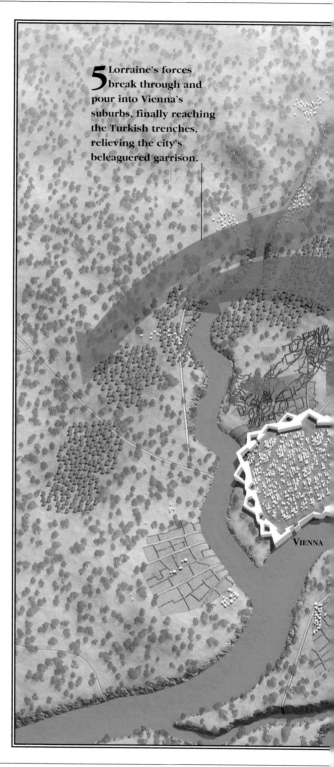

5 Lorraine's forces break through and pour into Vienna's suburbs, finally reaching the Turkish trenches, relieving the city's beleaguered garrison.

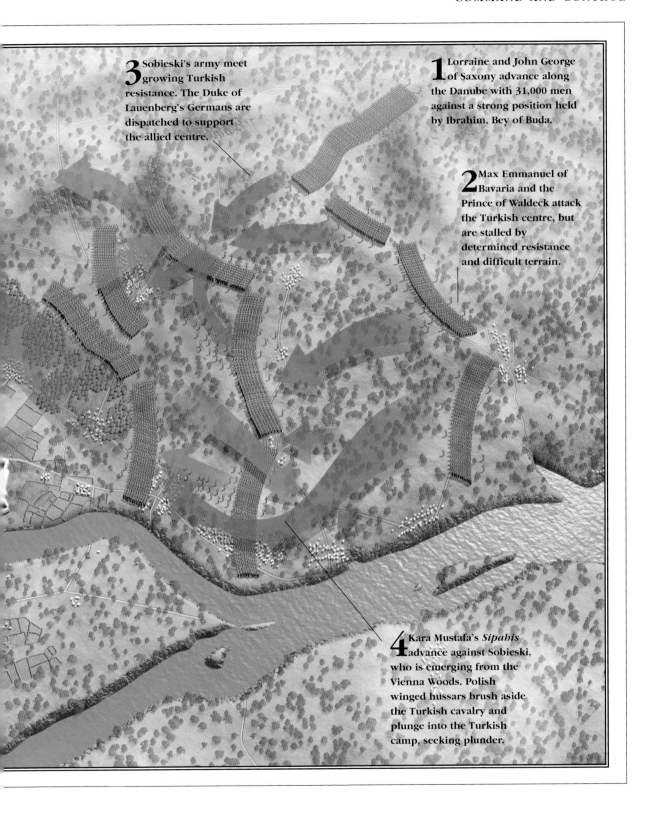

3 Sobieski's army meet growing Turkish resistance. The Duke of Lauenberg's Germans are dispatched to support the allied centre.

1 Lorraine and John George of Saxony advance along the Danube with 31,000 men against a strong position held by Ibrahim, Bey of Buda.

2 Max Emmanuel of Bavaria and the Prince of Waldeck attack the Turkish centre, but are stalled by determined resistance and difficult terrain.

4 Kara Mustafa's *Sipahis* advance against Sobieski, who is emerging from the Vienna Woods. Polish winged hussars brush aside the Turkish cavalry and plunge into the Turkish camp, seeking plunder.

in two lines. It was midday and Ibrahim's corps was collapsing. Shortly after noon the Polish king personally led an attack that cracked the Turkish troops opposed to him. He pursued them into the Turkish camp. Shortly thereafter Lorraine's wing led by Prince Louis broke the Turkish right and moved on Wahring.

The janissaries were kept in the trenches by Kara Mustafa to maintain the siege and when the Imperialists appeared they stood their ground. The Saxons and Bavarians lent weight to the renewed assault on the Turkish trenches. Kara Mustafa had terribly under-estimated his enemy's strength. He was so surprised he almost fell into Polish hands. The Poles halted their pursuit at reaching the Turkish camp and began plundering. By 5 PM the Ottoman resistance had collapsed and the city was saved. Turkish losses were between 10,000–20,000. The Imperialists and their allies lost 4000.

The relief of Vienna was a central European effort. The difficulty of raising forces in the face of French military operations in Germany was balanced by the timely arrival of the Polish army. The distance between Passau, where Leopold set up his camp, and Warsaw, created great uncertainty about whether Sobieski would honour his agreements, and to what extent he was able to assemble an army.

For that matter, the size of the kingdom of Poland increased the time taken for Polish nobles and their troops to join the king. Sobieski left the capital still waiting for thousands of men from Lithuania. He assumed they were en route, when in fact they were never raised by the Lithuanian princes. It was extremely difficult for the duke of

Lorraine to plan a relief effort when he was unsure Sobieski would even arrive. Even dismissing the problems of coordinating with an ally at great distance, Lorraine still had to coordinate the movement of the Imperial army with that of John George of Saxony, who was marching through Bohemia. Messengers and envoys on horseback rode in all directions to enable Lorraine to assess when and where all the armies would be able to meet.

Kara Mustafa paid the ultimate price for his failure. On Christmas Day 1683 the Grand Vizier was executed at Belgrade on the Sultan's orders. He had enormous military resources at hand, but was so focused on Vienna that he under-estimated the significance of the relief force. Similarly, he did not try to delay Lorraine's advance, nor that of the Polish king, despite information on their approach. It was an error to send the Tatars en masse to south of the city on the day of the battle when they should have been in action in the west against Lorraine, harrying and scouting. The scant forces sent into the Vienna Woods did delay Lorraine, but in the absence of Kara Mustafa's superior numbers of cavalry they stood no chance against Sobieski's flanking manoeuvre. In the end it was a poorly handled affair.

By the late 17th and early 18th century uniforms were supplied to ever-expanding armies. Although the common soldier wore relatively plain apparel, officer's and non-commissioned officer's uniforms were a bit more polished. This allowed them to stand out in formation on the battlefield. Piping generally reflected the rank and station of an officer.

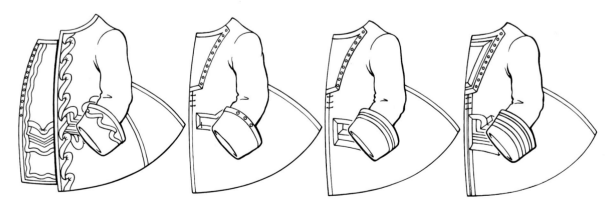

Supreme Command and Standing Armies

It was not until the 1640s that Richelieu and his successor Cardinal Mazarin hired armies led by French generals. These men, however, were still drawn from the grandees. Marshal Vicomte de Turenne took command in Germany in 1643, and despite having been a servant of the crown he led rebel forces during the first Fronde six years later. Similarly, Louis II, duc d'Enghien, later prince de Condé, responsible for the decisive victory over the Spanish at Rocroi in 1643, defended the monarchy during the first Fronde, fought desperately against Mazarin in the second, and went into self-imposed exile rather than return to royal service afterwards. Only after the passing of these experienced grand nobles was Louis able to elevate mid-level nobles to prominent military rank, binding their prestige to the military glory of the monarchy. Marshals Villeroi, Tallard and Villars were only promoted at the beginning of the War of

Spanish Succession, but they obeyed their sovereign despite disagreements over military strategy and occasional royal micromanagement of their campaigns. Louis' previous marshals tended to ignore him if they disagreed.

As the military entrepreneur had disappeared by the War of Spanish Succession (1701–1714), in central and eastern Europe generals of noble birth from military families replaced the military contractors. Soldiers of fortune with noble patents sought military service with foreign leaders too. At the Habsburg court the Stahrembergs retained a substantial presence in the *Hofkriegsrat* (High War Council) and among army commanders well into the eighteenth century. Raimondo Montecuccoli and Prince Eugene of Savoy were not subjects of the Habsburg emperors but commanded their armies from the seventeenth through eighteenth centuries. In fact, Prince Eugene initially approached Louis XIV for a

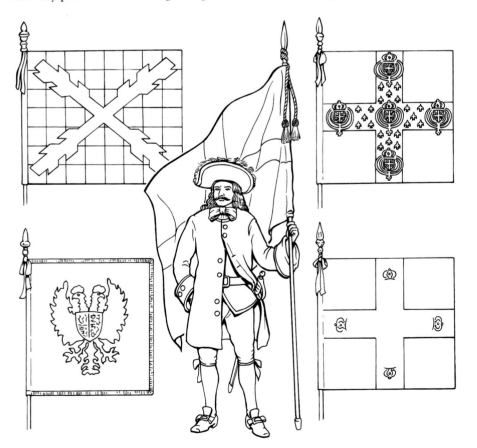

BANNERS WERE USED regularly on the battlefield to identify an individual or a unit in the midst of the chaos that is war. As armies grew banners and flags became critical for identifying regiments on the battlefield. Each was different, reflecting dynastic colours, coats of arms, regional character and eventually unit history. Top left is a banner from one of the Spanish Tercio of Flanders; top right is a Prussian regimental banner; bottom left is an Austrian banner; at the bottom right and centre are French flags.

153

commission and only took employment with the Austrian Hapsburgs after being rejected.

Leadership of the Swedish army changed more rapidly between the days of Gustavus Adolphus and Charles XII. Although the monarch retained personal command of the army, its officer corps followed similar patterns as their German counterparts. Whereas one-third of Gustavus' army was Swedish, one-third Saxon allies and the remainder recruited from Germany, Holland and Scotland, by the Great Northern War Charles XII's army was largely drawn from Swedish territories and led by Swedish generals. The army he led in Russia and Poland was almost exclusively drawn from the Sweden's Baltic Empire, while the army that confronted the Danes relied on allied and hired German troops.

Charles' opponent, Peter the Great, reformed the Russian army by eliminating the *Streltsy* (palace guard) and compelling the nobility to serve as officers in the line as was the custom in western Europe. Foreigners were initially recruited to train and lead the army, but as losses incurred through the years of war were substantial, necessity dictated the establishment of a reliable pool from which to draw military leadership. This too was terribly difficult and did not produce desired results. To meet this challenge Peter advanced the revolutionary notion of promotion for merit at the very moment he was constructing a standing army. This created an officer corps of veterans whose lack of social standing did not prevent them leading troops. In truth their elevation rarely extended beyond the ranks of junior officers, but it provided experienced leadership. By the end of the Tsar's reign meritocracy was so vital to his army and regime that he established the famed Table of Ranks (1722), giving graded social status to officers and civil servants.

Professional Armies

By the middle of the eighteenth century, it was normal to have professional armies. Even the Habsburgs, who disliked spending any more than they absolutely had to, had been compelled to raise a standing army by the War of Austrian Succession. Command of these standing armies varied. In some cases they were led by monarchs like Frederick the Great, although the soldier-king was initially guided by German princes in his service, such as Leopold I, prince of Anhalt-Dessau, or professionals like von Schwerin. Even Habsburg armies came to be led by military professionals such as Field Marshals Maximilian Browne, Daun and Loudon, though dynastic considerations might sometimes give command to incompetents like Charles of Lorraine.

Louis XV of France employed Maurice de Saxe, one of more than 300 bastard children of Augustus the Strong of Saxony. But by the Seven Years' War the quality of French military leadership had declined. On more than one occasion French generals were faced with demands from their colonels who were either their social superiors, or who had connections at court, including demands that their regiments receive posts of honour on the field of battle, or their refusal to serve alongside regiments of their rivals and inferiors. Soldiers of fortune and lesser nobles were reduced in status by this re-emergence of the court nobility. Competition among these powerful nobles often resulted in Louis XV appointing dual commanders to a single army.

Despite the enormous difficulties in forging a professional army, the nobility were a critical part of the enterprise for two reasons. First, they were the social elite. As descendants of the warrior class it was generally believed that they were naturally imbued with martial prowess. Only in rare cases were commoners or other non-nobles to be found among the senior ranks in continental armies. The other important factor was the financial capacity of the nobility because commissions were sold as a matter of course. The higher the rank the greater the cost of office. Royal commissions were a mark of wealth and prestige. The price was further determined by the regiment's reputation and status. Colonels were required to ensure their troops were properly equipped and trained. Though the state paid for basic maintenance, any shortfall was to be made up by the regimental patron (known, for example, as the *Inhaber* in Germany), and the colonel passed on his costs to his subordinates. Captains were responsible for the condition of their companies and lieutenants were

IN ORDER TO DEFRAY *the cost of maintaining large armies, monarchs often sold commissions. The more prestigious the rank and position, the greater was the purchase price. Although uniforms were standard by the 18th century, embellishments were initially permitted to reflect the individual's social and military stature. On the left is a British general, in the centre an officer of engineers and on the right a British Field Marshal. The latter appeared to prefer a less ostentatious display of his rank.*

expected to contribute as well. The fiscal responsibility was substantial and many nobles went into severe debt or bankruptcy in the course of their military career.

Of course not all colonels undertook their responsibilities equally. The unevenness of regimental preparedness was often evident at the beginning of a war. There was always a discrepancy between the paper strength and the actual strength of regiments. To prevent regiments being under-strength and badly equipped, Louis XIV created the rank of lieutenant-colonel to ensure that the colonel was taking his job seriously. In order to maintain uniformity, military inspectorates became commonplace into the eighteenth century. Whatever the apparent imperfections of the new standing armies, the monarchies had successfully imposed their authority at every level.

Blenheim, 1704: Bold Strategy

The Battle of Blenheim highlights well both the benefits and the difficulties of coalition warfare in the age of professional armies. It also illustrates the evolving nature of military leadership. John Churchill, duke of Marlborough and Prince Eugene of Savoy won a tremendously decisive battle against the Franco–Bavarian army, which knocked Bavaria out of the war. The political coordination between Queen Anne and Emperor Leopold I was surpassed by the operational cooperation of their respective military commanders. Conversely, the relationship between the French under Marshal Camille Count Tallard and the Bavarians under Elector Maximilian II Emanuel was faulty at best.

The Bavarian alliance was crucial for Louis XIV. In 1703, the French Marshal Claude Villars and Elector Max Emmanuel successfully cleared Bavaria of Imperial forces, but subsequently fell out with each other. In 1704 Villars was recalled and Marshal Tallard was appointed to lead another French army across the Rhine to reinforce the French and Bavarians.

THIS TYPE OF INFANTRY *formation was commonly used around the time of the Battle of Breitenfeld in 1631. Such a formation allowed the infantry to change its direction of fire in case of a cavalry threat, or in support of another unit. The pikemen in the middle of the formation were an added disincentive to cavalry. The unit's standard was protected in the centre and served as an identifier for the commanding general. In fact the infantry battle was usually fought separately from the cavalry battle. Once the cavalry battle had been won by either side, the victorious cavalry would return to help eliminate the enemy's infantry.*

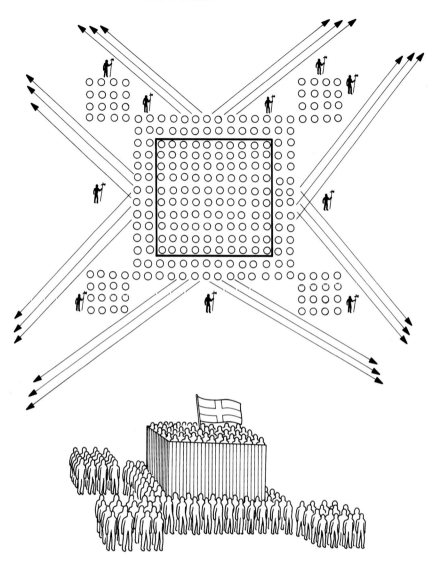

Marlborough led the Anglo-Dutch army. His appointment was the product of years of experience as a soldier, and in particular the fact that his wife was the queen's confidante. Although an English general, he was required by virtue of the Grand Alliance to consult with the Dutch States-General on matters of strategy. In 1704 it was clear that the Imperial effort in southern Germany was on the verge of collapse, and that Vienna was threatened from Bavaria and Hungary. Marlborough decided he would march to Austria's aid. Two factors made this a difficult affair: he would never gain permission of the Dutch States-General to leave with his army and secondly, the Dutch ran his logistics.

The duke misled his Dutch allies by appearing to conduct his operations on the River Moselle. But on 19 May he took 20,000 troops and marched up the River Rhine instead, crossing at Koblenz and arriving at Heidelberg on 7 June. During his march through Germany he was re-inforced by almost 15,000 troops from Hanover, Prussia and the Hesses. Turning east he reached Launsheim two weeks later where he joined Prince Eugene with his Imperial army.

Marlborough moved 402km (250 miles) in almost a month. It was not an unprecedented feat, but impressive nonetheless. He solved his logistical dilemma by leaving his Dutch contractors behind and sending officers in advance of his march to arrange for supplies in those cities he would pass. Because it was all Allied territory, this was not a difficult task.

Logistics

Marlborough's march from the Lower Rhine to Bavaria was truly remarkable, not for the distance travelled nor its speed (the army moved less than 16km/10 miles a day) but for the logistical achievement of detaching his army from its base of supply and redeploying to a new theatre. Logistical considerations had always played a key role in military operations, but as the size of armies increased, the cost and practical difficulty of providing sufficient supplies became paramount strategic considerations. Movement along navigable rivers, or metalled roads passing through major cities was preferred.

Marlborough forewarned Prince Eugene of his intentions to march to the Danube. The Habsburg general sent Prince Louis of Baden with more than half his force to Bavaria while he shadowed Tallard, who crossed the Rhine in early July. Eugene beat Tallard to Bavaria and with Marlborough crossed the Danube to pillage the region. This was done largely to deprive the Bavarian elector of precious resources, and provide for his own army at his enemy's expense. The ravaging of Bavaria forced Max Emmanuel and Tallard to react by moving on Augsburg. Upon their concentration Marlborough and Eugene moved back across the Danube. Tallard and Max Emmanuel pursued moving east along the river to Blenheim where they camped on 12 August. Beyond Blenheim was the Nebel stream and on the other side, Marlborough and Eugene's army.

Tallard was confident in his position. It was anchored by the Danube on his right, and to his front was the Nebel, with marshy banks, dotted by several small towns. It was a strong position and he did not think Marlborough and Eugene would chance an attack. But he deployed his army for battle. Max Emmanuel held the left between Lutzingen and Oberglau with 42 battalions of infantry and 67 squadrons of cavalry. Tallard himself personally directed the centre and right with 33 battalions and 76 squadrons. The marshal placed his infantry in the towns with his cavalry deployed to cover the open ground. Nine of his battalions were allocated to Blenheim, supported by 18 in reserve and a dozen squadrons of cavalry. In the interval between this town and Oberglau, more than 2.4km (1.5 miles) in distance, he had two lines of cavalry supported by a third line of infantry. There was no reserve.

On 13 August Marlborough and Eugene surveyed Tallard's position. They determined to attack the Franco–Bavarians that day. Eugene would keep Max Emmanuel occupied while the duke attacked Blenheim and Oberglau. All of these pinning attacks would prevent Tallard from using his superiority in infantry. Into the centre across the Nebel, Charles Churchill, the duke's brother, would lead the *coup de main*. The centre consisted of four lines, seven battalions in the first followed by two lines of 72 squadrons in all. The fourth line comprised a further 11 battalions in reserve. The hammer would fall after Lord Cutts' 20 battalions attacked Blenheim and General Holstein-Beck's Germans stormed Oberglau.

At 12:30 the army was in place and Marlborough ordered the advance. Cutts' battalions stormed the defences of Blenheim, causing the French to commit their entire reserve deployed behind the town. Across the field the Germans met determined resistance. At 2 PM the French cavalry in the centre charged Charles Churchill's lines when a gap appeared between his command and Holstein-Beck. Keeping a close eye on his centre, Marlborough sent a rider to Eugene asking for support. Fortunately the messenger found his man and the Imperial general quickly dispatched squadrons of Austrian *cuirassiers*. They did the trick and the English centre was saved. Churchill continued his advance.

The cooperation between Eugene and Marlborough was critical to their success. If Eugene had failed to dispatch cavalry to support the English centre it would have been disastrous. By 3 PM the Germans wrested Oberglau from the French though Holstein-Beck was killed in the process, and Blenheim was contained. Marlborough moved his centre forwards against Tallard's cavalry and re-inforced it with the cavalry that were no longer needed to support Cutts. Tallard opposed them with 64 squadrons and nine battalions. The duke released his now 81 squadrons and 18 battalions at 4 PM. Their overwhelming numbers broke the French line. Eugene's attack upon Max Emmanuel's wing was

Battle of Blenheim

1704

John Churchill, duke of Marlborough, marched his
army more than 402 km (250 miles) from the
Netherlands to Bavaria, to come to his Austrian ally's
aid. Marlborough and Prince Eugene of Savoy, his
Habsburg counterpart, engaged French Marshal
Tallard and Elector Max II Emmanuel of Bavaria at
Blenheim. The Franco-Bavarian army held a strong
position with the Danube to their right, and their
front guarded by a stream with marshy banks,
fortified by several villages and towns. Despite the
strength of their position, Tallard disposed of his
troops poorly, leaving his cavalry to guard the
centre, while his infantry was isolated largely in
Blenheim. Marlborough attacked the town, pinning
Tallard's battalions there, and launched a determined
assault upon the French centre. Prince Eugene
advanced in coordination with his ally, and
prevented Max Emmanuel from coming to Tallard's
aid. The French centre collapsed, Tallard's infantry
were trapped in and around Blenheim and Max
Emmanuel withdrew with the remnants of his army.

*Blenheim is located on the north bank of the
Danube in Bavaria. Several Bavarian cities,
including Donauworth, were the scene of pitched
battles during this campaign.*

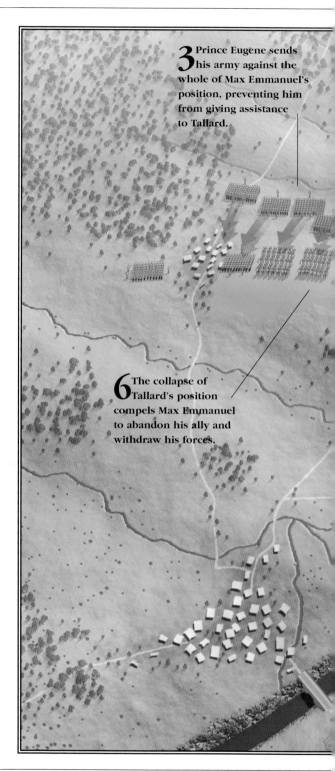

3 Prince Eugene sends
his army against the
whole of Max Emmanuel's
position, preventing him
from giving assistance
to Tallard.

6 The collapse of
Tallard's position
compels Max Emmanuel
to abandon his ally and
withdraw his forces.

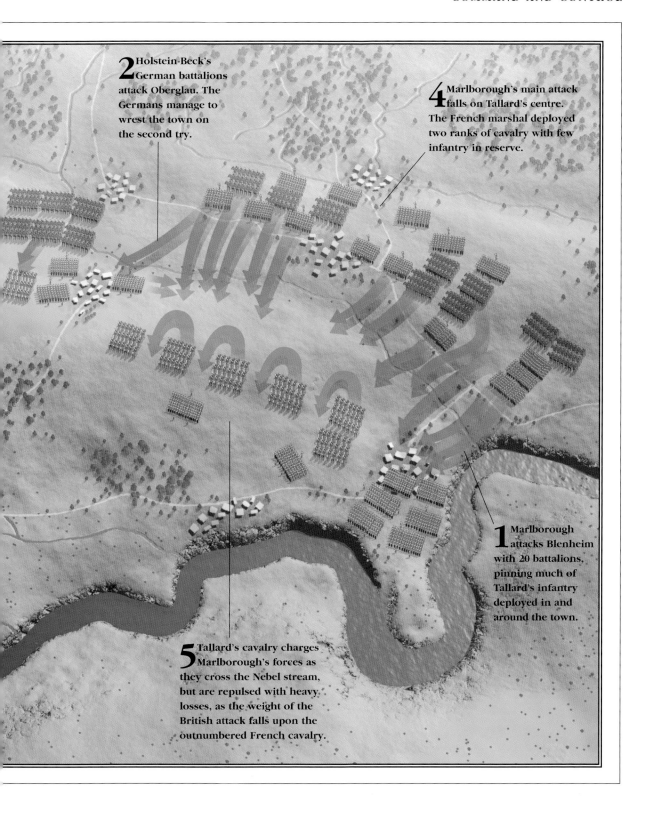

2 Holstein-Beck's German battalions attack Oberglau. The Germans manage to wrest the town on the second try.

4 Marlborough's main attack falls on Tallard's centre. The French marshal deployed two ranks of cavalry with few infantry in reserve.

1 Marlborough attacks Blenheim with 20 battalions, pinning much of Tallard's infantry deployed in and around the town.

5 Tallard's cavalry charges Marlborough's forces as they cross the Nebel stream, but are repulsed with heavy losses, as the weight of the British attack falls upon the outnumbered French cavalry.

pressed so effectively that the Bavarian elector was unable to support Tallard when John Churchill's attack fell on the French centre. In a matter of less than two hours Tallard's army collapsed and fled. The battalions and squadrons at Blenheim were surrounded and compelled to surrender. Max Emmanuel extricated his wing after suffering terrible losses.

The entire French military effort in Bavaria collapsed in a single afternoon. Tallard and his Bavarian allies lost 20,000 casualties, and 14,000 prisoners: more than half his army. The English and Imperialists took 13,000 casualties - a price they could afford, considering the results. Max Emmanuel was cut off from his electorate and withdrew towards the Rhine River. Eugene proceeded to invest the Bavarian fortresses and occupy his lands. Tallard lost several thousand more men during his retreat, leaving scant French forces on the upper Rhine. Louis XIV began the year with Vienna under threat and the entire Imperial cause in jeopardy. On 13 August he lost an army and in November he lost his ally. Bavaria withdrew from the French alliance. For the remainder of the war Louis' armies were forced to operate from bases on the left bank of the Rhine. That put them at a strategic disadvantage because the Austrians and Imperialists could threaten France much more easily than French armies could threaten the heart of Austria.

Generalship on Campaign and on the Battlefield

War in the early modern era was a costly affair. Raising an army and supplying it put enormous strain on state and personal resources, as Marlborough and Max Emmanuel were both to experience in 1704. As the wars of this period tended to be dynastic in nature acquisition of territory was paramount. Possession was nine-tenths of the law and the ability to arrive at the negotiating table having seized substantial territory, towns and cities guaranteed the right to keep some after the peace. Territorial acquisition promised financial reward, compensating for the cost of conflict. Battle was not as cost effective or as beneficial as outmanoeuvring the enemy and taking territory without battle.

The preference for manoeuvre and siege over battle prevailed throughout the early modern era.

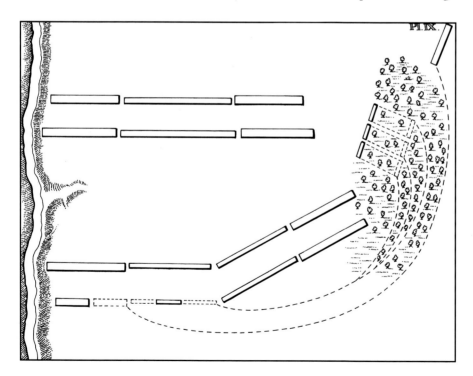

FREDERICK THE GREAT'S *work, entitled* Military Instructions, *includes this diagram. It illustrates the oblique attack, an enfilade advance upon an enemy line. Frederick employed this tactic at Leuthen with great success, crushing the Austrians in Silesia in December 1757.*

Maurice of Nassau only fought two major engagements throughout his career, at Turnhout (1597) and Nieuport (1600). The ability to achieve victory by outmanoeuvring the enemy without engaging in battle, was seen as a higher form of war. Manoeuvre also offered substantial territorial gains as the enemy could be forced from an entire region. Wallenstein's march from Bohemia to Nuremberg in 1632 forced Gustavus Adolphus to abandon Bavaria and move north to prevent his lines of supply and communications being cut. Wallenstein's subsequent movement into Saxony compelled Gustavus to abandon Franconia. During the Wars of Louis XIV, Marshal Sebastien le Prestre de Vauban's successes at siege warfare did more for the extension and securing of French territory than the military feats of his generals.

Generals consciously operated within this framework and pursued state objectives in this manner. The lack of decisive battles led to wars of attrition, where state resources would have to be exhausted before an enemy would come to terms. This was the rationale for Gustavus' scouring of Bavaria in 1631–32; for the deliberate devastation of the Palatinate in 1674 and 1688; and the duke of Marlborough's ravaging of Bavaria in 1704. These examples illustrate the vital importance of logistics. A hungry army becomes unruly and loses discipline and cohesion. Soldiers tolerated irregular pay, but only for short periods. Mutinies were commonplace in armies of the sixteenth and seventeenth centuries. The aphorism, 'point d'argent, point de Suisse,' (no money, no Swiss) applied equally to the military contractor who neglected soldier's pay. The problem continued in the professional armies of the eighteenth century, though in a different form.

> *'The functions of a general are infinite. He must know how to subsist his army...how to place it so that he will not be forced to fight except when he chooses; how to form his troops in an infinity of different dispositions; how to profit from that favourable moment which occurs in all battles and which decides their success.*
>
> – MAURICE DE SAXE, REVERIES

Desertion was a terrible problem and contributed to the brutal discipline imposed by officers and non-commissioned officers. The notion that a soldier in the Prussian army was more afraid of his sergeant than the enemy was true.

When battle was accepted the traditional deployment since ancient times was the placement of cavalry on the wings and infantry in the centre. Cavalry remained the *arme blanche* into the eighteenth century. Its manoeuvrability and the gradual adoption of firearms made it formidable on the battlefield. Infantry, much more slow-moving, needed to have its vulnerable flanks covered by cavalry. Battles commonly began with the advance of cavalry on the wings with the intention of turning the enemy flanks.

Armies grew in size in the seventeenth century, so generals deployed in greater depth. Two or three lines several hundred metres apart let the general sustain a battle by feeding units into the first line. The second and third lines also ensured that the collapse of the first line did not translate into the total destruction of the entire army. This deployment was stressed by Vegetius and reflected a strong Roman influence.

The emergence of cannon by the fifteenth century transformed the nature of siege warfare and gradually altered the shape of the battlefield. In the sixteenth and seventeenth centuries most artillery was heavy and difficult to manoeuvre. Its initial emplacement on the field was its final one. Gustavus Adolphus was the first to experiment seriously with lighter regimental guns. Heavier calibre weapons could normally only bombard the enemy until their own troops' advance obscured the line of fire. Regimental guns could move more easily but remained too cumbersome to keep up with the infantry in the course of a battle. There were few occasions until the eighteenth century that generals were able to employ artillery in reasonably mobile fashion. In most cases then, heavy guns prepared the enemy position for a general attack, while lighter cannon supplemented regimental fire and were most effective defending a position.

Command and control of an army was anything but scientific. As army size grew and depth and breadth of the line of battle increased it became problematic. Generals divided their armies into wings and appointed subordinates or allied generals to command one of them. While generals were not required to lead attacks personally, it was part of their martial culture to do so. Officers led by example. It became less common as time passed and by the late seventeenth and eighteenth centuries army commanders tended to direct the action from a vantage point.

Regimental banners allowed the general to identify his units and observe their progress in battle. Banners also provided rallying points for soldiers confused and lost in the heat of combat. As gunpowder weapons became prevalent smoke obscured larger sections of the battlefield. Messengers were crucial in receiving and dispatching orders and information from one part of the line to another, and from the commander to his reserves. When riders failed to get the general's orders to units in a timely fashion, generals might lead units into action themselves. At the Battle of Prague in 1757 Marshal von Schwerin, seeing Prussian infantry waver, grabbed their standard from his horse and shouted, 'Come on my children!' Unfortunately, he was blown away by a cluster of grapeshot shortly afterwards.

Throughout the early modern era an army's strength was committed at the beginning of a battle. Defence in depth and the maintenance of a

COMPARE THESE GENTLEMEN *to the British officers on page 155. On the left is a Saxon officer of cuirassier (heavy cavalry) with breast and back plate and helmet. The figure in the centre is a Marshal of France, holding the esteemed baton, and to his right a French general. Note the distinguishing features of their uniforms, particularly when compared to the British Field Marshal in the earlier illustration.*

reserve was likely to be advantageous, but did not guarantee victory. Often grand battles devolved into a contest of small unit actions and a general's ability to coordinate them decreased as time went on.

Choosing one's ground and the construction of field-works were also crucial. In either case it created what is today referred to as a force multiplier. If a general was outnumbered or inclined for other reasons to take up a defensive posture, he would choose ground that would protect his flanks, break up the enemy advance and/or funnel the enemy army into a killing zone.

While this promised better chances of success, nothing was certain. Peter the Great used field-works and entrenchments regularly from his first battle with Charles XII at Narva (1700) to his victory over the Swedish king at Poltava (1709). At Narva the Russian infantry fled in the face of a determined Swedish attack. At Poltava, the Russian army stood its ground in its fortified camp, using outlying forts to wear down the Swedish assault, and then sortied from its position to counter-attack, successfully.

Battles were not fought in a vacuum but within the context of a campaign. A general had to consider the risk and determine whether the net gain was worth the commitment of valuable men and material. Among the list of great captains of the early modern era, most fought few battles and it was possible for a campaign season to pass without a serious engagement. By the eighteenth century the scope of the conflict and the size of armies made fighting battles less risky. In the end, a general had to understand what the great Prussian general Helmuth von Moltke said after his victory over Austria in 1866, 'Great success in war is not achieved without great risks.'

FRENCH UNIFORMS *were much like those of other European armies of the period. This illustration shows a private of the Mestre-de-Camp cavalry regiment (mounted) and an officer of the La Reine cavalry brigade. Both formations fought at Rossbach.*

Rossbach, 1757: Prussia Triumphant

Unlike many of his contemporaries, Frederick the Great did not shy from battle. In 1757 alone he fought four major engagements: at Prague, Kolin, Rossbach and Leuthen. All but Rossbach were very costly in lives. Historians have often debated whether Frederick sought a war of annihilation through battle or one of attrition. Prussia was, after all, surrounded by enemies. In the 1750s Maria Theresa, the Habsburg empress, convinced the major continental powers to join her efforts to defeat the Prussian monarch and divide his possessions.

In 1757 Frederick faced the enmity of Austria, and counted Russia and France among his other enemies. The Prussian kingdom lacked the men and money that his opponents could muster. England sided with the soldier-king, but its commitments were largely focused in Hanover and north Germany. Two of the battles Frederick

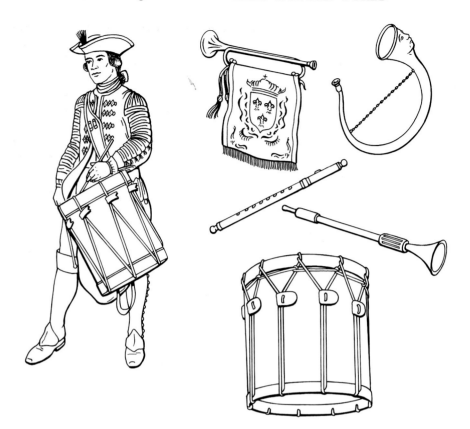

MUSIC WAS CRITICALLY *important to European armies. Pipers, drummers and trumpeters provided the cadence for an army's march. On the battlefield drums and trumpets were used to convey orders over the din of cannon and shot. Musicians were generally young boys, whose uniforms marked them as separate from the rank and file.*

fought in 1757 were not of his choice. Both Prague and Kolin were the products of Austrian efforts to raise the siege of Prague. But Rossbach and Leuthen were deliberate engagements designed to eliminate strategic threats. The Battle of Rossbach plays a particularly important role in the conduct of the campaign. Frederick's victory there re-invigorated the demoralized monarch and ensured the defence of his realm.

1757 began well enough. Frederick's occupation of Saxony the previous year allowed him to invade Bohemia in the spring. The first months of the campaign found him before the gates of Prague, yet by summer the tide of war had turned. In May an Austrian relief army under Marshal Browne approached the Bohemian capital. With few troops to spare, Frederick marched to meet Browne and defeated him after a bloody day's combat that cost him the life of a dear friend, Marshal von Schwerin.

A month later Daun, at the head of a second Austrian army advanced to the relief of the city.

Once more, Frederick detached troops from the siege and moved to engage the Austrian marshal. The Battle of Kolin was a desperate affair in which Frederick himself narrowly escaped capture. It was here that the soldier-king supposedly harangued a regiment of infantry, sword in hand, shouting 'Rogues! Do you want to live forever?' After suffering 14,000 casualties, Frederick left the field of battle to his enemy, raised the siege of Prague and limped back to Saxony. The situation worsened. France entered the war in the spring of 1757, sending a huge army into Germany under the Duc d'Estrees.

This would have been devestating enough but Frederick soon found that Prussia had been compromised even further by the Swedes and Russians. Sweden joined the alliance in the spring and landed a small army in Swedish Pomerania. Tsarina Elizabeth also contributed a large Russian army to the war effort. In the summer Marshal Apraxin advanced upon East Prussia with 100,000 men, where Frederick had only 30,000.

Surrounded

The Prussian king looked for an opportunity to strike at his enemies where he could inflict a significant blow. After their victory at Kolin the Austrians were moving forces into Silesia to retake the province Frederick had stolen a decade earlier. Although he could march to the relief of the meagre Prussian army there, a better opportunity presented itself when a second French army of 24,000 under Charles de Rohan, Prince de Soubise crossed the Rhine. Moving through Hesse-Kassel into Franconia, Soubise was to meet General Joseph von Saxe-Hilburghausen commanding the *Reicharmee*. The Austrians called for *Kreise* contingents to be raised against Frederick in 1757. The Imperial army numbered more than 32,000 men by the end of summer and combined with the French outnumbered Frederick's field army by two to one.

The Allied plan was that Soubise and Hilburghausen were to push into Saxony while the French army in Hanover moved into Brandenburg, the Russians into East Prussia and the Austrians into Silesia. By October the French and Imperial armies had moved into the Saxon Duchies. Frederick benefited from the lack of cooperation between the two generals, reminiscent of Villars and Max Emmanuel in 1703. According to the Austro-French military agreement, Soubise was to act as an auxiliary to Hilburghausen's army. The prince chafed at the notion. He had little military experience and he owed his rank to his social standing. He was not yet a Marshal of France, and his appointment in 1757 was due to his friendship with Madame de Pompadour, mistress to Louis XV. Frederick had offered Pompadour a bribe to

'When a general conducts himself with prudence, he can still suffer ill fortune.... Weather, harvest, the officers, the health or sickness of his troops, blunders...exposure of your spies...and finally, betrayal. These are things that should be kept continually before your eyes so as to be prepared for them and so that good fortune will not blind us.

— FREDERICK THE GREAT,
MILITARY INSTRUCTIONS

reconsider the French war effort but it failed. He received a warmer response from Richelieu, the new commander of the French army in Hanover.

At the end of October Frederick moved his army west towards Soubise and Hilburghausen, whose army was afflicted with terrible desertion. There was inadequate logistical preparation for the campaign, the soldiers were hungry and had not been paid. Regardless, the disparity in numbers was substantial if only they could coordinate properly. However, Soubise preferred to manoeuvre against Frederick and not offer battle.

The disunity between Soubise and Hilburghausen offered Frederick greater opportunity to catch one of the wings of the French or Imperial army. As the Prussians crossed the Saale River, Soubise and Hilburghausen, whose armies had temporarily separated, rejoined to find safety in numbers. By the evening of 4 November the Prussian army camped near the town of Rossbach, not far from the combined army's position. Intelligence had correctly informed Frederick that the French and Imperialists were low on supplies. He also found out that his enemies controlled no more than 41,000 men. Only one-third of Hilburghausen's army, 11,000 strong, was with Soubise, whose own forces included several thousand German allies.

Hilburghausen and Soubise decided that morning to attack the Prussian king. Instead of an advance head-on, they would screen their camp, and move their columns around the Prussian left flank, catching Frederick unawares. It was a sound plan and uncharacteristically bold. Frederick would do the same the following month at Leuthen. There was, however, a difference. It took most of the

Battle of Rossbach
1757

A French army under the Prince de Soubise marched through Franconia to join with an Imperial army under General Joseph Saxe-Hilburghausen in the Saxon duchies. Frederick thought the close proximity of the Franco-Imperial army gave him a chance to strike. On 4 November he camped at Rossbach, opposite Soubise and Hilburghausen's army, inviting battle. The next morning the two generals decided to attempt a flanking manoeuvre around the Prussian left. Screening their positions with battalions, the Franco-Bavarian army began its circuitous march. A mile to the front of the allied columns rode their vanguard. Frederick's outposts warned the king who quickly redeployed his entire army and sent his battalions forwards in an enfilade attack. To head off the Allied cavalry, Frederick dispatched General Seydlitz with the Prussian cavalry. Seydlitz scattered the enemy squadrons and moved round the Allied right. Frederick's battalions appeared before the Franco-Bavarian army and blasted them as they tried to adjust their formation. Seydlitz's appearance on the French flank alarmed Soubise's army and it was shattered in a short time.

1 Soubise and Hilbughausen move their columns around the Prussian left flank, preceded by a large contingent of cavalry that formed the vanguard.

Frederick chose Saxony as the place to rest his army after the retreat from Bohemia because it offered him a central position in Germany to react to his enemy's numerous thrusts.

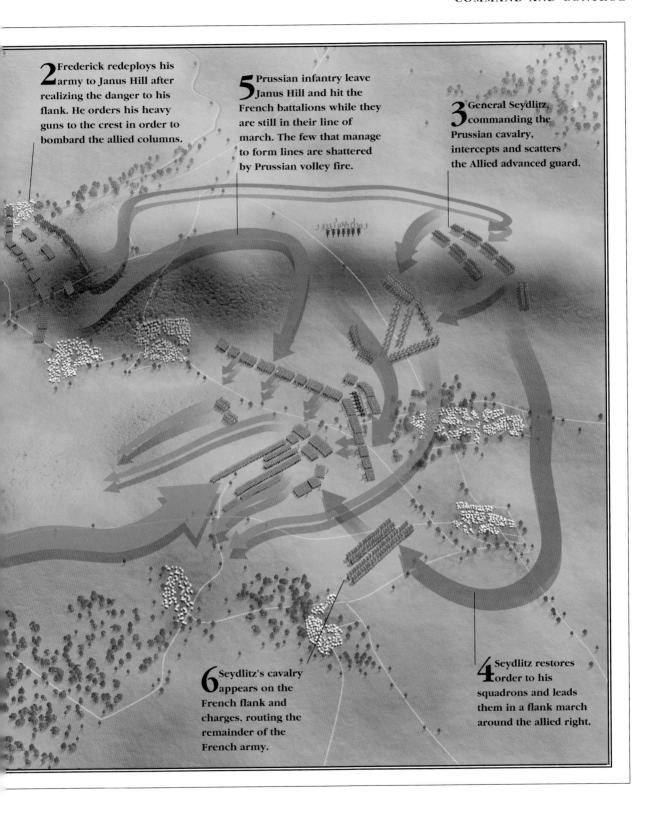

2 Frederick redeploys his army to Janus Hill after realizing the danger to his flank. He orders his heavy guns to the crest in order to bombard the allied columns.

5 Prussian infantry leave Janus Hill and hit the French battalions while they are still in their line of march. The few that manage to form lines are shattered by Prussian volley fire.

3 General Seydlitz, commanding the Prussian cavalry, intercepts and scatters the Allied advanced guard.

6 Seydlitz's cavalry appears on the French flank and charges, routing the remainder of the French army.

4 Seydlitz restores order to his squadrons and leads them in a flank march around the allied right.

morning for the French and Imperialists to organize into three march columns. The advanced guard were Austrian and German heavy cavalry. The first two Allied columns comprised the French army, while Hilburgshausen led the third.

Swift Reactions

Prussian reconnaissance indicated that several French battalions were screening the enemy camp, but clearly there was great activity there. By noon there was still no suggestion of the Allied movement. A Prussian captain interrupted Frederick's lunch. While observing the French battalions screening their camp, he had spotted the Allied columns to the Prussian left. Frederick dismissed the captain's report, but as others came to the king with similar information he was stirred. Seeing that the Prussian position was already compromised and the advance guard of Austrian cavalry was moving perpendicular to his left and rear, Frederick ordered General von Seydlitz, his cavalry commander, to take all the

cavalry and head off the Allied advance. The redeployment of the Prussian army shows the critical importance of decisive leadership, and the benefit of having a well-disciplined, professional army that could respond quickly in a crisis.

As Seydlitz led his cavalry away, the Prussian infantry marched. Frederick benefited from the local geography. To his immediate rear and oblique to the Allied columns was Janus Hill. He ordered his heavy guns to the crest and proceeded to bombard the French more than a mile off. His battalions wheeled left with meticulous precision and marched to their new position on the hill. Fewer than 90 minutes passed between

FREDERICK THE GREAT *addresses his generals on the morning of the Battle of Leuthen, 2 December 1757. The difficulties communicating orders during the course of a battle meant that orders issued the night or the morning before had to be clearly understood. There was little opportunity to alter a plan once the army was disposed and set in motion.*

Frederick's interrupted lunch and the redeployment of his entire army. Prussian artillery opened up at 3:15 PM and Seydlitz's cavalry emerged from around Janus Hill soon after. Ahead was the Allied cavalry still in column. Seydlitz unleashed his 38 squadrons. Surprised, only some of the Austrian cavalry were able to meet the charge. The fighting was sharp, but the Prussian cavalry succeeded in scattering the Allied squadrons. With the enemy in flight, Seydlitz recalled his regiments, illustrating the superb training of these troops and the skill of their general. As the Prussian infantry moved down the slope towards the French, Seydlitz re-formed his regiments and sent them on their own wide flanking march to the French right beyond the towns of Posendorf and Tagewerden.

After the Prussian battalions descended from Janus Hill the Allies were unable to observe their progress due to a dip between their position and the Prussian army. The first sight of Prussian infantry was to their front, when the left-most battalions wheeled right facing the French front. The centre and right of Frederick's army appeared not long afterwards. Only seven French battalions could deploy before the Prussian infantry attacked. Disciplined volleys poured into the head of the Allied columns. The French battalions faltered.

Timing is everything. As the infantry attack developed, Seydlitz's cavalry emerged on the French right. The charge of Prussian heavy squadrons took apart the already shaken army. Whatever control Soubise had disappeared in moments. Hilburghausen was luckier as the Imperialists were in the rear. He had more time to bring his battalions into line and resigned himself to covering the French rout. Prussian infantry fire and artillery salvoes tore holes in Hilburghausen's line. The battalions from Hesse-Darmstadt stood under withering fire while covering the retreat. Seydlitz ordered his cavalry to charge again, completely unnerving the Imperialists who fled.

By 5 PM the field was cleared of French. Hilburghausen moved off with the remnants of his small force. Frederick had not only won the day, but the victory transformed the strategic situation that had depressed the Prussian king through the summer. The battle cost Frederick 500 men. For the French and Imperialists it was much more expensive: 5,000 killed and wounded and another 5,000 captured. Instead of moving into winter quarters, Frederick decided to move rapidly eastwards against the Austrians in Silesia. A month later he was ale to shatter the Austrian army at Leuthen. Frederick could now consider 1757 a good year for Prussia. Oddly, it proved to be not too bad of a year for Soubise either, who blamed the defeat on Hilburghausen. The prince was granted a marshal's baton the following year and was given another command. In the age of Louis XIV he might have been disgraced, as was Tallard after Blenheim, but this was the age of Louis XV, and Madame de Pompadour's friendship counted for more than a mere lost battle.

Conclusion

Generalship had evolved considerably since the sixteenth century. The nature of war, the composition of the armies, technology, increased state revenue, growth in population and the formation of the modern state all brought huge changes. The establishment of military institutions and the evolution of leadership at once created a bureaucracy to wage war, and the other a military administration to direct it. The Military Revolution embodied all of these factors, and redefined the European nobility as a service class.

By the middle of the eighteenth century the institutionalization of war brought about a growing demand for systemization and regimentation. It also became clear that in the Age of Reason marshals, generals and officers must consider military education a fundamental part of their trade. Military academies and the study of military history were already beginning to emerge and Frederick the Great produced several works to enlighten his officer corps. But the military professional found in German armies was still a relatively rare breed. The perseverance of Prussia, and the abject defeat of France in the Seven Years' War led Louis XV to conduct significant military reforms. The result was the opening of the officer corps to non-nobles, trained in new military academies. The product was a well-educated, professional officer corps that would eventually become the military leadership of Revolutionary and Napoleonic France.

CHAPTER 4

SIEGE WARFARE

The siege cannon made its first appearance in Europe in the middle part of the fourteenth century and revolutionized warfare, especially siege warfare, over the following centuries. Complex systems of bastions and outworks were designed in response to this new artillery and increasingly sophisticated new theories of siege warfare were expounded.

The appearance of the first siege cannon would not have struck a professional artillery officer of a later age as particularly impressive. Early siege guns were simply hollowed-out barrels made of iron, mounted on fixed wooden platforms, firing cannon balls of iron or stone. Range, accuracy and rate of fire were all equally feeble. Hence there was little reason to improve or change the building of fortifications in

FRANZ GEFFLER'S PAINTING *depicts the siege of Vienna in 1683 in which Turkish troops under the Grand Vizier attempt to take this heavily-fortified and heroically-defended city. With the timely arrival of King John Sobieski's Polish relief army, this last Ottoman attempt to conquer Europe ended in spectacular and ignominious failure.*

171

the fourteenth or early fifteenth centuries. The walls of fortresses and castles remained high, relatively thin and built to resist storming by ladders or the use of siege towers.

A medieval cannon was a clumsy beast transported on a cart and then actually carried to its firing position by horse or human muscle. It was not a gun that could be used easily in a fluid war of movement and its role had been limited to laying siege to castles and fortified towns. That all changed when the French created an improved siege train capable of mobility and immense firepower.

The French Artillery

The French gun design was revolutionary. The barrel, made of solid bronze, was 2.4m (8ft) long. It was mounted for easy transportation on a wooden carriage that could be pulled by a fairly small team of horses. This mobility gave the French an unprecedented advantage when they took the offensive, as they did in Italy in 1494.

But that was not all. The barrel could be elevated or depressed around the fulcrum formed by two trunnions or prongs, which were cast into the barrels just forwards of the centre of gravity, almost directly over the axle of the two-wheeled gun carriage beneath. For traversing, the trail of the carriage was lifted from the ground and swung to the right or left. Unlike the fixed and clumsy medieval 'iron pipe', this was a modern gun and its basic design was not to change until the late nineteenth century. The French type of cannon could be transported with ease across enormous distances in a relatively short period of time by a small horse team and be in a position upon arrival to be ready for immediate service. The cannon could be used not only to hit the base of a castle's wall like the medieval gun but, if placed in a highly elevated firing position with the barrel elevated, it could fire on the towers and the lip of the curtain walls.

But the French – displaying the professionalism and thoroughness that would characterize the rise of the engineer corps two centuries later – believed that the cannon had to be matched by men specially trained in their use. Here, again, was a departure from the old methods and ideas. In the French army, gunners or artillerists were a specially-trained and led corps of professionals.

Charles VIII invaded Italy in late 1494 with a good-sized army that included a large, modern and

TYPICAL BRONZE CANNONS *used in European warfare for much of the 16th century had barrel lengths of 1.25m (4ft). An improvement on the guns of the previous century, they were fairly ineffective, inaccurate, crude weapons with no capacity to traverse or elevate the barrel.*

THE ITALIANS PIONEERED *an entirely new form of fortress, shown in this drawing of 1561 by G. Zanchi, to meet the 'French' style artillery, which was not only capable of devastating fire power but also mobile. The walls were built at an angle and sloped downwards at a gentle gradient to deflect cannon fire. Behind the walls massive interior masonry buttresses were built to support the walls to withstand artillery fire.*

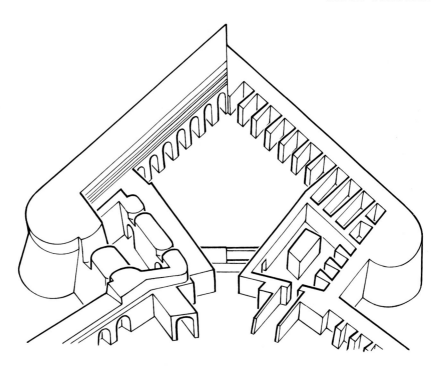

numerous siege train led by specialist troops and officers who were well trained in the use of their guns. The Italians were astonished to find that forts and fortified cities had no chance when confronted by this foe and sieges that would have taken days to accomplish using the equipment and methods of the previous century took the French no more than a few hours. Charles VIII took Florence, Rome and, finally, Naples by January 1495.

The 'Italian' Fort:
Response to the New Siege Artillery

The Italians, once the initial astonishment of the invasion by 'northern barbarians' wore off, responded robustly by overhauling their forts and modelling their own artillery along French lines. The shock of the 1494–95 campaign had swung the advantage entirely over to the side of the besieger. By designing new fortifications the Italians now evened the odds considerably.

Medieval walls were thin and tall. For the new heavy-calibre guns these large, tall targets were simply too good to be true. A short-term solution was to throw up massive, low earthen breastworks that could absorb the artillery fire and protect the higher castle walls. To prevent storming parties

mounting and occupying breastworks these earthen embankments were crested with wooden palisades and held by hand-picked troops.

Fieldworks of this kind were only a temporary solution and, unless regularly maintained, were likely to subside and collapse while the palisades rotted quickly. Obviously the old medieval stone castles had to be replaced by modern fortifications, but this called for an enormous effort in terms of engineering skill and costs.

Italian engineers rejected the circular medieval tower in favour of a four-sided angular bastion with two flanks and two outward faces. The bastion had several advantages. It could bring heavy cross-fire to bear along the ditch, and eliminated the patch of dead ground in front of the medieval circular tower. It was also possible to place a huge number of artillery pieces along the angular walls and thus provide supporting fire to neighbouring bastions. It was no longer necessary, as with many previous fortifications, for each bastion to provide its own close-range defence. These hammer-shaped bastions were to become massive and powerful fortifications in their own right. Grouped closely together they could sweep the intervening ground with concentrated artillery fire.

THIS DUTCH EARTHENWORK fortification, imitating the Trace Italienne model, dates from the early 17th century. It includes a number of levels, with features such as ravelins, or detached bastions (A), demi-lunes (B) and hornworks (C).

The newly-built fortified city of Verona was viewed as a model. However, the Italian engineers were not slaves to a particular model or system of fortification and they adapted their designs to the surrounding topography and landscape. When Venice built its main fortress at Choggia, at the southern end of the Venetian lagoon, the fortress was, unlike Verona, surrounded by a wide water-filled ditch and not massive stone ramparts.

By 1497 the Genoese had designed a triangular earthen fortification, called a ravelin, to cover gates and weak points in the walls – the same role the medieval barbican had had in its time. It soon became apparent that the ravelin could also be used more generally in defending a fortification's walls. Hence ravelins could be built either to protect or give bastions cover fire or be placed at regular intervals in front of curtain walls to give these added protection. A third line of defence was provided by a covered way, behind a dry or wet moat. This gave cover for musketeers who would keep up close fire against attackers,

and protect infantry that would make sorties. The fortress was once again made formidable and stood ready to resist a besieging army's artillery.

The new Italian fortification system worked. In 1500 a Franco-Florentine army laid siege to the city of Pisa, which had been expected to fall with ease once the French artillery began to fire against its walls. The attackers made a breach and the French expected to storm and sack the city with little effort. But the defenders had a nasty surprise in store for the French. They had dug a ditch behind the breach and behind the ditch they had erected a so-called *retirara* – a free-standing rampart or Pisan double rampart. When the French stormed through the breach they were dismayed to find a new wall. Several attempts to take it failed since the infantry, musketeers and artillery huddling behind it proved impossible to dislodge.

Demoralized by this unexpectedly harsh resistance, high casualties and no hope of taking the *retirara* the French – hitherto seemingly invincible – quit the siege. Nine years later, when the defenders adopted the same measures, the French tried and failed to take Padua. It was now certain that the new forts had neutralized the initially devastating effect of the new artillery. The defeated French took due note of these developments and in 1543 the French king,

Francis I, imported a hundred Italian engineers to construct their new style forts for him along his huge kingdom's sprawling frontiers.

The Turkish Art of Mining

If the Turks' siege artillery left something to be desired, that did not apply to their mining operations. Experienced civilian miners, especially Serbs, were recruited by the Ottomans to head mining operations. In the night the miner would take a stone with a string attached, throw it to the foot of the wall, cut the line and pull it back. He would then measure the length of string to calculate how long and deep the tunnel had to be in order to reach the wall. The mine gallery was kept to a correct, straight line by aligning a plumb line suspended from a peg stuck into the ground at the entrance of the tunnel with a with a candle placed at the working-face of the tunnel.

HERE THE BESIEGERS *have breached the defences of the fortress only to find, to their alarm, that the defenders, following the 16th-century Italian technique of siege warfare, have constructed a new improvised line of defence, called a* retirara. *As illustrated, this is made up of earthen ramparts held together with wooden covers and topped by bags.*

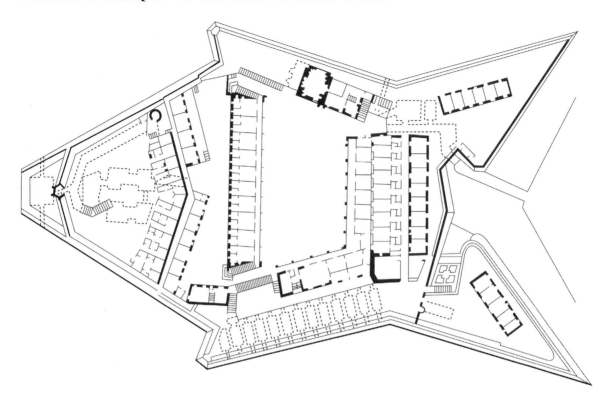

THE SMALL FORTRESS of St Elmo had been built in 1552 by the Spanish military engineer and master architect, Don Pedron Padro as the lynchpin of the Maltese defences of the Grand Harbour. It was well designed but lacked outer defences and was highly vulnerable to Turkish mortar fire.

The Europeans were also keen miners and learnt from the Turks. In 1500 the Turks occupied the Venetian island of Cephalonia in the Ionian Islands and put a strong garrison inside the fortress of San Giorgio. Pedro Navarro, a Spaniard in the service of Venice, having learnt his trade by observing and learning from the Turks, used mines to blow up the fort's bastions. Navarro joined his countrymen in Italy fighting the French and in 1503 he built and set off a massive mine underneath the walls of the Castello Uovo outside Naples, which caused the French to panic.

Over the following two centuries the Europeans made mining an integral part of their siege strategy but under the influence of the great French engineer, Sébastien le Prestre de Vauban, the siege train and the trench predominated.

Malta 1565: The Siege that Saved Europe

From 1453 and the fall of Constantinople to the siege of Vienna in 1683 Europe faced a constant threat from the formidable Ottoman Empire. The Europeans reacted with supine indifference to the advance of the Turks across the Balkans and not even the fall of the Kingdom of Hungary to the Turks at the Battle of Mohacs in 1521 could shake the western Europeans out of their apathy.

Some resistance was offered, in the Mediterranean, by the Catholic League of the Pope, Spain and Venice but above all by the Order of the Hospitaller Knights of St John. They had been based on the rocky island of Malta since the fall of Rhodes in 1522 to the Turks. The order proved a persistent and serious threat to Muslim shipping in the Mediterranean.

Sultan Suleyman 'the Magnificent' was determined to crush the order as a threat to his lines of communications in the western half of the Mediterranean Sea by invading and conquering Malta. As a strategic base in Turkish hands the island, south of Sicily and Naples, would be ideally suited for invading Italy and creating trouble for the infidels in the Sultan's Holy War against Christian Europe. If the Sultan thought he was in for a walkover campaign of only a few weeks while his hitherto invincible troops seized yet another fortress, then Suleyman was in for a surprise. In warfare, especially siege warfare, the side that wins is the one that is determined to fight to the bitter end – up to, or even beyond, the usual limits of human endurance. To hold out the besieged would need exceptional leadership and rare human qualities in their commander. The Knights and the population of Malta had just such a man in the Grand Master of the Order: Chevalier Jean Parisot de la Vallette. As a young man La Vallette had taken part in the siege of Rhodes and was determined to die rather than surrender Malta to an enemy he feared and loathed in equal measure. He had determination and indomitable willpower and he would need every ounce of these qualities as he faced the world's most formidable war machine.

'When you want to take a fortress of any strength, you have to think of taking along twenty-four heavy cannon, six or seven powerful culverins... and 200,000 pounds of powder.'

— DUKE OF GUISE

Trusting in his Knights and the Maltese the Grand Master set to fortify vulnerable points on the island and modernize existing fortifications. La Vallette focussed his attention on defending the Grand Harbour on the southeastern coast. The main fortification, where the heaviest fighting was to take place, was the fortress of St Elmo on the tip of the Sciberras Peninsula. Built and completed in 1552 by a Spanish engineer, St Elmo not only defended the peninsula but also covered the entrance to the harbour and the bay of Marsamuscetto. It was a small, four-pointed, star-shaped fortress with high walls built of sand and limestone blocks. It stood on solid rock.

But St Elmo's weakness was its position, on low ground beneath Mount Sciberras, from where the Turks would be able to dominate the fort with artillery. The fortress itself was built with low-quality stone due to lack of time and lack of foresight on the part of its builder. It also lacked outer works, a ditch, a counterscarp or a ravelin to protect its inner core. As soon as he took over command, La Vallette had ordered the building of a counterscarp and ravelin connected by a drawbridge to the fortress proper.

Across the Grand Harbour lay the main Maltese fortifications. Birgu was the main fortress where food and supplies were stored for a long siege. Its most powerful defences faced south: a large stone ditch protected by four bastions and half bastions. Cut off from Birgu by a narrow watery ditch lay Fort St Angelo, containing a mass of artillery that dominated Grand Harbour. Across the narrow Dockyard Creek lay Senglea. Like Birgu Senglea was a fortified town covered to the south by Fort St Michael. Just in the nick of time La Vallette repaired and improved the defences of Birgu and Senglea. He increased the garrison to 600 Knights and 7000–8000 Maltese irregulars to man and defend these extensive defences. As a last measure of defence La Vallette demolished all buildings outside the walls, and stripped the countryside of peasants and food to prevent the Turks getting supplies and labour.

These measures did not come one day too early because the massive Ottoman fleet of almost 200 ships carrying 40,000 troops (including 6300 elite Janissaries) was spotted off the coast on 18 May 1565. The following day the Turks landed on the southern coast of Malta unopposed.

Mahmud Pasha and his naval colleague, Admiral Pali Pasha, committed three fatal strategic blunders at the beginning of the siege of Malta. They landed too far from the main forts and since they never captured poorly defended Mdina they allowed the Christian defenders to harass and interrupt their exposed lines of communications and supply routes from the bridgehead to the siege works. Their gravest mistake, however, was to attack St Elmo instead of concentrating their massive resources against Birgu and Senglea. The Turks

Siege of Malta

1565

The Ottoman commanders made a serious error by not concentrating their huge army of 40,000 men against Malta's main defences – the forts ringing the Grand Harbour – at the onset of the battle rather than being bogged down for weeks on end trying to reduce the small outer fortress of St Elmo. Through over confidence they failed to prepare for the eventuality that the garrison would resist with all force by erecting a similar artillery post on Gallow's point. What should have been a side-show taking no more than a few days turned into the most savage and protracted part of the battle for Malta. This allowed the Order to gain time preparing their main defences and grind down the Turkish morale through a gruelling and time-consuming siege that lasted for two long months. By the time the Turks shifted their attention to Birgu and Senglea – the main fortified towns – it was too late in the season, morale in their army had slumped and the massive assault on 18 August failed.

The island of Malta lies in the very centre of the Mediterranean Sea almost equidistant between Spanish-controlled Sicily to the north and the Ottoman province of Tripolitania (present-day Libya) to the south.

2 The Turks move up the peninsula leading to Mount Scibberas, where they erect an artillery post to bombard St Elmo into submission.

1 The Ottoman Turkish army lands on the southern shore of Malta, leading to extended lines of communications and delaying the assault of the forts surrounding the Grand Harbour.

3 When finally, in late August, St Elmo falls the Turks moved their artillery to the shore line to bombard St Angelo fort, protecting Birgu – the main fortress at the Grand Harbour – from an attack.

ST ELMO

ST ANGELO

5 Having sustained 30,000 casualties in total the demoralised Turks withdraw from the Grand Harbour in September. The siege is over.

4 The Turks make a land attack with Algerian and Turkish troops against both Fort Michael and Castile, but to little effect.

expected to take St Elmo in a matter of days. They were in for a deeply unpleasant surprise.

The Ottomans constructed a parapet on the heights above St Elmo and placed two 60 pounders, ten 80 pounders and a single massive mortar that fired 73kg (160lb) of solid shot inside this battery. The Turks used marble, iron and stone cannon balls to bombard the fort, beginning on 24 May. Their fire made little impression.

Suleyman, having formed a low opinion of the progress so far, sent the 80-year-old Dragut Pasha, Bey of Algiers and commander of the North African pirates, to take charge. Dragut was appalled at the mistakes made by Mahmud and Pali, especially the attack on St Elmo. Judging it too late to pull out, Dragut erected a Turkish battery on Gallow's Point to lay crossfire on St Elmo, and built a screening wall to protect his own troops.

Mustapha was not pleased at being sidelined by the Algerian and sent a massive Janissary assault against St Elmo. The defenders threw their entire defensive siege arsenal against the Turks, including Greek Fire – thin pots filled with a hellish brew of saltpetre, pounded sulphur, pitch, ammonia, resin and turpentine. Lit by a cord the pots were thrown at the enemy. The sticky, burning contents worked like modern napalm, sticking to clothes, skin and hair. The defenders also made use of Trumps – hollowed-out tubes of wood or metal filled with flammable liquid – that were either thrown or dropped on the Turks. Finally, there were firework hoops. These were made of light wood, dipped in brandy, rubbed in oil, then covered with oiled wool and cotton, and sprinkled with saltpetre and gunpowder. The flowing robes of the Janissaries proved an ideal target and the air filled with the stench of burning human flesh. The attack cost 2000 Turkish lives.

Under relentless fire senior officers urged the Grand Master to evacuate St Elmo but this only made La Vallette more determined to hold the fortress at all costs. He sacked fainthearted Knights, sent reinforcements and admonished the fort's commandant Luigi Broglia to fight to the death. La Vallette knew that every day that St Elmo held out meant more time for the main forts and more time for relief to arrive. On 7 June the Turkish artillery opened a massive barrage that went on for hours,

and three days later Mustapha unleashed his Janissaries again. This time it seemed they had their own secret weapon. They threw fire grenades – *sachettis* – that stuck to the Knights' heavy armour. The Christians had anticipated this trick and had placed water barrels for the Knights to plunge themselves into. After the attack ceased 60 Knights and 1500 Janissaries lay dead. Morale among the defenders remained high.

Mustapha, knowing a silk cord around his neck awaited him if he failed, grew quite frantic as St Elmo held out week after week. He decided to send in waves of *Iayalars,* or volunteers, armed with scimitars. Encouraged by Mullahs shouting verses out of the Koran, by the howling din of the Ottoman Music Corps and supported by the fire of 4000 musketeers the *Iayalars* threw themselves at the walls only to be thrown back by the defenders' fire and weapons. This time 150 defenders lay dead, but also more than a thousand *Iayalars.* Two days

THE IDEA BEHIND *the petard was quite simple and devastating: fill a mortar with gunpowder mounted on a wooden platform, rest the mortar against the besieged gate or a selected section of the wall and blow a huge hole. But the operation went wrong more often than not and gave rise to the expression 'boist by his own petard'.*

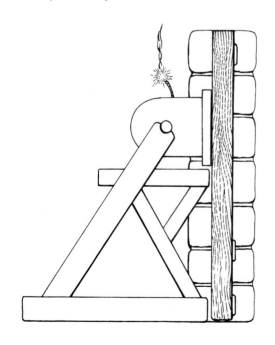

after this assault Dragut was fatally wounded by a cannon ball. But now the screening wall was complete, St Elmo encircled and communications across the Grand Harbour had been cut. On Friday 22 June the Turks launched another massive attack, but they were beaten back. After six hours of hand-to-hand combat the garrison had lost 200 men and the Turks ten times that number. The following day every man in the Turkish army attacked. They were beaten back by 100 defenders initially, but their second assault succeeded. The Sultan's blood-red flag flapped in the wind above the walls of St Elmo. It was a Pyrrhic victory for the Turks. It took nearly one-quarter of their number – 8000 men – to take this, the smallest and weakest of the Maltese forts. Now the Ottoman assault turned to Senglea.

Mustapha sent 1000 Janissaries in boats across the harbour to attack Senglea's northern tip, while another force attacked the southern wall. However, the defenders had erected a concealed battery of five guns at the water line. These opened fire on the boats at point-blank range, sinking many and killing 800 Turks. Those that reached shore were instantly killed. Meanwhile the land assault was also beaten off.

Mustapha switched his attention to Birgu and the massive Ottoman bombardment could be heard all the way off in Sicily. Five days of intense bombardment opened up a breach but when, on 7 August, the Turks stormed through they met a second wall behind it. They were stopped dead in their tracks and then found themselves pursued by a Christian counterattack.

On the morning of 18 August the Turks began a massive bombardment against Senglea, but this was a diversion. A Turkish mine went off under the walls of Birgu, and a large slab of wall crashed down, leaving a gaping hole. The Turks, howling at the top of their lungs, rushed into the breach but they soon faced Knights and Maltese defenders led by La Vallette in person. La Vallette was wounded in the leg but only had it dressed when city wall was safely back in Christian hands.

Next the Turks tried to take Birgu with a massive wooden siege tower, but it was set on fire by the Knights using their arsenal of inflammables. By the end of August the Turks were demoralized by their casualties, they were running out of supplies and autumn was approaching. They made a half-hearted attack on 1 September but this again failed. A week later there were no Turks left outside the fortress, and a small Spanish relief force had arrived at the north end of the island. The Knights and Maltese celebrated with a thunderous *Te Deum* and rang their church bells for hours as they celebrated the greatest and most unexpected victory in the annals

WHEN ARTILLERY WAS *not available in sufficient quantity the troops were forced to improvise. The Greek Fire pot (from a contemporary drawing) was a simple but deadly weapon that could either be dropped on or thrown at an attacker. The noxious content would stick to clothes, skin and weapons. The musket-fired incendiary was just as nasty. This was a thin-walled clay pot filled with Greek Fire shot at attackers or the besieged from the end of a musket. It was used against wooden palisades and buildings, but it could be utilized to devastating effect against troops as well.*

of the Holy War between Christianity and Islam. Malta was safe and the Turks would never return. The Turks had lost, including to disease, a staggering 25–30,000 men in their attempt to take Malta and a year later Suleyman was dead. His great enemy, La Vallette, died in July 1568.

Siege War: The Eighty Years' War

When Philip II inherited his father's lands in the Netherlands he faced an immediate rebellion by his northern Dutch subjects who had by the middle part of the sixteenth century converted to Calvinist Protestantism. His response was to send the ruthless and able duke of Alva to crush what Madrid perceived, quite wrongly, as a mere rebellion. It would turn into the longest war in modern European history and would last until

1648. By that time Spain was an exhausted giant and the Dutch Republic, Northern Netherlands, was the richest and most powerful maritime power in the world. This lengthy conflict saw the birth of modern siege warfare and set the pattern for the next three centuries.

The duke of Alva arrived in 1567 and set about to build strong stone fortifications or citadels in all the southern Netherlands cities like Brussels, Valenciennes and Namur. This saved the region, which eventually became the Spanish Netherlands (i.e. Belgium). But the advance of the Spaniards was tougher further north where the Dutch erected field fortifications of great intricacy and strength behind lakes, swamps, dykes and canals to stop the hitherto invincible Spanish *tercios*. It would take years before the Spaniards realized that

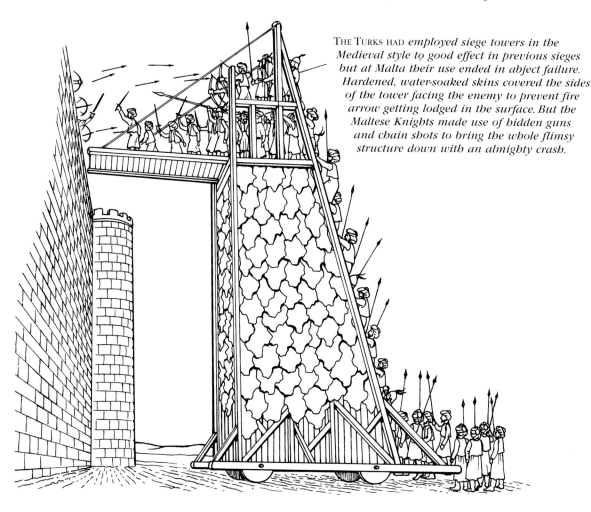

THE TURKS HAD *employed siege towers in the Medieval style to good effect in previous sieges but at Malta their use ended in abject failure. Hardened, water-soaked skins covered the sides of the tower facing the enemy to prevent fire arrow getting lodged in the surface. But the Maltese Knights made use of hidden guns and chain shots to bring the whole flimsy structure down with an almighty crash.*

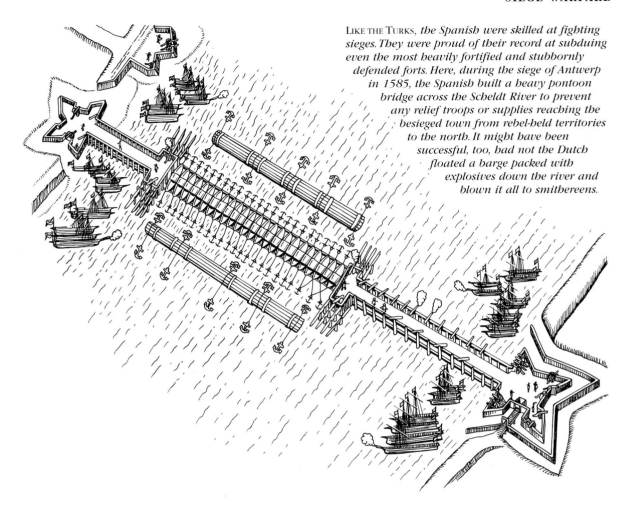

LIKE THE TURKS, the Spanish were skilled at fighting sieges. They were proud of their record at subduing even the most heavily fortified and stubbornly defended forts. Here, during the siege of Antwerp in 1585, the Spanish built a heavy pontoon bridge across the Scheldt River to prevent any relief troops or supplies reaching the besieged town from rebel-held territories to the north. It might have been successful, too, had not the Dutch floated a barge packed with explosives down the river and blown it all to smithereens.

they had to be patient and persistent in their pursuit of a besieged city or fortress. In 1572 their methods, having matured with a more persistent style of conduct, paid off. They built continuous lines around the cities to keep defenders in and relief forces out. That year Mons and Haarlem fell to the Spaniards.

Six years later Alexander Farnese, duke of Parma, took over command in the war and his methods aimed to avoid sieges altogether. This he would do emptying the surrounding countryside, leaving the rebel-held cities isolated and unable to get either relief or supplies. This would compel them to surrender sooner or later without a costly siege.

He was, therefore, reluctant to stage sieges. At Maastricht the city was taken in 1578 but only at the cost of the lives of 2000 precious troops. At Antwerp Parma put in place a far more sober and logical plan of attack. He blocked the Scheldt River with a boom – a pontoon bridge – to deny the city supplies and reinforcements from the rebels in the north, and constructed a battery across the river to pound Antwerp's weaker riverside walls. The defenders floated two rafts filled with explosives down the river and blew up the boom with the loss of 800 Spanish troops. But no relief came and the city capitulated in August 1585.

The longest siege of the war was conducted by the Spaniards against the port city of Ostend, which was considered impregnable because it was heavily fortified and surrounded by waterlogged swamps, canals and lakes. But no fortress, however

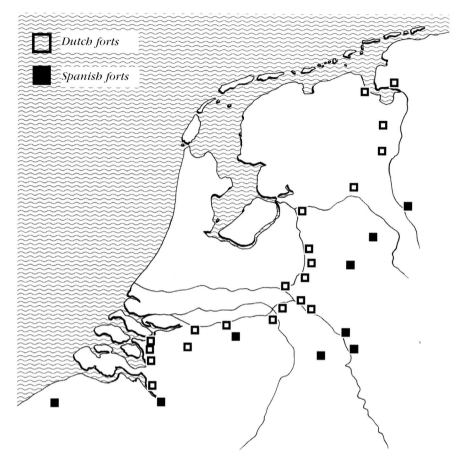

Dutch forts

Spanish forts

THE WAR BETWEEN *Imperial Spain and the Protestant Dutch was the second-longest European war. Lasting 70 years, it was conducted by way of protracted and often bloodily-fought sieges. The Low Countries, with their canals, embankments, rivers and flat ground, are ideal for siege warfare and slow deliberate advances where both sides built a massive number of forts and redoubts to keep the enemy at bay. The Spanish held a line of forts along the great Rhine and Maas (Meuse) rivers but also inside Germany, to cut off the Dutch from their main European supply base. Meanwhile the Dutch built forts that protected their main cities, such as Rotterdam, Utrecht and Amsterdam, from a Spanish attack.*

strong, is ever impregnable in the face of a determined foe. In this case it was the Spanish commander-in-chief, Don Ambrosio Spinola.

The only way to reach Ostend was via the coastal sand dunes but even once this had been done the Spaniards confronted a formidable defence line consisting of a wide and deep ditch behind which lay eight large earthen bastions filled with troops and artillery. Behind this defence line lay the city's own fortifications.

In January 1602, after a failed assault that cost 2000 men, Spinola identified the weak point of the defences and gave orders that the waterlogged marshes be filled with heavy fascines (bundles of straw or sticks) and that a line of gabions (huge wicker baskets filled with earth) be erected to give the attackers protection. Spinola inspired his men by leading the work in person.

By April 1604 the outer defences had fallen to the Spaniards, who laid siege to the inner line of defences. By late September 'impregnable' Ostend had capitulated. The siege had lasted over three years and cost as many as 40,000 lives. Despite the fall of Ostend and a 12-year truce from 1609, the war dragged on for another 44 years.

This long conflict was conducted mainly as a series of deadly and protracted sieges rather than as a war of mobile field armies coming to grips with each other on the battlefield, and gave birth to a range of sophisticated siege methods, fortifications and equipment.

The Hispano-Dutch Experience
Artillery at the beginning of this period consisted of a mass of guns of every conceivable calibre and range, that were used simply to batter a besieged city or fortress into submission by sheer weight of fire. Facing multiple wars the Spaniards were the

first to standardize their artillery and in 1609 the Spanish Quarter Master General announced four basic categories of gun: the huge 48 pounder ('wall-basher' or full gun); the 24 pounder (demi-gun); the 10–12 pounder (quarter cannon) and finally the light 5–6 pounder (eight gun). This was a remarkable achievement of rational standardization that in essence held its own until late in the nineteenth century.

The most effective siege gun was the 24 pounder, which did the job of pummelling walls as well as the wall-basher itself, but did it much more efficiently. The 24 pounder, compared to his elder brother the 48 pounder, weighed only half that weight and took up much less space in a gun line. Furthermore the 24 pounder could be loaded far more quickly and only used half the amount of gunpowder of the 48 pounder. It remained the main artillery piece in use in sieges for the next 250 years, and was an excellent all-round gun. In 1620 Spain's enemies, France and the Netherlands, adopted the Spanish system.

Cannon could be used, quite literally, to bash holes in fortified walls and create breaches. But their limitation was that they could only be fired horizontally and at city walls. But what about the buildings within those walls where ammunition and gunpowder were stored? High-trajectory artillery was needed and the solution came in the course of the seventeenth century in the shape of the cannon's stubby-nosed cousin, the mortar.

Once again it was the Spaniards who were the innovators since they were the ones who had used the mortar for the first time in combat during the siege of Wacthendonck in 1588 against the Dutch. The Spaniards were slow to apply mortars to more general use and some came to the erroneous conclusion that the mortar was a defensive weapon, which improved the chances of survival for a fort. In fact, the very opposite was true since

'Nowadays the Spanish and Dutch officers have made the capture of towns an art and they can predict the duration of resistance of a fortress, however strong, in terms of days.'

— MARSHAL DE TAVANNES

the mortar was the most dangerous beast a besieged fortress had to contend with. Heavy stone walls provided a city or fortress with a modicum of protection against normal artillery fire, boosting the morale of the besieged population and garrison. But walls were no protection against the high-trajectory mortar shot, which was capable of hitting any target within the fortress.

This insecurity and the damage the mortar could cause to buildings and the population within made it a fearsome siege weapon. Many forts, especially as the Vauban system won ground and use, sued for capitulation as soon as the first rounds of mortar shells hit them. A mortar round was made of iron or stone with a hollow interior packed with an explosive charge. The shot had to weigh at least 63–68kg (140–150lbs), to enable it to crash through the roofs and floors of houses, ending up in the basement where it would explode. As a contemporary French observer noted with unsavoury enthusiasm, the mortars exploded 'smashing and roasting the people within'.

A entirely new style of fortification was needed by both sides to meet the new artillery that had been standardized and improved upon during the Eighty Years' War. In Italy the earlier response had been to build solid stone forts but in the Netherlands neither side had the time or money to indulge in such luxuries. Fortifications had to be cheap, easy to build and moulded to the terrain.

The Dutch, as the side on the defensive during much of the war, perfected the building of such earthen bastions to back up the permanent medieval-style walls around their cities, such as Antwerp or Haarlem. In addition the Dutch would erect small earthen redoubts called *Schanzen* (ramparts) to command river crossings or dykes. In 1599 Prince Maurice erected a line of these *schanzen* along the Waal and Maas rivers to guard against a Spanish offensive. In addition the towns

A DEADLY WEAPON *in sieges, the trajectory of the mortar made it virtually impossible for the defenders to protect themselves from its heavy rounds. This monstrous beauty was made of bronze and so was expensive to produce. Weighing almost half a metric ton (445kg), it had a calibre of 127mm (5in) and shot a massive stone or solid-iron ball through its half-metre (20-in) barrel.*

of the two main provinces, Zeeland and Holland, were heavily fortified and re-inforced, after 1589, by a second line of defence from the Zuider Zee to the Rhine called the New Dutch Water line comprising forts, block houses, ditches, dykes, lakes and canals. The Dutch defence system was strengthened during the winter of 1605–6 against a Spanish surprise attack from Hertogenbosch.

A Dutch earthen fort was made of thick earthen ramparts, with the outer face sloping down to a bank. It was protected against escalade by horizontal palisades called storm poles. Along the foot of this rampart ran a low outer earthwork known as a *fausse-braye* that gave defenders complete command of the ditch. Defences were built with muskets in mind, not artillery, and thus bastions were rarely placed more than 229m (250 yards) apart. These bastions were long and faces met in narrow salient angles. The Dutch copied the Italian ravelins but added demi-lune (half-moon redoubts)

and hornworks to give bastions further defence or flanking fire. These Netherlands fortifications (used by both Spaniards and Dutch) gave formidable defence in depth to the besieged side. In 1587 a French military expert, La Noue, admitted the Italians had made fortification into a science but that the Dutch beat the Italians when it came to the speed and cost of fortification. He pointed out that it had taken the Dutch two years and 300,000 florins to fortify Ghent when it would have taken the Italians 20 years and ten times the money to fortify the city according to their methods. In Germany the main cities were built according to the Dutch system and even Venice fortified Corfu according to the Dutch model despite the obvious climatic differences with soggy Holland.

But there were major weaknesses with the Dutch system. To be defended properly they required an inordinately large number of scarce troops. Once the outer works had fallen they gave the enemy comfortable accommodation and sites for the stationing of siege artillery.

Furthermore, while posing formidable problems for the attacker, the wet ditch created almost as many headaches for the defender as concerns supplying and re-inforcing the outer works. If the defender built a wooden bridge across, eliminating the problem of crossing by rafts or boats, then this would provide an excellent avenue of invasion for the enemy. If the weather turned severe then the ditch froze and offered no defence at all. Both Spanish and Dutch garrisons spent much time and energy in winter keeping ditches open and free of ice.

Finally, these fortifications were in fact only temporary measures. They needed constant and costly maintenance to prevent the earth embankments sliding and subsiding. The wet ditches needed clearing of mud and silt and the wooden palisades and storm poles rotted easily in the wet climate. In the long run it was better both from an economic and military point of view to build permanent stone forts instead of trying to maintain the wood and earth ones forever.

Laying Siege

A first priority among the techniques applied by a besieging army was to build a strongly fortified camp. Then it had to build a continuous line of wooden fortifications – a line of circumvallations (facing the surrounding countryside) and countervallation (facing the besieged city) to prevent relief or supplies getting through to the besieged garrison.

Again it was the Spaniards who pioneered these siege techniques – Alva using them against Mons in 1572. Parma developed Alva's techniques and their enemy, Prince Maurice of Holland, perfected them in the early seventeenth century. At the siege of Grave in 1602 the French ambassador noted that Maurice had given each redoubt its own wet ditch and drawbridge. It took him five hours to make the circuit of the impressive Dutch siege lines.

Once the siege lines were completed and the commander had settled upon a point of attack a base for closer operations would be built in the shape of a redoubt. Some 500 troops would be used during the night to advance within musket range of the fort's outer works. With luck this advance by

stealth would go unnoticed by the defenders. A deep trench was dug with a earthen parapet in front for additional protection. Where there was insufficient soil, or if the ground was too wet, gabions would be erected instead. The trenches would be widened until they could accommodate cannon and steps were made on the side facing the enemy.

The next step was to dig a sap in a zig-zag pattern towards the enemy, if the ground was clear. If it was not, as at Haarlem, a straight sap was dug, protected by sap roller. This was a re-inforced, heavier gabion pushed in front of the work party. By now the countervallation was too far away to lend the work parties any support, so the besiegers

A FORT'S ENTRANCE *could be protected by a complex system of sentries (S), which prevented it being surprised by the enemy. The first checks were at a guard point outside the fort. Then there were more guards in the ravelin in the moat, followed by a sentry on the drawbridge (D) before a further sentry inside the fort. Numerous guardhouses (G) also protected the entrance.*

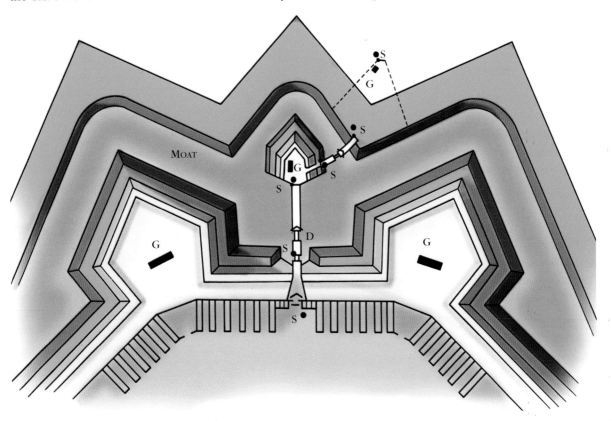

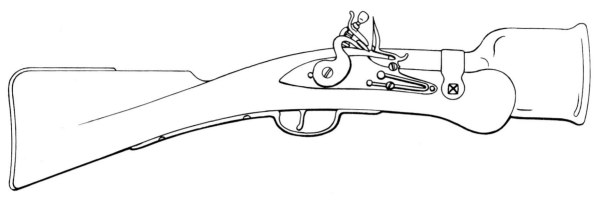

THIS STRANGE-LOOKING *weapon was a development on the attached musket grenade discussed earlier. A specifically modified musket was developed to launch grenades from the cup-like barrel. It was light, easy to handle and an excellent support weapon for siege infantry when artillery did not suffice.*

erected covered ways, and each trench was studded at regular intervals by redoubts. As the head of the sap came closer to the walls sap rollers or wooden screens were put up to protect the labourers. It was reckoned that as many as two-thirds of the working parties were killed but they were well paid to do this dirty, dangerous and exhausting work. The sap came to an end some 27m (30 yards) from the covered way. Then the besiegers dug trenches to both the right and left and erected a *cavalier de tranchée* or *Kantze* (a rampart). This would serve two purposes: first, as a safe position to attack enemy positions with artillery and musket fire; second, as an assembly point for storming parties sent against the covered way and the fort's walls. At Hertogenbosch in 1629 the Dutch had four saps going at the same time.

In the sixteenth century normal practice had been to place a general battery in a single position but the evolution of fortifications during the subsequent century required major changes. After 1600 the general batteries were reduced in size and supplemented by smaller batteries on either flank to bring fire against the flanks of the bastion being attacked or cross fire on a breach. To increase effectiveness the siege batteries moved ever closer, and by 1620 the accepted distance was only 200 paces. The accepted wisdom was now to attack bastions. If an attacker opened a breach in a curtain wall then his troops, as they moved closer, would be under flanking fire from the adjoining bastions. Instead it became the habit to plant four or more heavy guns opposite the salient angle of the bastion. Supplementary batteries were placed on either side to knock out enemy guns in adjacent bastions.

Meanwhile the sap had reached the covered way. The garrison would make attacks to try to remove the defenders from this position, using hand grenades made of cast iron, wood, bronze or thick glass. At this juncture the besieged realized the city was already half-taken and few defenders were willing to make a last stand once the breach had been made. By this time the defenders' artillery would have been silenced and the enemy would have erected a bridge or causeway (of weighted fascines) across the wet ditch.

The 'Swedish Method' – Storm Assault

In eastern and northern Europe the Dutch-Hispanic model was never accepted or practised with any skill or enthusiasm. It was too costly and slow for the kind of fast and mobile war the regional powers preferred. A typical example was Gustavus II Adolphus who conquered much of Germany without having recourse to either sieges

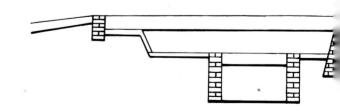

or heavy siege artillery. He defeated his Imperial Catholic enemies through field battles rather than the slowly and laboriously conducted sieges that were usual in the Low Countries.

Charles X, his nephew and successor, shared his uncle's disdain for sieges and encumbering siege trains. In 1657 Charles X quit Poland, which he had invaded for no other reason than lust of conquest, marched on Denmark and crossed the ice of the Great and Lesser Belts. He reached the formidable walls of Copenhagen by late 1657 and laid siege to the Danish capital. But what was he to do next – rapidly running out of time, without powerful artillery or a proper siege train?

The answer was to attempt to storm Copenhagen's defences. On 11 February 1658 Charles sent two columns of troops, totalling 5800 men, across the icy surfaces surrounding the capital. The first assault column was spearheaded by seventy musketeers and 150 men carrying scaling ladders. Since the attacking Swedish force had brought with them no artillery they had to settle for grenades shot from muskets instead. This was their only form of 'artillery' support, although the Danish defenders had plenty of artillery on the walls above.

To begin with the assault carried all before it. The Swedes stormed and captured two Danish gunboats that lay frozen fast in the harbour. The desperate Danes realized that if they lost this fight Denmark's independence was at an end. Meanwhile, some 100 troops made a diversionary attack on the fortified suburb of Christianshavn but this offensive failed completely despite three desperately brave attempts to scale the walls.

Charles' harebrained gamble depended completely on inaccurate intelligence, which had been provided by his chief spy, Erik Dahlberg. This claimed that along Copenhagen's southern (sea) wall there was an undefended gate, located between the main city wall and the Citadel. Some 3000 Swedes, primed with *brännvin* (spirits) and with war cries, swept across the ice towards this supposed weak spot only to find that there was no gate or doorway in the wall. Instead the Danes had placed their strongest artillery and musketeer contingents in this exposed sector and now gave their hated foe a warm Danish welcome: grape shot, cannon balls and a hail of bullets from 100 guns and more than 1000 muskets. The Swedes threw grappling hooks up towards the top of the

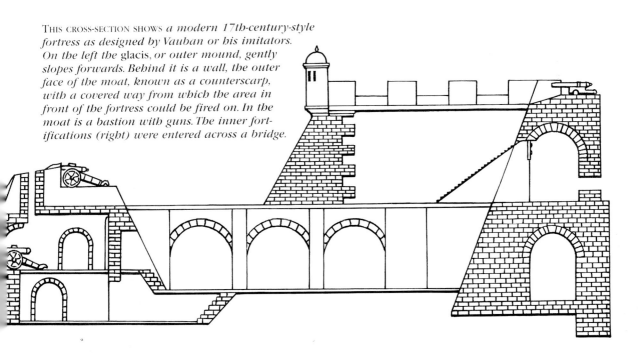

THIS CROSS-SECTION SHOWS *a modern 17th-century-style fortress as designed by Vauban or his imitators. On the left the* glacis, *or outer mound, gently slopes forwards. Behind it is a wall, the outer face of the moat, known as a* counterscarp, *with a covered way from which the area in front of the fortress could be fired on. In the moat is a bastion with guns. The inner fortifications (right) were entered across a bridge.*

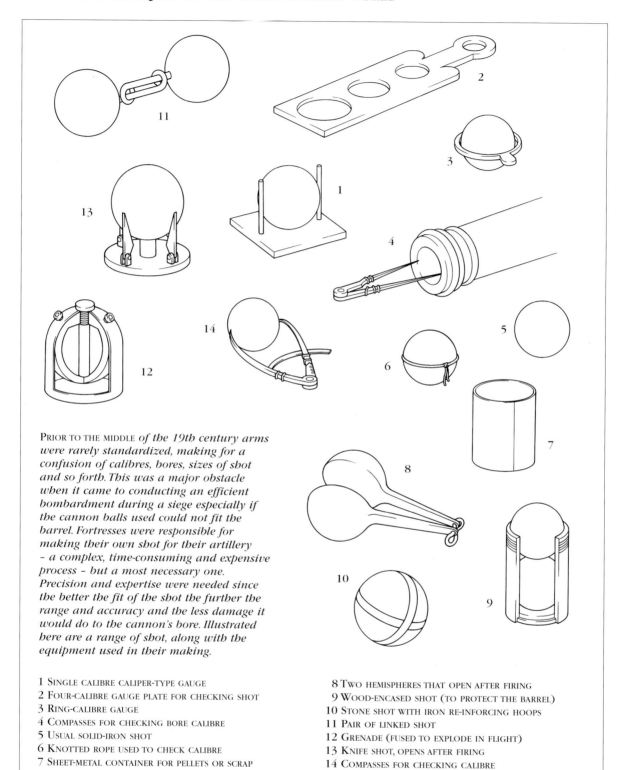

PRIOR TO THE MIDDLE *of the 19th century arms were rarely standardized, making for a confusion of calibres, bores, sizes of shot and so forth. This was a major obstacle when it came to conducting an efficient bombardment during a siege especially if the cannon balls used could not fit the barrel. Fortresses were responsible for making their own shot for their artillery – a complex, time-consuming and expensive process – but a most necessary one. Precision and expertise were needed since the better the fit of the shot the further the range and accuracy and the less damage it would do to the cannon's bore. Illustrated here are a range of shot, along with the equipment used in their making.*

1 SINGLE CALIBRE CALIPER-TYPE GAUGE
2 FOUR-CALIBRE GAUGE PLATE FOR CHECKING SHOT
3 RING-CALIBRE GAUGE
4 COMPASSES FOR CHECKING BORE CALIBRE
5 USUAL SOLID-IRON SHOT
6 KNOTTED ROPE USED TO CHECK CALIBRE
7 SHEET-METAL CONTAINER FOR PELLETS OR SCRAP

8 TWO HEMISPHERES THAT OPEN AFTER FIRING
9 WOOD-ENCASED SHOT (TO PROTECT THE BARREL)
10 STONE SHOT WITH IRON RE-INFORCING HOOPS
11 PAIR OF LINKED SHOT
12 GRENADE (FUSED TO EXPLODE IN FLIGHT)
13 KNIFE SHOT, OPENS AFTER FIRING
14 COMPASSES FOR CHECKING CALIBRE

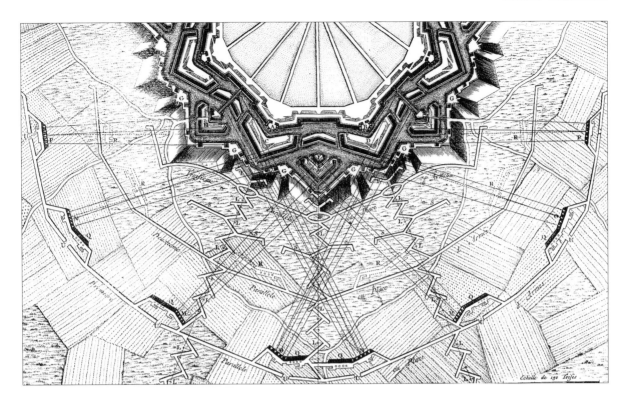

walls and tried to set up scaling ladders. Some managed to mount the ladders and perhaps one or two even reached the top only to be stabbed or shot by the defenders. Their comrades below were sitting ducks and the Swedes did not die in pairs but by the hundreds – shot up by musket and artillery fire or blown to bits by grenades thrown down by the defenders. Bloody piles and heaps of bodies lay scattered across the ice below the walls.

The assault had been a total failure, due to Charles X's rashness and Dahlberg's faulty intelligence. The Swedes suffered more than 2000 casualties, almost half the attacking force. The Danish casualties were low: only 20 men killed and less than 100 wounded. It showed that fortifications could save a nation from destruction and exemplified the dangers of storming a well-defended and heavily fortified city.

Charles X died before he had time to learn from his mistakes. Dahlberg, the bungling spymaster, learnt his lesson well. As Governor of the Baltic states, he built a formidable line of forts to protect the region against a Russian invasion that arrived in 1710–11.

Fredriksten 1718: Siege That Saved Norway

The Great Northern War had been going on for 16 long years when Sweden's formidable warrior king, Charles XII, laid plans to invade Norway in 1716. This country was only a stepping stone in his grandiose plans to invade Britain, dethrone George I and crown James Stuart, before moving on to deal with Denmark and Russia.

Charles' plan in 1716 was for a blitzkrieg-style attack on Norway with only a small army of 7700 men, in three columns. The Swedes hoped that by treating the Norwegians with silk gloves they would welcome their 'liberators'. The Swedes knew that their small invasion army faced a Norwegian army twice their size. But it consisted of poorly equipped, badly trained peasant recruits. As the aggressors the Swedes held the initiative, which ensured that the Norwegian army was strung out along the long frontier not knowing where or when the Swedes would strike. Norway was similar to Canada, built like a natural fortress, especially in winter with frozen lakes, rivers, marshes, wooded hills and endless forests sparsely sprinkled with small peasant settlements. It was not an easy country for an invader to stage a European-style campaign.

The Norwegians could also rely on the support of the Danish Navy. Danish and Norwegian vessels led by Norway's 'Nelson', Admiral Peter Tordenskjold, disrupted Swedish coastal communications and prevented vital supplies reaching the invading army. Sweden's naval weakness was a major problem for the plans Charles had laid. The Norwegians had also built a formidable line of six major fortifications along the main river barrier in eastern Norway, called the Glomma Line. To add further defences to this Glomma Line the Norwegian commander, General Lützow, constructed field fortifications at the two main hill passes blocking the entrance to Christiania. These field forts were held by 1500 cavalry and 5600 infantry.

When Charles, who had crossed the frontier in early March, reached this line his attack against one of these forts failed and he was forced to retreat south. He then turned north but was surprised by the speed with which his enemy erected a barrier of logs and felled trees

that his troops could not force. Like the Canadians, the Norwegians were adept at throwing up defensive lines. But Charles marched his men across frozen ice on the Oslo fjord to outflank his enemy, and by 21 March he was outside the empty Norwegian capital.

Once news arrived of the Lion of the North's approach the population fled westwards. Christiania's garrison of 3000 regulars had plentiful supplies and was under the command of a tough German officer in Danish service, Colonel Jörgen von Klenow. The Swedish invasion began to run into difficulties with the Norwegian fortifications. Charles occupied Christiania on 22 March, but the town was built with its streets perpendicular to the fortresses' guns so that the guns could shoot straight down the street and onto any Swede foolish enough to venture out. The Swedes tore up paving stones, houses and anything else they could find to erect breastworks or dig trenches to protect themselves. Assaults on other forts were

GALLEYS HAD BEEN *used in the Mediterranean Sea during the 16th century but a lesser-known fact was that both Russia and Sweden used them during the Great Northern War. Here teams of horses and men are pulling one such galley across greased logs from the North Sea coast overland to the dark waters of the Iddefjord, near Fredrikshald, in 1718.*

beaten back with heavy losses. Charles did not give up hope but his officers were pessimistic and a defeatism that had marred the Swedish army's morale since the catastrophic defeat at Poltava in 1709 now surfaced. The officers feared they would be cut off and starved into submission due to their long supply lines. Charles marched south and took the town of Fredrikshald (present-day Halden) in July. However, he could not take its fortress, Fredriksten, or the city's inner defence wall, which was held by an armed force of the town's inhabitants.

When Charles invaded Norway again in 1718 his approach was very different. If the Norwegians would not greet the Swedes as liberators then they would be bludgeoned into submission and crushed by sheer military might. Bearing in mind his experiences in 1716, he was determined to take Fredriksten first. It was Norway's most formidable fortress and it straddled Sweden's supply routes and the lines of communication all the way back to Sweden.

The first step in this plan was to get a galley flotilla into the Iddefjord in order to reduce Sponviken fort and then bombard Halden from the fjord as well from the land side. The flotilla would avoid having to run the gauntlet of Fredrikstad's fortress batteries and the deadly attentions of Tordenskjold's fleet hovering off the coast. Charles ordered 800 troops and 1000 horses to haul his galleys and gunboats across the peninsula between the North Sea and Iddefjord.

Fredriksten, meaning Frederick's rock, was built on top of a massive granite mountain above the city of Fredrikshald on the Norwegian side of Iddefjord, which connected in the west with the waters of Svinesund. On three sides this eagle's nest was protected by water, cliffs or deep valleys and it was only to the south-east that it was open to attack. Even on that side the approaches were protected by marshes and three forts.

'The attack and defence of fortifications is one of the most essential components of warfare...a war conducted by sieges exposes a state to fewer dangers and holds forth better hope of victory.' — VAUBAN

This time Charles was taking no chances. He created a huge, well-supplied army of 40,000 troops accompanied by a well-equipped siege train led by a professional fortification officer with a wide experience of sieges. The French colonel of fortification, Philippe Maigret, had been trained by Vauban and now prepared to conduct a siege in this northern wilderness according to his illustrious teacher's masterly system. Fredriksten would be completely encircled and cut off from the outside world. Parallel trenches would be dug to surround the fortress in concentric circles. *Approches* would be dug to close in on the fort and in such a way that they avoided its artillery. Then heavy siege mortars and guns would be used to make a breach in the walls. Meanwhile, Maigret told the Swedes, the garrison would become demoralized by their isolation, the absence of news and the growing lack of supplies. Once this had been done the Swedes could storm the fortress.

Swedish preparations had been so painstaking that the invasion of Norway only began in late October. Charles arrived ahead of schedule with 900 cavalry forcing the Norwegians to sink their transport flotilla on Iddefjord. Nevertheless it was only by 20 November that the siege artillery was in place. In total Charles had 35,000 men in southern Norway while Colonel Landsberg, the Norwegian commandant of Fredriksten, admitted that the fortress was totally cut off by the siege, and that he had only 1400 troops. Charles could not resist taking risks and personally commanded a daring attack on 27 November, which stormed and then took the outlying Gyldenløve fort.

The Swedes were now engaged in the tedious and unusual task of digging trenches to approach Fredriksten. Hard and unpleasant work in the rocky soil around the fortress, the troops dug in the face of Norwegian fire from the main fort and the two remaining outer works. On 30 November the

Siege of Fredriksten

1718

In October 1718 Swedish king Charles XII invaded southern Norway with 35,000 troops, determined to reduce the lynchpin of the enemy's frontier defences at Fredrikshald to rubble through a regular siege, led by a hired professional French artillery officer, Colonel Maigret. The Swedes, commanded in person by the king, stormed and captured the outer fort of Gyldenløve on 27 November. Three days later the Swedes, facing only 1400 enemy troops holding the fortress of Fredriksten, dug a parallel trench to the fortress, followed by an approach trench (to a second parallel), and seemed to be on the verge of a great – and relatively easy – victory. Once the siege artillery had the fortress within range it could be forced through bombardment to capitulate, as Colonel Maigret had assured the king. But on 30 November Charles XII was killed in the most mysterious of circumstances in the forward trenches, saving the Norwegians from what would have been a humiliating defeat and eventual occupation by their neighbours.

Fredriksten was the key fortress along the frontier with Sweden and located just next to the border town of Fredrikshald (present-day Halden) in southeastern Norway.

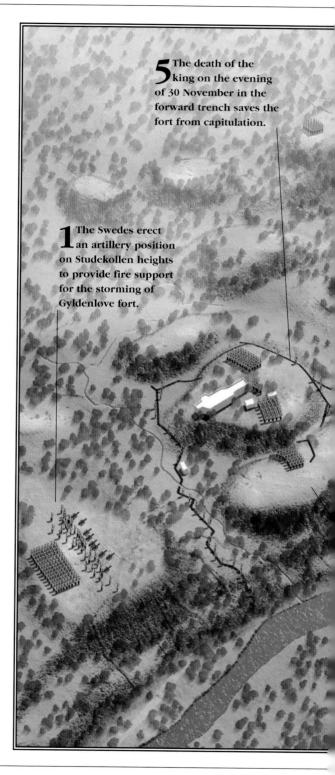

5 The death of the king on the evening of 30 November in the forward trench saves the fort from capitulation.

1 The Swedes erect an artillery position on Studekollen heights to provide fire support for the storming of Gyldenløve fort.

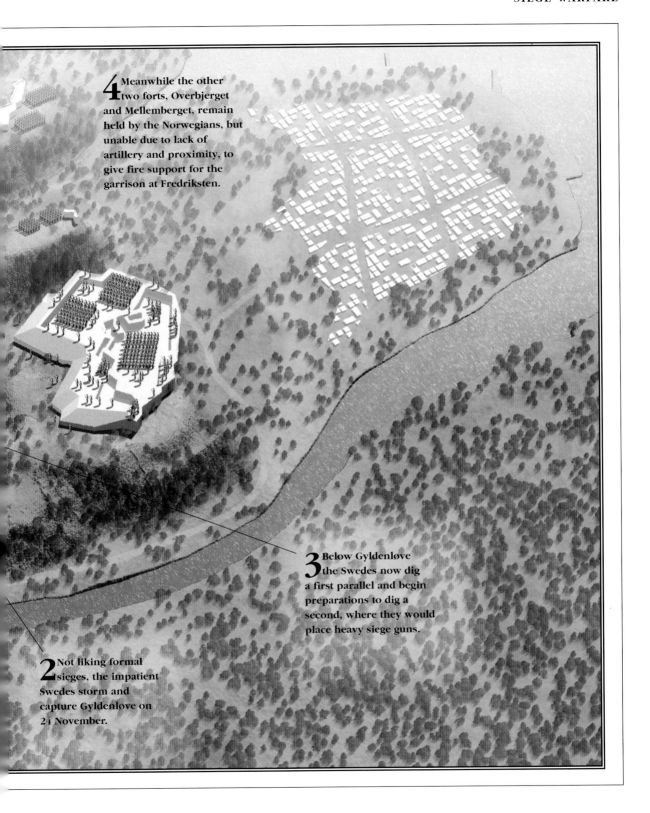

4 Meanwhile the other two forts, Overbjerget and Mellemberget, remain held by the Norwegians, but unable due to lack of artillery and proximity, to give fire support for the garrison at Fredriksten.

3 Below Gyldenløve the Swedes now dig a first parallel and begin preparations to dig a second, where they would place heavy siege guns.

2 Not liking formal sieges, the impatient Swedes storm and capture Gyldenløve on 24 November.

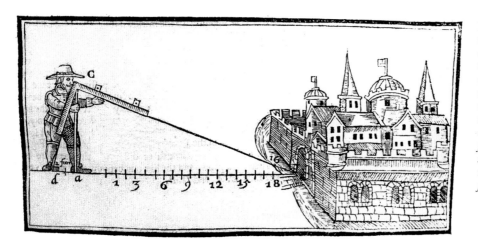

DESPITE PRIMITIVE INSTRUMENTS *the accuracy of siege lines, tunnels and trenches were remarkable. Here a siege engineer is using an unidentified instrument to calculate the distance from where he is standing and the moat surrounding the fortified town.*

first parallel was completed and a sap had been dug. Charles wanted Maigret to begin digging the second line as soon as possible. Earlier Maigret had assured the impatient king that the fortress would fall within eight days and even Fredriksten's commander, Colonel Landsberg, admitted that Fredriksten could not hold out longer than a week.

As the soil was thin the Swedes had to re-inforce their trenches with 600 fascines and 3000 bags every day. Once the second parallel had been dug and re-inforced with breastworks Maigret's siege artillery of 18 heavy pieces (six 16-kg [36-lb] howitzers and six 34-kg [75-lb] mortars) would bombard the walls and make a breach. Landsberg knew that the walls had not been properly embedded in the rock and that they would fall apart at the first Swedish barrage.

Fortunately for the Norwegians Charles, always in the front line, was in the sap during the evening of 30 November when, supposedly, a stray bullet hit him in the head and killed him instantly. The Swedish officers in command immediately ordered a retreat and all dreams of empire vanished. Today it is thought that the bullet was probably fired by a hired assassin, paid by the king's ruthless and ambitious brother-in-law, Prince Frederick of Hesse, who later became King Frederick I of Sweden.

The Master Fortifiers: Vauban and Coehoorn
France adopted the Dutch or Spanish systems of fortification, artillery and siege techniques in the early part of the seventeenth century with varying

degrees of success. The French found that Dutch countervallations required almost entire armies, yet the approach to the actual fortification was both narrow and isolated, which increased casualties and risk for the besieging force. The French had noted the Turkish use of parallel trenches but the French commanders, like the observant Marshal du Plessis, proposed to use the parallels to station siege artillery. This would give close support for storming parties and bring the artillery closer to the defenders' fortifications. This predated Vauban's improvements of the French siege train and techniques that would come during the second half of the century.

Sébastien Le Prestre de Vauban (1633–1707) had been a young artillery officer in the middle of the seventeenth century. He believed that the chaos and disorder that reigned in all armies, including the French, during a siege was due primarily to the lack of experienced engineers and a proper engineer corps. A professional engineer was a rare bird in the French army of Vauban's youth, and the engineer corps lacked permanence or status in the army. French commanders like Plessis, Condé or Turenne, saw themselves as jacks-of-all-trades, who conducted their own sieges without expert advice or professional siege engineers. It was Vauban who created and nurtured the engineering corps and its officers into a highly professional, proficient body of proud specialists who ultimately became indispensable to the French army. Vauban – the most famous fortification expert of all times – was born to a

poor Burgundian noble family in 1633. He became Commissaire Général des Fortifications in 1678 and was promoted to Lieutenant General in 1688 and finally, in 1703, he was made a Marshal of France. He died four years later at the respectable age of 78, having built or projected some 160 forts, conducting 48 sieges and receiving eight wounds. His contemporaries remembered him as a workaholic who was either in his Paris offices poring over maps, schemes and plans or constantly on inspection travels. His greatest achievement was to build a continuous line of fortifications, the famous *frontière de fer* stretching from the English Channel to the Swiss border. Wherever he could Vauban built a double line of fortifications.

It was this precaution that ensured that, even in the years 1709 to 1711, the darkest phase of the War of the Spanish Succession, the fortified line of iron was never pierced. These forts saved the struggling French Republic from invasion in the

VAUBAN'S OWN TEXTBOOK *on siege warfare, from which this drawing is taken, shows a thematic, simplified system of parallel trenches connected to each other by sloping. They come closer to the actual walls by the use of trenches dug in a zig-zag shape.*

1790s and stood up well even to the Prussian artillery in 1870-1871.

But Vauban, despite his merits as a builder of fortifications, is perhaps better remembered for destroying or taking forts than building them. Before Vauban introduced his logical, methodical and rational system of the *siège en forme,* there was a labyrinthine confusion of works, trenches and batteries. Under Vauban's system there was a central plan. The besieger would dig a trench, parallel to the wall that he was attacking, called the first parallel. Once this was completed a so-called *approche* (or sap) would be dug in a zig-zag pattern to prevent the enemy's artillery shooting *en enfilade* along an open, straight trench which, if the shot was well aimed, could wreak bloody havoc. A second parallel was then dug halfway to the wall, and the artillery moved closer. Then another *approche* would be dug, as before. Once this had been done a third and final parallel would be dug and the mortars and howitzers, capable of hurling shot over the walls, would open a hellish fire that inevitably brought on a capitulation. Usually it was understood that a breach and storming, leading to plunder and massacre of the defenders, should be avoided. The system worked in most cases and the besiegers rarely had to storm through breaches in the walls.

Vauban had, like some alchemist of an earlier age, created a brilliant and exact textbook system for reducing fortresses without major casualties or bloodshed for the besiegers – or even the besieged, if they had enough good sense to capitulate in time. But the technique was copied by France's enemies and Vauban also failed to make the French artillery a smoothly running cog in the siege system. It was his dislike of mining, however, that set French mining efforts back until Belidor invented the supercharged mine in the middle of the eighteenth century. Vauban never held command of a besieged fort and he had no new ideas of how to defend a fortress under siege, other than to put a mass of artillery in the forts. In the end Vauban's system was turned against its inventors with devastating effect.

Vauban's Dutch counterpart Menno von Coehoorn (1641–1704) remains a far more obscure character. He held Namur against the French in 1692 and recaptured it from them in September 1695. King William III of England and the Netherlands made him General of Fortifications and he set about modernizing the fortifications of Breda, Grave, Zwolle and Groningen. His masterpiece was Bergen-op-Zoom. He set up a Dutch Engineer Corps of 70 officers, and invented a light, mobile siege mortar that could be pulled by two men and easily placed in siege trenches, and was named the Coehoorn mortar after him. His work, like Vauban's, stood the test of time well.

Vauban's Heyday: The Sun King's Wars

Louis XIV came to the throne of France in 1661 and saw his primary duty as king as that of commander-in-chief of the army. Towards the end of his life he warned his successors not to love war as he had. If his passion was war then his special favourite was the siege, because it was orderly and, under Vauban's leadership, led inevitably to victory.

Louis XIV was at Vauban's side when, in 1673, he laid siege to the Dutch-held fortress city of Maastricht. Vauban dug broad, spacious siege trenches with re-inforced firing steps from which musketeers could keep up constant and accurate fire against the city's walls, and meet an enemy

THIS LIGHT MORTAR *was constructed by and named after the Dutch fortification expert Menno von Coehoorn for use as a mobile support weapon for infantry during sieges. It had a calibre of 143mm (5.63in), weighed a 'mere' 74kg (160lb) and had a range of about 1km (1200 yards). The barrel, which had a length of 457mm (18in), could be elevated from anything between 20 and 70 degrees.*

sortie on a broad front. He dug parallels to place artillery and made the saps in a zig-zag pattern to reduce casualties. He concentrated his artillery at one exposed point, in this case a city gate, and Maastricht capitulated on 1 July. Vaubans' greatest legacy was the *frontière de fer* that provided France with an unprecedented line of defence during the Spanish War of Succession, but he pointed out to the aggressive king that it came at a major cost to France. Too many troops were tied up in passive garrison duties in these forts when they could be better utilized in the French field army. The money spent on the forts not only exhausted the Crown's treasury but reduced the money available for the French field army as well.

Vauban Applied: The Seven Years' War in North America

That Vauban's textbook siege technique could be applied outside Europe was shown during the Seven Years' War when some of the most interesting sieges of that war were fought in North America between France and Britain. Britain held the trump cards with a strong navy and a large

A CONTEMPORARY VIEW *of battle in Quebec shows British troops in striking scarlet uniforms crossing the deceptively calm-looking St Lawrence River in rowing boats. They land and immediately scale the sheer cliffs of the northern shore before mounting an attack on the Plain of Abraham.*

colonial militia to back up her regular troops. If numerical strength and resources alone had decided the outcome of wars then the French should have been crushed with ease by their old foe. The main reason they were not, besides British bungling at the outset of the war, was the formidable French fortifications defending every possible route into Canada.

The Marquis de Montcalm, the French commander-in-chief in North America, sensibly took the initiative against the far stronger British by sending a raiding party in March 1757 against Fort William Henry. The French burnt the lake flotilla there leaving the fort bereft of communication and unable to stop a French advance across Lake George. Montcalm landed near the fort on 3 August without any resistance from the British garrison. Montcalm set up an artillery post west of the fort that same day and immediately began to dig saps and parallels to approach the fort, in the classic Vauban style, step by step. Three days later the French opened fire with their artillery from the parallel and then, a day later, opened fire with mortars. The mortar fire destroyed the buildings inside the fort without the British being able to reply in kind, while the walls began to crumble under the onslaught of the conventional artillery. Morale slumped. On 9 August the fort's commander, Colonel Munro, capitulated.

The following year saw the British better organized and thirsting to avenge their setback at the hands of the French. General James Abercromby, aptly nicknamed 'Granny' by his own troops, sailed across Lake George with 12,000 troops and a huge siege train to attack Fort Carillon (Ticonderoga). Abercromby should have captured Rattlesnake Hill one mile south-west of the fort, placed his siege artilery there (16 guns, 11 mortars and 13 howitzers) and pounded its feeble walls to pieces.

Instead Abercromby dithered, giving time for Montcalm to erect an *abattis* line to defend the fort. This consisted of a shallow entrenchment of logged breastworks topped by sandbags and fronted by a hundred metres of felled trees (*arbres abattus*), where trunks and sharpened, tangled branches formed an impenetrable barrier.

Abercromby obliged his enemy by sending 7000 splendid redcoats in closely-packed lines against the *abattis* line, where they blundered into the undergrowth and were shot to pieces by French musket and artillery fire. The British lost 2000 troops in dead alone and made a humiliating retreat back to their flotilla while the French shouted and jeered.

Further east on the continent a very different siege, more reminiscent of Vauban, was being conducted by the British against the strongest French fort in North America – Louisbourg. General Amherst, with 14,000 troops, began to land on Cape Breton Island on 8 June and threw a trench line in an arc around the city's walls. Louisbourg's defences consisted of two massive bastions (*Le Roi* and *La Reine*) and two smaller demi-bastions (*Dauphin* and *Princesse*), and contained a garrison of 6000 troops and sailors. By North American standards it was a huge fort. This siege proved beyond doubt that the British had mastered

Vauban's techniques in a most masterful way. They began digging on 8 June, had driven the French from the outer works by 12 June and began their bombardment a week later. By 3 July the British batteries, containing the lethal mortars, were only 550m (600 yards) from the city's walls and poured mortar shells into the interior of the fortified town with devastating results. On 24 July, with the French naval squadron incapacitated and a British fleet entering the harbour, *Le Roi* bastion was hit by accurate mortar fire and burst into flames. Louisbourg capitulated. The road to Canada's heartland lay open.

Quebec 1759: Beginning of the End for the French in North America

The British reduction of Canada's outer defences and the capture of Louisbourg left the river route up the St Lawrence open to a British invasion of the heartland of New France. General James Wolfe, the commander of the Quebec expedition, left British-occupied Louisbourg and sailed up the St Lawrence with 8500 British regulars. He faced the greatest challenge of his career: to reduce and capture the fortress of Quebec.

In locating their capital and the main fortress city of New France at Quebec the French appeared to have excelled themselves in the art of Vauban-style military architectural engineering. Quebec was ideally sited at the top of a powerful rocky headland a few hundred metres above and protected on three sides by the waters of the St Lawrence and St Charles rivers.

Basing their thinking on the failure of earlier British expeditions in 1693 and 1711, the French believed the British would have great difficulties navigating the St Lawrence and assumed that their fireships would prevent the enemy boats coming near Quebec. Should the British attack the city the French were sure it would mean a landing to the north. From this bridgehead the British would no doubt blunder south and attack across the St Charles. If the enemy attacked from the south, the French believed that the massive solid bluffs along the northern shore of the river would form a formidable obstacle to a landing and assault. If the British came from the west then the continuous city wall built with two massive bastions and two half-bastions would halt their advance. The French were confident but, unfortunately for them, their confidence was misplaced. Facing the land wall of Quebec may have given the onlooker a false sense of strength but the fortress was merely a bluff. There were several problems with the seemingly formidable land wall. It had only been completed in 1749 and it lacked a proper ditch in front of it. After the fall of Quebec, British engineers were highly critical of their enemy's work. The ground was so rocky that a ditch had to be blasted to make it of sufficient depth and width. But because the walls had been built first, they were liable to cracking and collapse. The British inspection revealed that a proper ditch and outer works only existed outside the northern St John's Bastion. Elsewhere it was incomplete. Where it did exist it was only a shallow ditch of about 1.5-1.8m (5-6ft) in depth.

A modern fortress of the time needed wide and powerful outer works to protect the city wall from direct artillery fire and escalade. These were lacking completely at Quebec and the city wall itself had further problems. The ground sloped downwards from north to south. This meant that each bastion from south to north was lower than the next, which prevented the bastions giving one another the mutual supporting fire they were designed for. In addition, the entire wall was exposed to enfilading (flanking) fire from across the St Charles and the northern end of the wall was commanded by higher ground outside the wall. One final problem with the land wall was that its builder, de Léry, had failed to mount any guns in the wall or create any embrasures there that faced the Plains of Abraham. The four bastions in the wall were not built to enable firing towards an enemy on the plains, and in any case could only fire the 52 guns along the wall in case an attempt to storm the walls was attempted. However, if the enemy did reach the walls - given their weaknesses - then Quebec would inevitably fall.

'Siegecraft offers the means of taking and holding territory; a battle may leave the victor in control of the countryside for a while, but he cannot master an entire area if he does not take the fortress.' — VAUBAN

Once Quebec was theirs the British immediately cut the embrasures facing the plain.

The French had committed one more omission that would cost them dear. In 1702 the French had made plans to build one, or possibly two forts at Point Lévis across the St Lawrence, opposite the Lower Town of Quebec. If the British took this area they could erect batteries that would not only provide cover for a British fleet to proceed upriver and strike Quebec from the south or west, but these guns could also bombard the city into submission.

In the autumn of 1758 Montcalm and his chief engineering officer, Colonel Pontleroy, made their own plan of defence. They had no confidence in the fortified lines of Quebec and planned to make a stand along a line of field fortifications outside the walls. But they assumed the British fleet would have to anchor and stay in the Beauport Basin until they could make a landing between the mouths of the rivers St Charles and Montmorency. So Montcalm decided to build his main defence line along the Beauport shoreline, with a second fall-back line along the St Charles. They did not take into account the weaknesses of Quebec, at Point Lévis and on the plains of Abraham. If the first fell to the British then the British would sail past Quebec and outflank the Beauport line and if they managed, against all French assumptions, to scale the almost perpendicular cliffs on the northern shore, then Quebec would fall.

By 11 June 1759 the Beauport line was completed, with three large redoubts, several smaller ones and three bridges across the St Charles river. Montcalm was not, as he later claimed, short of enough troops to build fortifications and man them. Through a major mobilization effort he had managed to form an army of 15,000 men, including Canadian militia troops. But Montcalm found that the St Lawrence River's main channel was too wide for the

Siege of Quebec
1759

The French authorities in North America had always hoped that they would never be called upon to defend their colonial capital anywhere near its vicinity and consequently miscalculated their enemy's moves. Montcalm placed his defences north of the St Charles river in the vaunted Beauport line but failed to fortify Point St.Lévis, opposite Lower Town. General Wolfe, the British commander, occupied this vital point, erected a battery there, then moved his flotilla under the cover of these guns and by doing so undermined the French completely by landing his army upstream from Quebec at l'Anse de Foulon. Wolf then gave battle on the Plains of Abraham on his terms. Montcalm made one more fatal error by committing his troops too early to battle, instead of taking up a more defensive posture. The French were cut to pieces by infantry volleys as they hastily attacked the British formations. After the bloody battle the British begun erecting siege lines but the city capitulated once its garrison had been defeated in the field.

Quebec not only controlled the St Lawrence River but lay in the very centre of the French colony of Canada. It was well fortified, making its capture by Wolfe and his British troops a difficult proposition.

5 Montcalm rushed into battle and his troops are cut to pieces by British infantry volleys.

4 The British moved rapidly to form their positions upon the Plains of Abraham outside Quebec's walls. Montcalm was forced to move his army to meet this new threat.

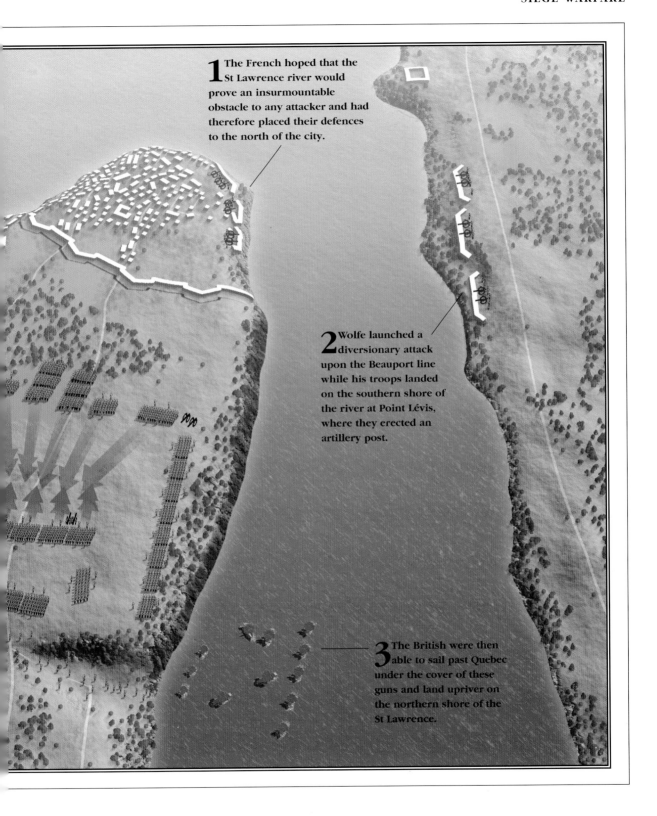

1 The French hoped that the St Lawrence river would prove an insurmountable obstacle to any attacker and had therefore placed their defences to the north of the city.

2 Wolfe launched a diversionary attack upon the Beauport line while his troops landed on the southern shore of the river at Point Lévis, where they erected an artillery post.

3 The British were then able to sail past Quebec under the cover of these guns and land upriver on the northern shore of the St Lawrence.

blocking of ships to be effective, and when the fireships were unleashed prematurely, on 27 June, they were a spectacular failure.

On the British side the commanders were more alert to Quebec's weaknesses and the naval commander Admiral Saunders recommended that Wolfe immediately attack, seize and fortify Point Lévis. This vital area was taken on 29 June to prevent the French blocking entry to the Upper St Lawrence and the following day more British troops poured ashore. With Point Lévis in their hands the British could open fire on Quebec and sail upriver without having to take too much notice of any riverside batteries.

The British now held the southern bank of the river. Wolfe made a failed attack on 31 July that cost him 443 troops. In August he sent troops to ravage the surrounding countryside, destroying 1400 farms in a savage attempt to goad Montcalm to come out and fight in the open. But Montcalm remained behind his ramparts.

Then Wolfe had a lucky break. A British officer, Captain Robert Stabo, had been a prisoner of war in Quebec, but he had escaped in the spring of 1759. He told Wolfe that there was a narrow, precipitous track leading up from the shoreline to

the Plains of Abraham at L'Anse de Foulon. At this stage Wolfe had nothing to lose by acting like a gambler and landed his army at this point. Meanwhile to trick the French into thinking that this was only a feint Admiral Saunders staged a showy diversionary attack against Beauport. At L'Anse de Foulon Wolfe sent troops ahead to take a small French camp at the top of the cliffs and then placed his army on the plains. The French took the bait, responding to the attack at Beauport, and it was only quite late in the day that Montcalm took in the dreadful news that the enemy now threatened his vulnerable rear.

Montcalm should have waited some three hours until Colonel Bougainville with his 1500 regulars could reach the plains from Cap Rouge. Instead he made one final error of judgement. He

THE SIEGE GUNS *in this gun emplacement were protected by massive defences made of earth and stones. Although these gave superb protection they restricted the field of fire for the guns. Trenches were dug behind the emplacement and the powder store lay at the bottom beneath a thick layer of earth and wooden beams. These were kept at a safe distance from the emplacement to protect it against an explosion if the store was hit by enemy gunfire.*

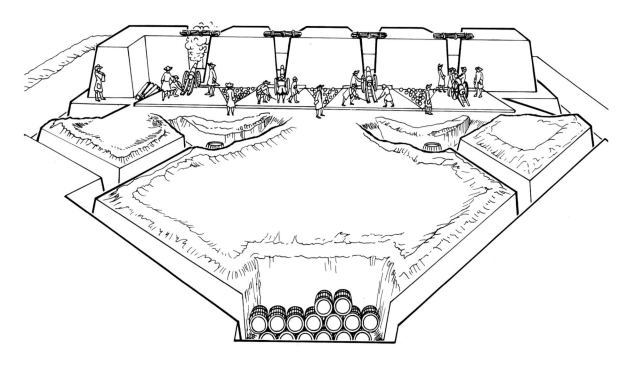

decided to attack immediately, despite his lack of regular, disciplined troops. The brave but tempestuous Canadians rushed at the British line and fired scattered volleys at them with no great effect. The British line opened and concentrated deadly fire at a close range of 12-20m (40-60ft). The impact of this fire on the French was shattering and their wobbly lines collapsed into a panic-stricken mob heading towards the walls of Quebec. The Highlanders set after the fleeing soldiers with heavy swords. The only consolation for the French was that Native and Canadian snipers shot both Wolfe and his colleague Monckton dead.

Montcalm was also fatally wounded and died on 14 September. That same day the British began digging a siege line outside the walls. Over the next three days they continued this work, hauling more artillery to the line. By the afternoon on 17 September the English fleet were ready to bombard Quebec from the riverside, and the land force from the siege line, concentrating their fire on the St Ursule Bastion. On 18 September Quebec capitulated.

Havana 1762: The Siege That Humbled Spain

Havana was the most powerful fortified city in the Americas in the eighteenth century, and the lynchpin of the Spanish Empire in the New World. The city was not only the capital and main port of Cuba and the centre of Spanish power in the West Indies, but also a vital port where the silver fleets made rendezvous before sailing across the Atlantic to Cadiz. The Spaniards placed their most powerful fleet there to protect the strategic port, naval base and shipyard. The capture of Havana dealt a massive blow to Spain's imperial prestige, slowly undermining her grip upon her mainland American colonies over the next 60 years, and was comparable in its effects to Japan's capture of Singapore from the British in 1942.

Early in 1762 the British collected 16,000 troops and a massive transport fleet at Spithead. They set sail on 5 March, arriving off St Domingue's (Haiti) northern coast on 25 May. To catch the Spaniards off guard the British Fleet braved the narrow and treacherous waters of the Old Bahama Channel, and took the Spaniards completely by surprise when they arrived off Havana on 6 June.

This element of surprise was essential, because the British needed to take Havana before the sickly season began in the autumn if they were to avoid the ravages of yellow fever and malaria. But reducing Havana was no simple proposition as the Spaniards viewed the fortress city as impregnable. Guarding the entrance to the harbour and the walled city itself lay the massive fortress of El Morro. The huge land walls of the fort were re-inforced by a deep and wide stone ditch. The ground outside the fortress was devoid of soil to dig siege trenches or fill sandbags, furnished no cover for an enemy and had no source of fresh water. The entrance to the harbour was also blocked by the fortress of La Punta on the western side, by a boom and by the ships of the Havana squadron. The city, its outer forts and the harbour were an interlocking defence system of great strength – no mean task for a besieging army to overcome. There was also a garrison of 5000-10,000 including sailors from the squadron to contend with. But the Spanish defences had one fatal weakness that the British could exploit – the commanding heights of La Cabana had not been fortified. British batteries placed here could rake El Morro, Havana and the harbour with deadly fire.

The British, commanded by Lord Albermarle, decided to concentrate their efforts to attack and take El Morro, but this condemned them to a protracted siege that would expose their unseasoned troops to all the horrors of the local climate and diseases. On 7 June the British landed 4000 troops at the mouth of the Bacuranao River and captured a fort there without much resistance. Once the British had created a bridgehead it was clearer than ever that the Spaniards should have fortified La Cabana. On 10 June Colonel Carleton and his light infantry captured this vital height. With speed and determination the British began building a road from the bridgehead to La Cabana, and batteries there opposite El Morro.

Once these were complete heavy mortars on La Cabana sank vessels in port and bombarded Morro with single-minded determination. The Spaniards, hoping to prolong the campaign into the hurricane and disease season, changed the garrison of El Morro at regular intervals and the Governor picked

Siege of Havana

1762

In June 1762 the British caught the Spanish off guard by landing at the mouth of the Bacuranao river and moving swiftly to occupy the strategic heights of La Cabana and the village of Guanabacoa. Albermarle, the British commander, was criticised for his slow but methodical strategy. La Cabana gave the British a commanding position above the Bay of Havana, where they could position artillery before moving to take control of the fortress of Morro. To distract Morro's defenders the British staged a diversionary attack at Correa to the west of Havana. Unexpectedly Morro, fiercely defended by the Spanish, held out until 22 July and the delay cost the British dearly in numbers of sick and wounded in the unhealthy tropical climate. However, it meant that Albermarle could finally march with his troops around the south of the Bay and lay siege to the city itself, which eventually capitulated on 14 August 1762. The siege was over and Britain had won a great victory over her colonial rivals.

Cuba, the pearl of the Antilles, is a strategically placed island controlling shipping lanes into and out of the Mexican Gulf and Florida Straits. Havana was the main port and fortified base on the island.

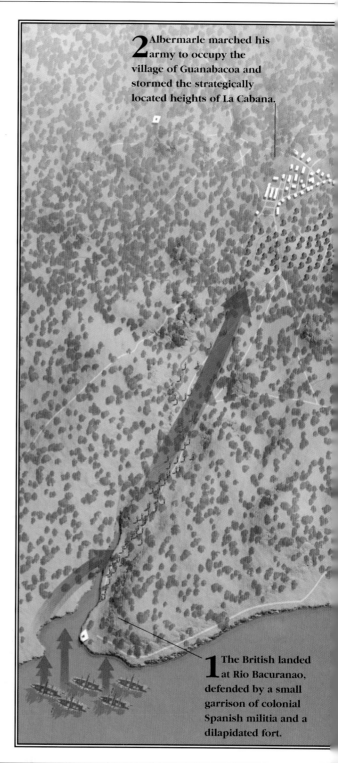

2 Albermarle marched his army to occupy the village of Guanabacoa and stormed the strategically located heights of La Cabana.

1 The British landed at Rio Bacuranao, defended by a small garrison of colonial Spanish militia and a dilapidated fort.

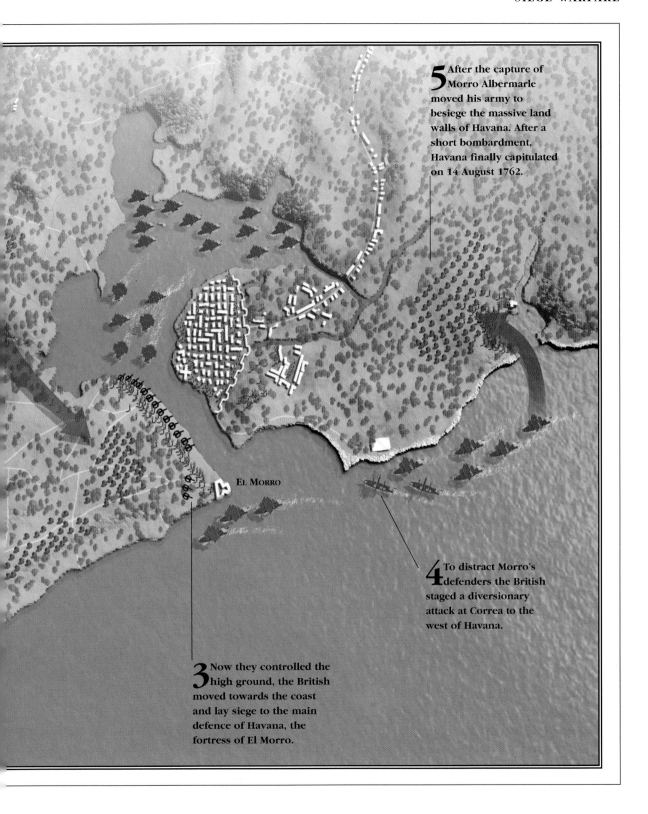

5 After the capture of Morro Albermarle moved his army to besiege the massive land walls of Havana. After a short bombardment, Havana finally capitulated on 14 August 1762.

El Morro

4 To distract Morro's defenders the British staged a diversionary attack at Correa to the west of Havana.

3 Now they controlled the high ground, the British moved towards the coast and lay siege to the main defence of Havana, the fortress of El Morro.

THE BRITISH FLEET *are shown giving artillery support to the troops disembarking in large rowing boats just east of Fort Morro and the city in this engraving. Both of these are shown as being fired upon by the heavy guns of the fleet. In fact that only came much later and most artillery fire came from land-based British guns and mortars.*

a determined commander for the fort, Don Luis de Velasco. The British realized that Don Velasco would hold out at all costs and that Morro needed to be softened up with a massive and prolonged bombardment before a breach could be made.

In the first week of July the British troops were suffering from the intense heat and lack of water. One battery, after two weeks without a drop of rain, self-ignited. Morale, already low, slumped further still. Sailors from Admiral Pocock's fleet (some 800 men) were recruited to fill sandbags and fascines. Every day fire from 24 and 32 pounders, accompanied by 28- and 33-cm (11- and 13-in) mortars, pounded El Morro so intensely that the batteries were beginning to run out of shot. Nevertheless, British batteries sprayed the inside of El Morro with shell fragments that

knocked great hunks of masonry from the stone walls. By 17 July El Morro that was left with only two working guns and the British were able to make an approach. The British built a line running north-west towards the right-hand bastion, next to the sea, but since there was no earth to use this line had to be protected by a continuous line of breastworks. On 20 July the breastwork line was completed, enabling the British to fire with small arms against the top of the walls and set up a battery opposite the bastion. It was here that they hoped to make a breach. But the British changed their plans when they discovered a narrow stone ridge crossing the ditch, and decided to place two mines there. One would be positioned under the wall to make a breach, and they hoped to explode the other so that a barrier of stone and rubble debris would fill the ditch, enabling the columns of assault to cross unhindered.

Mining operations began on 20 July and were completed two days later. On that day (22 July) the Spaniards made desperate efforts to spike the guns of the batteries and destroy the mines with 1300 troops attacking at three separate points including La Cabana. All these attacks failed.

When the mines were set off, the breach was made, but the ditch was not filled as planned. Lt Colonel James Stuart of the 90th Regiment led the assault of 268 infantry and 150 sappers. The British attack came through the breach with such force, speed and numbers that it only took them an hour of savage hand-to-hand fighting to win the fortress of El Morro. The Spaniards lost 130 killed, 37 wounded, 326 prisoners and another 213 killed or drowned when they tried to swim across the entrance of the harbour to safety in Havana. One of the many killed was the brave, resolute commandant, Don Velasco. The Spanish Governor of the city, Don Juan de Prado, would now probably have been justified in capitulating to Albermarle, but the Spaniards wanted to fight on.

At this moment much needed reinforcements arrived: some 3188 American auxiliaries and British regulars from New York. This enabled the British to expand their bridgehead and erect additional batteries to bombard La Punta and Havana itself. Again Spanish sorties failed to dislodge the British or destroy the batteries. By 31 July Albermarle had completed a siege line running along the entire western (land) front of Havana and had erected batteries along the entire harbour shore from El Morro to La Cabana. By 10 August he had ten mortars, five howitzers and more than 40 guns ready to pound the city's defences to pieces. He sent an ADC to ask Don Prado to capitulate but the Governor refused.

On 11 August the final British bombardment commenced upon Havana and the remaining Spanish-held outer forts of La Punta and La Fuerza with deadly effect. After several unpleasant hours under the intense fire La Punta was silenced and the Spanish garrison withdrew to Havana. By noon most guns on the city's walls were out of action. It was now only a question of time before the city was stormed and sacked. At 2 PM Prado ran up the white flag and sent an adjutant across the lines to negotiate terms. After fruitless discussions Albemarle and Pocock sent a joint warning to the Governor threatening to level the town unless Prado agreed to British terms immediately. On 14 August the British occupied La Punta and marched into Havana.

The victory at Havana was a triumph of logistics and siege warfare under difficult climatic conditions. Pocock had lost 1200 of his men, mainly to disease, and Albemarle lost more than 5000 troops. In the end the costly and protracted siege of Havana contributed not only to the fall of the Spanish American Empire but also to that of Britain in North America. When the American auxiliaries returned to New York they were racked by disease. The British were unable to stem Native American attacks. This fuelled the American colonists' discontent with Imperial rule, culminating in the rebellion of 1776.

A 1769 MODEL *of a British land-service mortar had a bronze barrel, trunnioned at the rear into a wooden bed. This gave it stability for fire but made it somewhat awkward to transport, especially along jungle routes around Havana. Elevation of the mortar was controlled by wedges. This type of mortar was also used by the Royal Navy for shore bombardment.*

CHAPTER 5

NAVAL WARFARE

Tactics, technology and terrain determined the failure or success of combat at sea. This was an era of innovation in technology and tactics, the two areas human intellect could alter – and tactics and technology influenced the effect of the third essential factor, terrain.

B y the end of the early modern era, the Europeans found that their improved vessels and arms had given them a weapons system that could project force to any coastal point on the globe. No major area of the world would henceforth be entirely isolated from Western influence. Throughout the era, successful tactics determined the future direction the technology would take, while at the same time the technology of the ships, their equipment and weapons directed what sort of fighting techniques admirals and ship masters could employ at a given point in time. The need to

TACTICS, TECHNOLOGY AND TERRAIN *framed the maritime struggles of the dawning modern era. In the lack of modern power and communications, entire fleet actions could be determined by a basic plan of attack, the quality of ships and their weaponry, or something as simple as a fold in the coast.*

protect, attack or acquire distant possessions meant that the Europeans of the early modern era fought in waters unknown a generation earlier. Commanders sheltering in harbours thought secure would find improved hostile vessels braving forts, storms and shoals to attack them, with devastating consequences.

Tactics

An admiral from a later era summed up the oldest naval tactic of them all: Lord Nelson declared 'just go at them', as his basic order to his subordinate commanders. Getting at them was the problem, unless the enemy obligingly shared the same objective, as was the case at Lepanto in 1571. In other cases, aggressive commanders forced battle upon fleets that had hoped to escape it. Exactly how to bring an unwilling foe to battle was a persistent problem for commanders.

Ships unsuited to the conditions of the stormy North Atlantic would find it a challenge just to survive there, much less to fight and win in serious combat, as the unfortunate galleasses of the Spanish Armada discovered before, during and after the Battle of Gravelines in 1588. Ship designs subsequently changed, builders strengthening hulls both against the waves and the need to carry heavy guns. Finding an enemy that did not want to engage under unfavourable conditions posed another problem, leading to the construction of specialized lighter vessels for reconnaissance. The use of such vessels enabled the Dutch admiral Maarten van Tromp to stay in contact with a more powerful enemy fleet until he could gather enough new ships to engage with decisive finality at the Battle of the Downs in 1639.

Communication was another problem that was slowly solved by technology. The Armada suffered terribly from difficulties of coordination, and

'It is said all this attempt at order on the sea is useless, for order can not be preserved. To that I answer that having equal arms, the fleet in the best order will win, for if the…sea throw an ordered fleet into confusion, the fleet without order will be more confused.'

— Alonso de Chavez, 1530

admirals-in-chief like Don Juan at Lepanto could do little to transmit their orders to their subordinates beyond the most rudimentary of signals. Orders to attack or withdraw were about the limit of tactical communication throughout the earlier portion of the period. More advanced communication by signal flag only came in at the end of the eighteenth century, and then was only feasible in conditions of good visibility. Prearranged signals could be sent by a variety of means, but they could not be changed to reflect changed conditions.

Other technologies were factors in communication and command. Admirals of the era lacked either telescopes or a flexible system of signalling to observe with them. More complicated signal systems using flags and cannon discharges were brought in as the years passed, but any detailed and interactive communication at sea relied on the physical movement of the individuals involved to speak face to face or within hailing distance. Such a meeting was at the mercy of small craft, weather conditions, and, in combat, personal survival. Pity the messenger in a small boat trying to find a given ship in the muddle and carnage of a battle at sea and then attempting to return with a reply. There were many more complicating factors in the era before modern military discipline. Supposedly subordinate officers were often insubordinate to commanding admirals, and chaos was often the result. Francis Drake during the first battle with the Armada left Lord Admiral Howard fuming when he sailed off to capture the crippled *Nuestra Senora del Rosario*; ignoring the demands of military duty in his piratical eagerness to seize a rich prize. At Lepanto each of the four 'rear admirals' – that is, admirals in the rear behind the supreme commander – largely fought their own battles once the action began. Tromp was fortunate at the Downs in that his subordinates

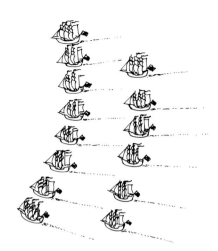

followed him and engaged, rather than wilfully refusing battle out of personal disagreement or temper, as was often disastrously the case among the Dutch. Hawke was much more fortunate at Quiberon Bay in 1759, by which time relatively advanced optics, weatherly vessels and a functional signalling system had been introduced. Even so, his ships and guns were only barely up to the tasks he set them.

The tactics of the era revolved around manoeuvres using the ancient, basic formations of line astern and line abreast – vessels moving either in line astern, bow-to-stern, one after the other; or in line abreast, ships travelling side-by-side in the same direction. The Greeks and Romans had used the same two basic formations on land and sea, and the same fundamental division of tactics would predominate even in the naval battles of World War II. The ships themselves and their equipment would determine which of the two formations would succeed in a given battle.

Technology

A ship is one of the most impressive manifestations of human technology – wood, later metal, rope and cloth floating safely upon the waters of the devouring sea. Ships are capable of taking travellers – or warriors – to any destination the world's waters touch. The shipwright's basic task is seaworthiness, yet even that becomes complicated by the nature of the waters his creation is meant to traverse. The relatively placid

LINE OF SIGHT *limited the formations of the era into two basic shapes: line of battle (ships side to side with their bows to the enemy) or column (ships proceeding bow to stern towards the foe). The ships in line of battle have the options, wind or sea permitting, to present their broadsides to the advancing foe. The ships in column are closing the range and may attempt to sail through the enemy's formation or they may turn suddenly to form a line of battle of their own.*

waters of the Mediterranean in the sailing season allowed long-range maritime commerce a thousand years before the birth of Christ, but the thought of one of the cockleshells of the Bronze Age braving the stormy Atlantic waters beyond the 'pillars of Hercules' at Gibraltar was the stuff of legend. By the end of the Middle Ages the art of ship construction had advanced to a point where vessels of commerce or war could usually survive their battles with the world's seas. The successful voyage of Magellan around the globe fifty years before Lepanto was the proof of that success, although the ships in those and the later great voyages all needed anchorages to perform repairs and maintenance, and their crews needed access to food and fresh water, factors that would always set limits to their capabilities.

Surviving the efforts of the enemy tasked a shipwright even further. The high sides that kept the seas out of cargo vessels made them natural castles of wood which could be moved and defended by archers and crossbowmen, as was

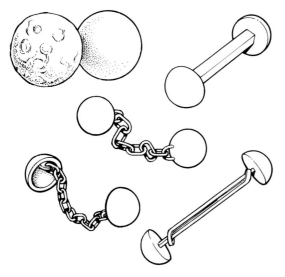

ROPES, SAILS AND MEN *could be chopped to pieces by special projectiles known as 'disabling shot' in later gunnery. Stone shot could shatter into lethal shards, but iron balls carried further and were easier and cheaper to make. Bar and chain shot whirled through rigging and tore rents in sails at close range, reducing a foe's mobility.*

their function at the medieval Battle of Sluys in 1340. Earlier, the Greeks and Romans had sharply differentiated between the 'Round Ships' of peace and the 'long ships' of war. The fact that galleys could carry cargo and early sailing vessels could take warriors did not make either class of ship particularly suitable for the other purpose. The ability to manoeuvre and to ram had made the rowed galley the dominant warship in the West

THE EARLIEST BREECH-LOADING *naval cannon spat fire around their breeches, which was potentially disastrous in the presence of black powder. The gunner would place powder in the hollow breech and the ball in the barrel itself, then use weights, wedges and prayers to hold the weapon together as it fired. The cumbersome system was slower to reload than the later muzzle-loaders.*

throughout the course of history up to the sixteenth century, and so it was for a final, spectacular time at Lepanto. But in that century it had become clear that the advancement of a new technology would have to be figured into the design of new vessels of war, and that was, of course, gunpowder and the cannon.

There had been primitive *pot de fer* iron bombards at Sluys, but there is no account of these unwieldy weapons having any dramatic effect at that battle. By Lepanto, however, cannon great and small were present and firing on any ship that could be expected to engage in combat. In galleys, three or five guns were positioned pointing forwards at the bow of the vessel, where they could be fired once, hopefully with devastating effect, immediately before the time-tested tactics of ramming and boarding could decide the combat. But as the design and use of naval cannon was refined, naval commanders realized that more could be achieved with artillery.

Cannon of the era, even as late as 1759 and after, were temperamental and often as dangerous to their crews as to the enemy. The phrase 'a loose cannon' survives as a legacy of the danger an unsecured gun rolling about a ship's deck posed

to the vessel and its crew. Unless perfectly cast, the guns could and did explode with horrific results for ships and crews, and, unless bored true, the most expensive cannon could be horrendously inaccurate, not justifying the resources and faith placed in their efficacy. Moisture in the powder could keep cannon from firing and make the powder itself dangerously unstable with, again, deadly consequences. It seems obvious today that the more cannon a vessel could carry, the greater its fighting power, but if a ship was neither seaworthy nor manoeuvrable as a result of its burden of ordnance, the ship and the cannon would end up at the bottom of the sea or in the hands of the foe.

Manoeuvrability versus Firepower

Hindsight makes it difficult for the modern reader to understand the true nature of technological progress in the early modern era. Sailing warships with many cannon eventually proved superior to rowed vessels with few guns, but admirals and captains alike were reluctant to forego the manoeuvrability oars provided.

The prospect of being becalmed by capricious winds as armed galleys drew near was not a pleasant one, as the Dutch pirate Carstens found when a squadron of Venetian galleasses bore down upon his galleon and annihilated him a few years after Lepanto. The design of the galleass itself attempted to combine the capability to mount a large number of cannon in broadside, with the manoeuvrability of oars, but this compromise was never truly successful.

HYBRIDIZATION PRODUCED RIGS *superior to the square sail of the Romans and Vikings, and the Lateen sails favoured by the later Mediterranean navigators, in which long triangular sails on single massive booms rotated easily around the masts to catch changeable winds. The 'ship' rigs combined the easy trim of a semi-triangular 'spanker' on the stern mast with superimposed square sails that pulled powerfully before a favourable wind.*

By the time of Lepanto, sailing ships themselves were a compromise, but in the long run were to prove a more successful one than the galleass. Triangular lateen sails were easy to shift to before changing winds, but quadrilateral square sails were more powerful pullers before a following wind. Combining the two forms of sails in a single design that could sail before and into the wind was the great innovation behind the successful carracks of the late medieval era. When the forecastle of the carrack was removed and other refinements to rig and sails were made, the result was the legendary galleon of the kind that bore Drake and Magellan around the world. Sailing vessels like these could carry cannon above the sea's damp and spray, their fields of fire unimpeded by waves or labouring oarsmen. There would be vital, even decisive refinements – such as gunports, which allowed additional levels of broadside guns below the ones on the main deck, and gun carriages, which could increase decisively a vessel's rate of fire. The four-wheeled gun carriage was England's second great secret weapon at Gravelines, but the mere opening of her gun ports sank a French vessel in stormy seas at Quiberon Bay – the cost of trying to use the ship's full firepower.

Without the filtering lens of hindsight, trends were not always clear to contemporaries. But there were some useful indicators, like that provided by an incident during the action at the Straits of Preveza in 1538, which served to show nations and admirals the potential of the sailing warship. During Andrea Doria's disastrous withdrawal from the straits, the flagship of the Venetian squadron of Charles V's allied fleet was cut off and flanked by the dreaded Turkish Admiral, Barbarossa. The 'Galleon of Venice' (perhaps one of the very first such ships ever constructed) lay becalmed while Doria's galleys escaped and the Turks approached.

It was a highly dangerous predicament, but under the capable command of Alessandro Condalmiero, the gunners of the monster warship's broadside batteries carefully ricocheted their shot off the sea and into the circling Turkish galleys. Despite the loss of her mainmast, and although Doria made no effort to relieve his rival city's flagship, the galleon repulsed every Turkish attack, killing many among the galleys' crews. Becalmed or not, a sailing ship had held her own against a fleet of galleys, and others would prove their ability to do the same. The failure of the galleasses at Gravelines in 1588, however, demonstrated the error of the Spanish attempt to hedge their bets with sailing technology. Ships that could manoeuvre quickly gave an admiral a new range of tactical options. Long-range cannon, or cannon that could be reloaded quickly (the two were mutually exclusive at first), offered further choices to the commanders of the early modern age, as did ships that could still fight their guns in

a rough sea where an opponent thought it safer to anchor in sheltered water, as was the case at Quiberon Bay and to an extent in the Downs. The devil, and the victory, would quite often lurk in the details.

Terrain

Men are not fish, nor, despite the increasing ability of seafarers and ships in the period, could the navies of the early modern age conduct themselves in any capacity at sea without reference to events and situations on land. The Armada at Gravelines and the French fleet under Conflans at Quiberon Bay both had invasions of the British Isles as their objectives. The battles of Lepanto and the Downs were straightforward contests of sea power. However, both were fought with the idea of preventing the enemy's fleet from interfering or assisting with terrestrial campaigns. Admiral Tromp's destruction of Spanish transports at the Downs was as effective a contribution to the cause of Dutch autonomy as any terrestrial engagement.

Matters besides theory and biology restricted the battles of this time and later to the coasts. The dependence of the ships of this era on land bases for repair and supply, the need for landmarks to aid in navigation and the objectives of friendly or hostile ports at the end of voyages or legs of longer journeys were all factors. The need for ports, and the need to support land campaigns kept fleets close to the shore – and kept fleets hoping to attack them likewise in proximity to the coasts.

The idea of encountering an enemy fleet in the midst of the vastness of the ocean, way out of sight of land, was almost inconceivable in the early modern era and a rarity afterwards. Surrounding

> '...if our fleet should be defeated our princes are not so weak but that they could not at least take sufficient measures for defense. Whereas, if we are victors, we might perhaps expect the rescue of Greece.... Besides, which...we cannot hope much to injure the Turk unless we first destroy his fleet...'
>
> — ASCANO DELLA CORNIA

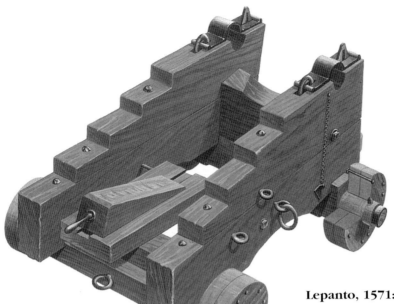

THE WHEELS OF this gun carriage allowed the cannon's recoil to expend itself in movement, rather than in damaging a vessel's timbers, while gunners could elevate the weapon by movement of the wooden wedge beneath the breech. Reloading tackles also allowed the cannon to be trained from side. Carriages of this design enabled the British to achieve a superior rate of fire during the Armada battles.

terrain could also make fighting possible in conditions that otherwise might have prevented it. The Gulf of Patras, where the Battle of Lepanto was fought, offered the calm waters that the Allied and Turkish fleets needed for their galleys to fight to their best advantage. The promise of safety offered by the anchorages of Gravelines and Quiberon Bay drew the Spanish and French fleets to them, and their enemies to the same location. The Downs offered shelter from sea and wind, and in theory the sanctuary of a neutral roadstead to the desperate Spaniards, already handled severely by the Dutch.

The hoped-for protection, even when supported by an English squadron, availed not at all before the determination and ability of the attacking Dutch. Shores and shoals determined the courses and fates of ships in the battles themselves, and in the circumstances leading up to them. All four of the following battles bear the names of terrestrial geographic features; features that themselves, along with tactics and technology, helped to bring the battles about.

Lepanto, 1571: Clash of the Galleys

Lepanto was a battle in which two great religions, each boosting their supporters' morale with promises of glory and paradise, fought it out in an area where the surrounding terrain allowed the galleys of both sides to engage with minimal interference from the caprice of weather and the sea. The tactics did show efforts at refinement, but the Christian order, 'Fire not until the blood of thine opponent will spatter you' succinctly embodies the shared desire of both sides to close and kill. Old weapons, the galleys, carrying much newer weapons, cannon, fought alongside a new and devastating secret weapon that gave the victory to the Holy League and left such an impression upon the vanquished Turks that to this day it is known as *Singin,* the crushing defeat.

Jihad in the name of Islam met revived Christian counter-attack when Pope Pius V proclaimed a crusade, along with special indulgences to lessen the after-life torments of those who fought for the Cross. The Ottoman Turkish Empire had centuries previously expanded their version of religious struggle into the waters of the Mediterranean with ships, commanders and cannon at least as good as, and sometimes better than those possessed by their Christian antagonists.

Among these numbered the ancient and formidable Republic of Venice which, since the

Ottoman state expanded to sprawl across all its trade routes to the East, faced the dilemma of maintaining good commercial relations with the Turks while at the same time resisting conquest by them. Philip II, the 'prudent' king of Spain, possessed a long Mediterranean coast and knew that the Turks considered a large part of his Spanish kingdom (the last parts finally reconquered less than a century before) as Muslim territory, to be reclaimed at the first opportunity.

The Pope himself was fighting a vigorous campaign against the Protestant reformation of

Christianity, but the older threat of aggressive Islam was not one that any inhabitant of Italy could ignore. The Venetians finally prevailed upon the Pope and the Spaniards to support them against the Ottoman threat only when their last outpost in the Eastern Mediterranean, Cyprus, was in imminent danger of capture and a powerful Turkish fleet was entering the Adriatic Sea.

In command of the allied forces of Spain, the Pope and Venice was King Philip's bastard brother, Don Juan of Austria. Don Juan was an inspiring, competent, decisive commander who had previous experience fighting Turkish raiders and understood the need to contest the apparent supremacy of the Ottoman fleet. The Pope's support, made tangible in the form of twelve galleys under the papal flag, was a vital psychological counter to the Turkish reputation for invincibility, which combined with Islam in giving Ali Pasha, his Turkish counterpart, confidence in an aggressive strategy and a willingness to fight it out.

ITSELF A GUIDED PROJECTILE, *galley engages galley with the ram striking into the hull as the attacker's heaviest cannon fire. Grappling and boarding follow as the marines of the attacking vessel attempt to swarm on board the target. Galleys manned by convicts or slave crews faced the danger at such a crisis of an uprising among their oarsmen. However, the chains used to prevent that meant their doom should a galley sink.*

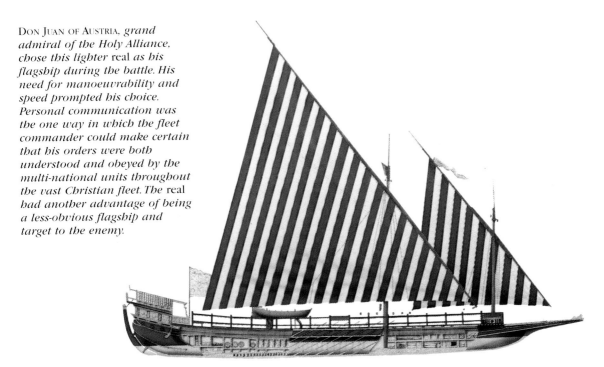

DON JUAN OF AUSTRIA, *grand admiral of the Holy Alliance, chose this lighter* real *as his flagship during the battle. His need for manoeuvrability and speed prompted his choice. Personal communication was the one way in which the fleet commander could make certain that his orders were both understood and obeyed by the multi-national units throughout the vast Christian fleet. The* real *had another advantage of being a less-obvious flagship and target to the enemy.*

The Christian forces numbered approximately 74,000 men in approximately 240 vessels, ranging from light *nefs* to the six great monsters that would decide the day. The Turkish fleet numbered approximately 210 vessels with crews totalling 75,000 men. Ali Pasha had risen to his command through royal favour, as had Don Juan, but his sub-commanders were all experienced men and the fighting men on board his vessels were the terror of Christian Europe. There was every reason for the Turks to expect to repeat the success they enjoyed in the Preveza campaign of 1538, when a similar coalition Christian fleet had been driven from the vital straits in disorganized defeat. Ali Pasha consolidated his forces in the Gulf of Patras on the western coast of Greece as the Christian fleet moved slowly eastwards, shadowed by the light, fast Turkish corsairs.

Several factors had altered, however, even in the short time between 1538 and 1571. For one thing, the Turks were no longer fighting just the wealth of Europe. The discovery of the New World had permitted large-scale exploitation of the new territories' natural resources, especially gold and silver. Most of the profit went directly into the

Spanish military, already formidable after centuries of struggle against the Moors in Spain, and, later, on the African coast. Philip's galleys were of the best design and quality, and his shipboard troops were equipped with new matchlock arquebuses, with which the Christians hoped to counter the dreaded Turkish composite bow.

Another factor working against the Turks was their own recent success. After the capture of Famagosta, a Venetian citadel taken at the cost of 50,000 Turkish lives, and with the fall of Cyprus imminent, the Venetian Republic could no longer discount the Ottoman threat against the profits generated for the mercantile families controlling the state by their eastern trade. The Turks were past the efforts of diplomacy. Accordingly, the Venetian fleet at Lepanto would be the largest yet put forth by the city-state, and the best equipped. The need for oarsmen was met for the first time by the addition of convicts (promised their freedom) and men from the Venetian subject territories to the crews of their galleys.

The ships themselves were the product of the most advanced and best-managed industrial plant in the Western world, the celebrated Venetian

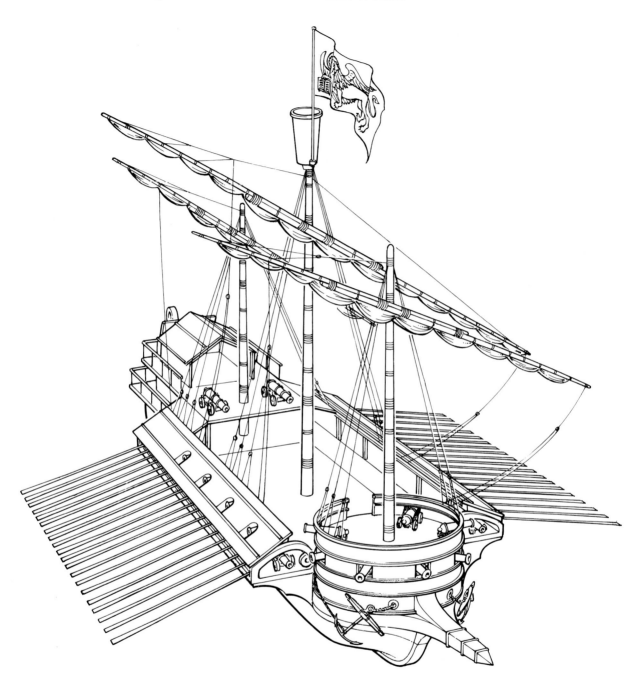

HASTY, DEADLY AND DECISIVE *conversions, the six galleasses the Venetian arsenal prepared and sent into the fury of Lepanto began their existences as large merchant galleys on the lucrative spice voyages to East Asia. These monsters freighted castles and cannon after their conversion, rendering them practically, but not completely, immobile. So successful was the new type that the commander of the galleass squadron received a special commendation after the battle, and later examples would be found in the fleets of two centuries later. Slow and unwieldy in comparison to ships under sail, the galleass could have a potentially telling advantage in the event of calm or unfavourable winds.*

Arsenal, the cauldrons and thousands of workers of which had informed Dante's descriptions of Hell. Trained specialists and standardized parts had been used in the months before Lepanto to produce and fit out a fleet of a hundred galleys by which the *Serenissima* meant to defend itself in this last great struggle. The Arsenal had provided ships for war and trade throughout the preceding centuries of Venice's seafaring. The dominant design was that of 'the great galley,' a large vessel pulled by as many as four men on an oar. Such vessels could carry cargo in divided hulls, or cannon, as noted, at the bow: the largest 'great cannon' on the ship's centreline with smaller 'dragons' or 'drakes' to the sides. Venetian cannon were simple, functional, standardized and lethal.

Secret Weapon

According to one account, six of the largest merchant galleys in the Venetian fleet were floating in one of the Arsenal's storage basins as the preparations for the impending battle reached a fever pitch. In an inspired moment the decision was made to freight these huge vessels with something more lethal than their usual cargoes of silks and spices. Workmen equipped each with heavy artillery and specialized fighting structures at the bow, the stern and along the sides. No other shipyard in the world could have produced the new hybrids so quickly.

Later versions of these hybrids were about 49m (160ft) long and 12m (40ft) wide, twice as wide as the lighter galleys. Six men pulled each of the vessel's 76 heavy oars, and the decks were protected from boarding by the high freeboard, the long distance from the water to her deck making a difficult obstacle for an attacker to surmount. Her gun battery probably contained

'...After gaining the day in the centre...I dropped the galleys I had taken and had in tow to go where help was needed. Some Venetian galleys coming behind boarded my prizes and had much booty, for these corsairs were very rich. I do not care, for I came not to rob but to fight and serve Our God...' – HONORATO CAETANI

five or so full cannon, which fired a 22.6-kg (50-lb) ball, two or three 11-kg (25-lb) cannon, some 23 lighter pieces of various sizes and shapes, and around 20 rail-mounted swivel guns, used to slaughter rowers and prevent parties boarding. Five normal galleys could have been armed with that assortment of weapons.

From every angle these novel vessels were fighting ships. Forward, the high, protected forecastle bristled with cannon, balanced by similar armament in the substantial aftercastle. Nine or more pieces were ranged along each side, mounted above, below or among the oarsmen, where on a galley such weaponry could not be accommodated. In later years, the heaviest Venetian galleasses could fire some 1147kg (325lb) of shot in every salvo. Above the grated deck, three huge lateen sails, each on its own mast, made up some 743m^2 (8000 sq ft) of canvas. We cannot be sure whether the six at Lepanto were this heavily armed or not, but we do know that they were very potent warships. The new leviathans needed towing to achieve any sort of speed at all, but such a necessity was not an issue in a fleet of large galleys.

Aside from the new galleasses, the galleys of the Holy Alliance were generally more heavily built than those of the Turks, and were consequently less manoeuvrable and slower, but they had built-up sides, or *pavesades*, giving protection to rowers and marines. The Turks had a major disadvantage in the presence of large numbers of enslaved Christians on the galley benches, men who might seize the chance of rescue at any moment, should the chaos of battle permit. Even the Turks' high morale and fighting élan proved to be an unexpected disadvantage. As the Christian fleet entered the Bay of Patras on the morning of 7 October 1571, the Turks still had the option to

Battle of Lepanto
1571

The terrain sheltering the waters of the Bay of Patras allowed the galleys, and deadly Christian galleasses of the Christian fleet, to fight at their best advantage without winds to disrupt formations and waves distracting the two fleets' marines from mortal combat. Turkish archery was accurate, rapid and deadly, but Christian armour and arquebuses proved a sufficient counter. Leaving the shelter of Turkish shore batteries, Ottoman admiral Ali Pasha moved forth to challenge Don Juan's collected forces of the Holy Alliance. Experienced Christian captains promptly put their vessels into battle formation while selected vessels towed forth the six monster galleasses which mauled the passing Turks and struck them from behind. The thrust of the Turkish advance in the Christian centre led to a near double-envelopment on the flanks, with most of the Turkish fleet destroyed or taken by day's end. Perhaps the most important result of the battle was its effect on men's minds: this emphatic victory, where most of the Turkish fleet was either destroyed or captured, ended the myth of Turkish invincibility.

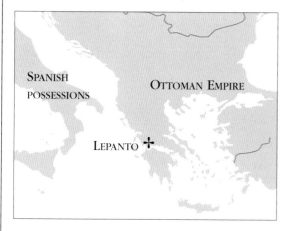

The gulf of Lepanto is situated east of the gulf of Corinth and near the port of Patras, in a long arm of the Ionian Sea that separates the Peloponnese peninsula to the south from the Greek mainland to the north.

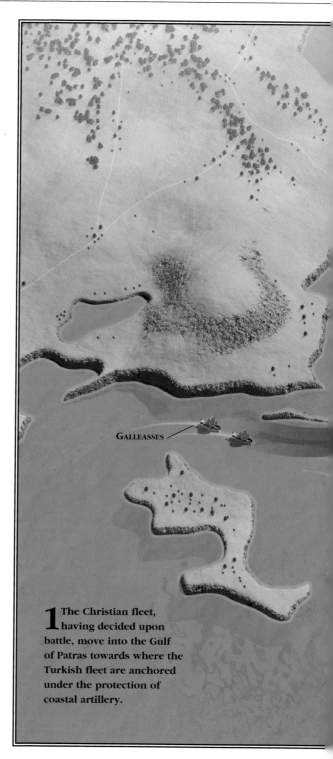

GALLEASSES

1 The Christian fleet, having decided upon battle, move into the Gulf of Patras towards where the Turkish fleet are anchored under the protection of coastal artillery.

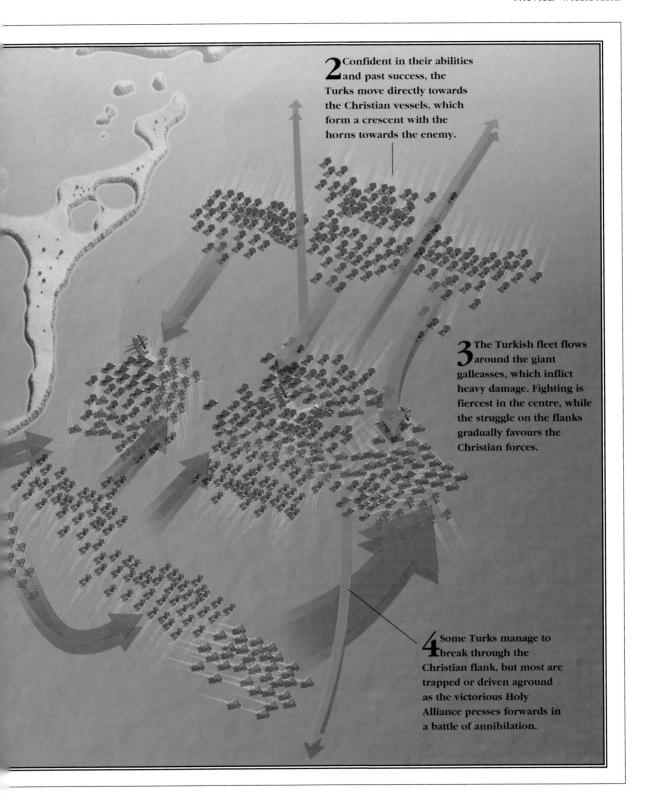

2 Confident in their abilities and past success, the Turks move directly towards the Christian vessels, which form a crescent with the horns towards the enemy.

3 The Turkish fleet flows around the giant galleasses, which inflict heavy damage. Fighting is fiercest in the centre, while the struggle on the flanks gradually favours the Christian forces.

4 Some Turks manage to break through the Christian flank, but most are trapped or driven aground as the victorious Holy Alliance presses forwards in a battle of annihilation.

refuse battle, and lie up under the protection of the guns of fortresses at the narrows of the Bay. Deciding instead to fight at once, Ali Pasha and his subordinate admirals sallied forth in line abreast to attack. The Turkish lookouts found the Christians in line astern as the sun rose behind them.

Some of Don Juan's rear admirals had urged retreat in the face of the Turkish force, but he replied 'It is too late for counsel, it is now time for battle.' At sighting the enemy, Don Juan raised a large flag blessed by the Pope and signalled with a gun and green pennant his order to engage. Don Juan's flagship was a fast, light vessel, and he moved around to organize and spur on the smaller flotillas of his command in the immediate prelude to the battle. The galleasses lurched forward in front of the formation by Don Juan's express order, each one towed by four of the standard galleys. Holding formation was a much easier task for oared vessels than for ships at the mercy of changeable winds.

A squadron of 12 galleys under a Genoese naval mercenary, the grandnephew and namesake of the celebrated Andrea Doria, led the Christian line as it surged forwards to form a crescent with

A MAN-KILLING 'MURDERER', *this breech-loading* falconet *earned its name due to its status as an anti-personnel weapon. Its tripod or rail-attached swivel mount allowed this family of weapon to kill sailors in the rigging, marksman in the tops or oarsmen or hostile gunners in the hold. At need, a ship's own deck could be swept with fire against the advance of a boarding party.*

its horns bent towards the advancing Turks. Such was the confidence of Ali Pasha and his captains that the cry went up as they sighted Doria's squadron that the Christian vessels were outnumbered and retreating before them, about to flee in disorder. Only as the sun rose higher in the sky did the Turks perceive the rest of the Holy Alliance's battle fleet moving forwards behind Doria. Ali Pasha, undaunted, signalled to engage.

Three squadrons made up the tactical components of each fleet as the two lines rushed together under the impetus of their oars. The sight of the six galleasses in the van of the Christian line posed a difficult dilemma for Ali Pasha. His galleys could have turned their bows and cannon upon the behemoths, and in so doing exposed their sides to the Christian galleys, who would have been certain to take cruel advantage. Instead the Turkish admiral chose to divide his own formation to sail through the galleasses' picket, enduring the cannon fire of their broadsides at the greatest possible distance. That strategy minimized the damage that the Christian leviathans could inflict upon the Turkish line at first onset, but it meant that the Turkish fleet would be separated into components that could not provide support for each other as they hit the main Christian line. It also allowed the galleasses ponderously to reverse course and loom up in their rear.

Clouds of smoke from the Christian *arquebuses* shared the sky with whistling Turkish arrows, and stranger weapons flew in both directions as the galleys met in close battle. Swivel guns called *versos*, man-killing 'murderers' in English, mounted on the rails of the Christian ships, fired all sorts of scrap iron into the enemy crews at close range, like over-sized shotguns. Special troops threw clay pots filled with flaming oil, animal fat or quicklime to burn the enemy boats or render the decks untenable, while a short-range incendiary called the *bomba,* essentially a huge Roman candle, showered sparks and hollow iron balls filled with burning matter upon the enemy's decks, hulls and men. The galleasses manoeuvred with their oars to bring stern or bow guns to bear as their broadsides thundered forth into Turkish galleys that were unable to board or inflict damage in return.

Fighting was particularly fierce at the ends of each line as each fleet sought to envelop the other, and the Christians gradually succeeded. Some of the Christian slaves on the benches of the Turkish fleet seized weapons dropped in battle and attacked their former masters. The heavier armour worn by the Christian fighting men proved an advantage, protecting them from the Turkish arrows but would prove fatal to any that fell in the sea. Ali Pasha's own squadron fought their way through to the 'Royal' galleys in the Christian centre, where many of the Christian commanders were, and boarded. The fate of the battle swung back and forth, and Ali Pasha himself bent a bow. On the Christian side, one septuagenarian Venetian nobleman with a heavy crossbow and an assistant to span and load it picked off Turkish boarders from the masthead.

A few days later anxious watchers on the jetty protecting the outermost waters of the Venetian lagoon observed a lone galley slowly pulling into sight out of the Adriatic mists. The vessel showed signs of severe damage, banners trailing and oars flailing wildly. Over the waters came the cry of the exhausted crew, 'Vittoria! Vittoria!' The trailing banners were Turkish. Over 170 galleys and lighter vessels of the Turkish fleet had been captured, and most of the rest destroyed. 30,000 Turks had perished in the carnage. The fleet of the Holy Alliance suffered a loss of approximately 7700 Christians and 12 ships.

It is fashionable today to discard the significance of this great battle on quite rational grounds: his viziers told the Turkish sultan that he could, if he wished, replace the fleet annihilated at Lepanto with one equipped with silver anchors, satin sails, and silken rigging out of the still-ample resources of his empire. Less than a generation afterwards the fading Venetian Republic recognized the hegemony of the Turkish Empire over the waters of the eastern Mediterranean by treaty. But the shock to the civilized world of the defeat of the Turks at the height of their strength by an alliance of only part of Christendom left an impression that remains to this day of overall Western military supremacy over Islam.

Gravelines, 1588: Wind and Tide

Philip of Spain could hardly be blamed, after Lepanto, for putting great faith in the galleasses, the secret weapon that had won the day for his half-brother. By 1588 Don Juan had been dead a decade, but the Spanish fleet still had the lustre of Lepanto and Philip's vast resources behind it when the King of Spain decided it was time to launch another great crusade, this time against the land and fleet of a heretic foe.

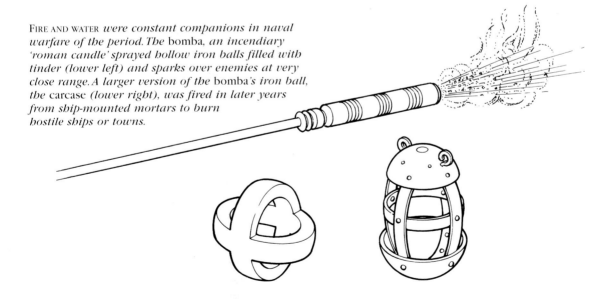

FIRE AND WATER *were constant companions in naval warfare of the period. The* bomba, *an incendiary 'roman candle' sprayed hollow iron balls filled with tinder (lower left) and sparks over enemies at very close range. A larger version of the* bomba's *iron ball, the* carcase *(lower right), was fired in later years from ship-mounted mortars to burn hostile ships or towns.*

But Elizabeth I of England and her 'sea dogs' were foes very different from the galleys of the Turkish Sultan. It is fortunate that historians and nautical archaeologists have been able to separate so many hard facts from the clouds of myth surrounding the events of 1588. Legends can no longer obscure the means by which the Spanish Armada faltered and English seamanship prevailed in another great struggle for national survival decided by the thunder of guns at sea.

Spain had felt herself dominant over England since the alliance of Henry VII, first of the Tudors,

THE FLAGSHIP OF THE *Invincible Armada, the* San Martin *carried Medina Sidonia, Philip's admiral, to battle and defeat. This 'Spanish galleon' originated with an Italian design that adapted very well to the wars and voyages of the Atlantic, with room for stores and heavy armament in her hull. The galleon dispensed with the lofty and dangerous fore and after castles of the earlier carracks.*

with Ferdinand and Isabella in 1501. Their daughter Catherine of Aragon married the future Henry VIII in 1502 and wrote letters to her father about 'these new lands of your Majesty's'. Henry's apostasy from Roman Catholicism in 1534 and mutual military difficulties had broken the alliance, but for a brief period Spain again had authority in England by the marriage in 1554 of Henry's daughter 'Bloody' Mary with Philip II himself. Philip liked neither England's queen nor England's climate, and by the accession of Elizabeth in 1558 the English and Spaniards confronted each other with well-acquainted dislike. Philip and Catholic Christendom declared Elizabeth a bastard child of an illegitimate marriage, and the Pope absolved her subjects of all oaths sworn to their queen.

Elizabeth proved a more formidable antagonist than anyone had expected. The last of the Tudors soon found an inexpensive, in fact a profitable

means of discomfiting the Spaniards and enriching her kingdom, ravaged by a series of wars with France. That was piracy, which the queen supported by ships leased or sold out of her own navy and funds from selected investors. Among these was often Elizabeth herself, as the raiding diverted the riches of the Spanish New World into English coffers. Francis Drake's raid on the port of Cadiz in 1587 was only the last in an increasingly painful series of thrusts against Spanish wealth and national prestige. Philip II had endured more than enough of English piracy, Protestantism and provocation by the following year, when he completed his preparations.

Trial and Error

Drake and his rival 'sea dogs' were well equipped in technological terms. The English by no means took as naturally to the sea as their later domination of it would indicate, but by the reign of Henry VIII some of the largest and most formidable ships of war ever built had slid off of English launching slips. There were failed experiments along the way, for example the capsizing and sinking of Henry VIII's 'great ship,' the carrack *Mary Rose*. This was a disaster for the watching king and the unfortunate crew, but a great revelation for modern underwater archaeologists. Later vessels would lack the towering forecastles of Henry's earlier ships, but a few matched or exceeded *Mary Rose* in size. A myth about the Armada that can be punctured at the outset is that of huge Spanish galleons confronted by nippy little English vessels. In fact, the largest ships engaged in the fighting were actually English ships.

With a string of suddenly hostile Catholic countries arrayed on the coasts opposite his island, Henry VIII had invested considerable time and treasure in developing the infrastructure for the independent production of ships and armaments of war. Imported Italian craftsmen had built the first great ships of his father's fleet. Their

sons taught and competed with English rivals in design of war vessels and the casting of bronze and iron cannon. Experiment and naval expansion had given the English the benefit of a number of refinements, which took the effectiveness of their vessels to a higher level than that of the Spaniards in several crucial areas, and would help to give them victory over Philip II's 'Invincible Armada.'

The most important manifestation of English expertise was the seemingly simple four-wheeled 'truck' gun carriage. Small vessels needed to fire rapidly to make up for the greater weight of large-calibre guns like those carried in the galleasses. In galleys rushing forwards into attack the idea of reloading artillery was impracticable. Soon after the galley was close enough to fire her bow guns at an opponent she would be ramming and her crew boarding over the ram to settle the issue with musket balls and cold steel.

> *'Whosoever commands the sea commands the trade; whosoever commands the trade of the world commands the riches of the world, and consequently the world itself.'*
>
> — SIR WALTER RALEIGH

That 'one-shot strategy' persisted in the sailing ships of Philip II's later navy, which carried cannons large and small on two-wheeled carriages either the same as used by field guns on land, or much resembling them. These were kept loaded (some have been recovered in that condition from the ocean floor centuries later) and trained forwards or backwards along the ship's side by their gunners, to be fired with hopefully shattering effect at close range immediately before boarding. Effective, rapid fire at long range was an aspiration for the Spaniards, not a reality. The excessively long barrels, heavy carriages and irregular bores of their cannon prevented it.

The English had done things differently. With the Spaniards and Portuguese controlling the trade routes to Asia and the mines and rarities of South America, English traders were driven farther afield in search of new trading opportunities and they sailed in ships that grew steadily more capable of long voyages. Huge one-shot guns were too massive for such extended voyages.

Light, movable cannon that fired twice as frequently, along with superior sailing qualities, were the advantages of the vessels Drake, Frobisher, Howard and the others would turn against the Spaniards. Innovation countered sheer size and expense. The huge stone shot fired by many of the Spanish cannon had murderous, shattering effect, but also took much more time to produce than England's cheap and ballistically superior cast iron balls. The English also correctly concluded that beyond a certain point, a longer barrel offered no gain to a cannon using black powder.

Spanish Preparations and Conundrums

What the Spaniards brought to the looming confrontation were the resources of a vast empire, and a king whose skills at organization and planning very nearly matched his objectives and aspirations. In terms of supply and procurement of ships and crews, what Philip II achieved still impresses. In combining the vessels of his own Mediterranean fleet with the deep-sailers of conquered Portugal and ships commandeered or leased from Italy into a united, powerful squadron, Philip produced a far more powerful threat more quickly than the English had anticipated or could, despite successful raids on the collecting forces by Drake, prevent. Among Philip's ships were also the secret weapons of Lepanto, galleasses improved to the extent of no longer requiring a tow to get into action and stuffed with veteran Spanish infantry.

The hammer of Philip's fleet was to complement the anvil of Philip's army, poised in Flanders and ready to strike under the command of the experienced Duke of Parma. The problem was the same one faced by all earlier and later would-be invaders of the British Isles: 39 km (24 miles) of open water. If Philip could combine his two powerful weapons of army and fleet against the English, there was no power in England

'It is of great importance that the Armada keep well together.... No ship belonging to the Armada shall separate from it without my permission.... Any disobedience of this order shall be punished by death.'

— *DUKE OF MEDINA SIDONIA*

that could have stopped a Spanish conquest of the annoyingly independent island kingdom.

Philip's prudence also manifested itself in the provision of supplies, small craft and armaments for his invasion forces. The Spaniards were fairly well provided with food and ammunition, provided they kept to the planners' timetables. Philip's ordnance experts had actually gone further than the English in attempting to standardize bores and limit the variety of shot required by differing guns, but in this they were thwarted by the very size of the Armada and its great variety of ships and cannon.

One indicator that achievement had not quite measured up to aspirations were the gunners' rules carried by Philip's gunners, a set of which has been found and analyzed by modern scholarship. The rules with precision and forethought informed their users of the trajectories of iron and lead shot of given weights but incorporated mathematical errors that made them entirely useless.

The war fleet had to protect the troop transports, and the troop transports had to be in position so that the fleet could escort them across the Channel and support the landing. Two great difficulties faced Medina Sidonia, Philip's admiral, and the duke of Parma. Coordination required communication, and the combined effect of wind conditions and the English naval forces were to make communication almost imposssible. Medina Sidonia had also been unprepared for his responsibility, having taken command when Philip's first choice of admiral died three months previously.

Medina Sidonia was an honourable, religious and fatalistic man – all qualities that would manifest themselves in the course of his command. His forces numbered 40 warships and an additional 90 support craft, carrying around 19,000 fighting troops, with the duke of Parma holding 300 invasion craft and an additional 27,000 veteran infantry in Spanish Flanders.

Checks and Delays

Soon after sailing from Lisbon on 25 May 1588 it became clear that circumstances were already not as anticipated. The fleet was making much slower progress than had been expected and a great deal of the food supplies had already spoiled. With misgivings, Medina Sidonia forged on until unanticipated gales damaged his fleet, demolished his timetable and kept the Armada refitting on the northern coast of Spain until July. Now that the threat had fully materialized Elizabeth was not idle, appointing Charles Howard, Lord Effingham, as Lord Admiral and giving him a fleet of 40 of her heaviest vessels. Accompanying them were about 160 lighter craft. These served as the fleet's scouts, pickets, couriers and supply vessels. When the Armada drew near the channel, the English battle squadron and about 60 smaller vessels awaited the ships and soldiers of Spain.

An English merchant vessel reported the approach of the Spanish fleet on 29 July. At this moment the English were at a disadvantage because their own fleet was refitting in Plymouth after an abortive plan to pre-empt the Spaniards with an attack on their anchorage at Corunna. Howard on board *Ark Royal* left port under the cover of darkness on the night of 30 July, moving with his hundred ships across the line of Medina Sidonia's advance and preparing to engage with the wind blowing his ships and powder smoke directly into the teeth of the Spaniards. The Armada readied itself for action by assuming the same crescent formation Don Juan had used over a decade before at Lepanto.

Fire Over England

Howard chivalrously fired a warning shot and moved to engage the awe-inspiring Spanish line, which stretched over 3 km (2 miles) from tip to tip. The Spaniards sailed on in their crescent formation, while Howard and his admirals exposed their broadsides to the Spaniards in line-ahead formation and began a furious cannonade. Howard was at this point tentative about closing the range and the English gunfire accomplished little as the

CONCEPT NOT YET PERFECTED, *the two-wheeled carriage and circular gunport of this wrought-iron Lombard foreshadowed later successful development. The two-wheeled carriages of the Armada's guns were slower to aim and train and they did little to protect the ship from the gun's recoil. Circular gunports were ill-suited for aiming and impossible to seal against the sea.*

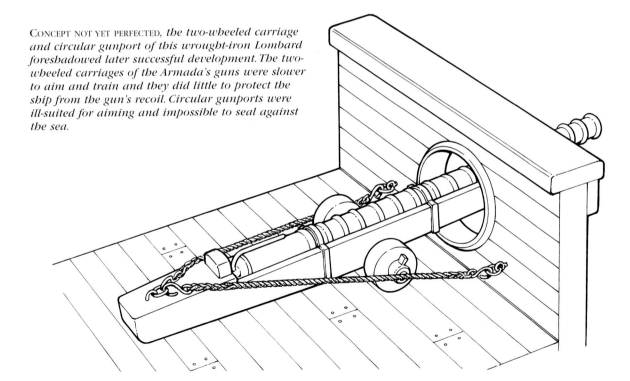

Battle of Gravelines
1588

Supplies going bad and coordination with the invasion fleet non-existent, the duke of Medina Sidonia anchored the 'Invincible' Armada in the neutral, but Catholic port of Calais in the hope of obtaining shelter and food, while the English returned to their own ports for more ammunition. Despite Spanish precautions, Admiral Lord Howard's fireships threw the Spanish fleet into disarray and the English ships closed to cannon range while the superior numbers of Spanish on board ship could do little besides perish from the effects of the cannonade. The Spanish guns were heavier, but slower firing and badly served. The day's end found the Spanish badly mauled and disorganized with all thought of escorting an invasion fleet to England forever vanished. Lord Howard's decision to convert his eight worst vessels into fireships has been called the best military expenditure in the whole of British history.

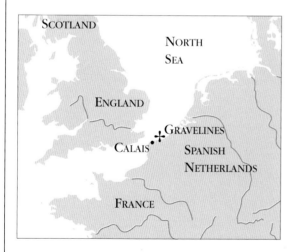

The battle of Gravelines took place in the English Channel just north of Calais. The decisive defeat of the Spanish Armada ended Spanish plans to launch an invasion of Britain, and marked the beginning of an era of English dominance of the high seas.

4 **Medina Sidonia attempts to re-form the Armada. The English press their advantage in a furious cannonade in which the Spanish suffer some loss and cannot resume their fleet formation.**

3 **The prepared Spanish elude the incendiary vessels but are thrown into great confusion.**

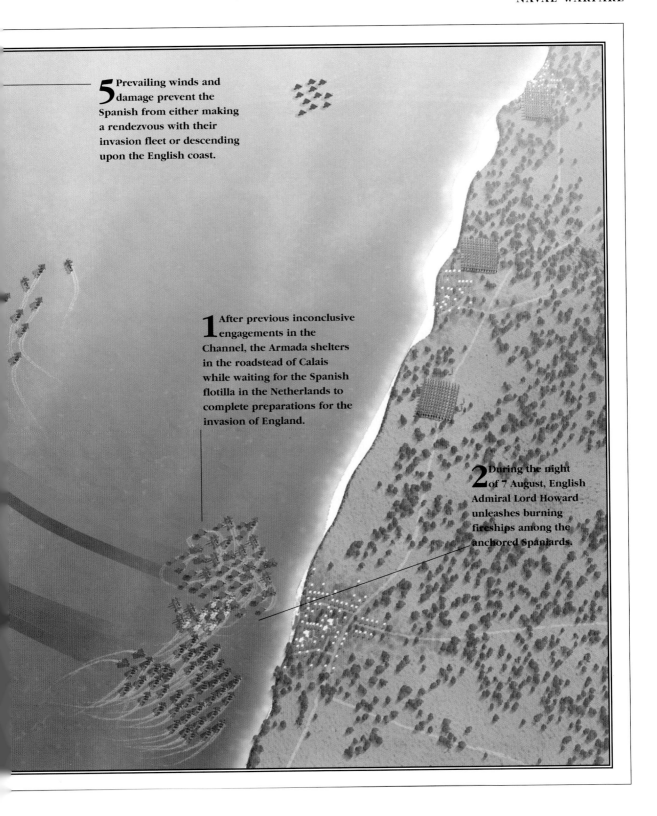

5 Prevailing winds and damage prevent the Spanish from either making a rendezvous with their invasion fleet or descending upon the English coast.

1 After previous inconclusive engagements in the Channel, the Armada shelters in the roadstead of Calais while waiting for the Spanish flotilla in the Netherlands to complete preparations for the invasion of England.

2 During the night of 7 August, English Admiral Lord Howard unleashes burning fireships among the anchored Spaniards.

Spaniards hesitantly responded. Inexperience can be a hazard in and of itself, and accidental explosions on board two of the largest Spanish ships, one the headquarters of the fleet's paymaster, swept confusion into the Spanish ranks. One of the damaged vessels, the *Rosario,*

'HELLBURNERS OF ANTWERP', *purpose-built fireships such as the one illustrated here in a 1630's manual, killed scores of besieging Spaniards. Carried by the currents or sailed close by selected crews, hulls such as this one brought fire or timed explosions into hostile fleets. Sinking or evading the fireship before the flames could spread was the only counter.*

drifted into the clutches of the piratical Francis Drake, who took himself out of the battle to secure the valuable prize.

Howard drew off, but having found the Armada, he was keen to maintain contact with the enemy while he and his captains prepared their next moves to counter the Armada's continuing advance up the channel. On 1 or 2 August off Portland Bill the Spaniards tried to implement a few of their own favoured tactics, and the swift *Regazona* made an effort to close and board with a large English vessel, but the English ship responded with rapid cannon fire and quickly sailed off.

The Spanish galleass squadron met much the same when it made for *Triumph*, the largest of the English warships, under Martin Frobisher, while the *Triumph* was briefly becalmed with a small consort. The *San Lorenzo* and her heavy battery gave nearly as good as she got from the English, but when the wind rose *Triumph* made better speed under sail and neatly escaped. The galleasses stalked the English behemoth again two days later in the narrow seaway of the Isle of Wight. Once again Frobisher replied with a hail of iron and outsailed the labouring Spanish hybrids to safety. What the galleasses could not catch, they could not destroy.

Respite

The English had used ammunition lavishly, and Howard had to withdraw his fleet to Dover to replenish powder and shot. For four days the Spaniards sailed without interference until they were a mere 40km (25 miles) from where the Duke of Parma was waiting in accordance with the stream of messages and updates Medina Sidonia had sent ahead of his fleet. The Spaniards drew into the neutral, but Catholic, anchorage of Calais to repair the damage while they waited for the signal to rendezvous and escort the invasion fleet to victory.

There the response from the duke of Parma reached the horrified Medina Sidonia that not so much as a barrel of beer was ready for the crossing. The vagaries of sixteenth-century travel had delayed the Armada's messages and it would be another six days before the army in Flanders was ready to sail across the Channel.

Howard was ignorant of these developments, but the sight of the Spaniards huddling in port prompted the obvious response. With his own ships re-supplied and ready for action, Howard mustered every available ship and attacked with the second of England's two special weapons.

Incendiary weapons had, as we have seen, been used at Lepanto and were among the weapons at the disposal of the Spaniards of the Armada: if they could get close enough to the swifter English vessels they would have thrown clay firepots and fired sparks and missiles from the *bomba*. Rhodian vessels had dumped flaming oil on their enemies from pots over their rams two millennia before, and the Byzantines had used Greek Fire many times against attacks on the city of Constantinople. Alexander the Great's siege works at the city of Tyre in 332 BC had been destroyed by fire weapons. The weapon the English were about to use was not new.

Fireships

The fireship was the only intelligently-guided munition of war before the twentieth century, guided, that is, until the last possible moment when their crews took to boats and escaped the flaming ruin they had steered against the enemy. The Spaniards had a justified terror of such a weapon, made all the more intense by the horrific losses their army had suffered when an Italian named Giambelli had sent his 'Hellburners of Antwerp' against them four years previously. These infernal machines were ships rigged to explode by fire, timer or contact, and had killed hundreds of Spaniards when they drifted down the current into the besieging troops. Medina Sidonia knew that Giambelli had afterwards escaped from doomed Antwerp to sanctuary in England. Despite these terrors, as a good commander, he had tried to take precautions against this kind of attack. He posted boats to grapple and tow away fire vessels, and gave orders that the larger ships were to slip their anchors and avoid the burning hulks as wind and tide bore them through the fleet.

Howard unleashed eight fireships against the Spaniards on the night of 7 August. The Spanish pickets managed to deflect two of the attackers, but when the remaining six drew close to the rest of the Armada, the result was panic, chaos and disaster. *San Lorenzo* drove herself aground where, with neither oars nor sails able to rescue her, she became an English prize. Other Spanish ships, cutting their cables, disappeared into the flame-shadowed darkness, with no anchors left to secure them against wind and tide. When dawn broke on 8 August at his anchorage, Medina Sidonia must have been shocked to find *San Martin* and a mere four other heavy ships facing the whole of the English fleet.

> *'The eight ships, filled with artificial fire, advanced in line...with the most terrible flames that may be imagined... the ships of the Armada cut their cables at once.'*
> — SPANISH SAILOR, SAN LORENZO

In the battle that followed, named after his anchorage at Gravelines, Medina Sidonia tried desperately in rough seas and adverse winds to re-assemble the scattered ships of the Armada. Meanwhile the English (taking care to stay beyond the reach of grapnels or boarders) closed to effective cannon range to pound the Spaniards with their rapid-firing guns until they ran out of ammunition. Medina Sidonia was unable to restore the Armada's cohesion.

'God breathed', as the English put it, and winds swept the surviving vessels past the Spanish army and Flanders, wrecked many on the Irish coast as they tried to return home, and left a mere 60 vessels afloat of the 200 that had left Spain. Only 4000 starving survivors of the 19,000 that had set forth to subdue the troublesome kingdom of England completed the miserable journey home.

The Downs, 1639: The Eclipse of Spain

The Dutch had been no mere onlookers in the struggles between England and Spain. The army

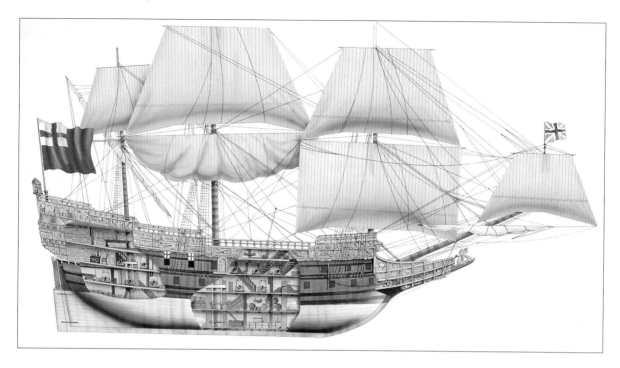

THE 'GILDED DEVIL' *to the Dutch she terrorized,*
Sovereign of the Seas *to Charles I and her English
sailors, this leviathan launched in 1637 had more
than 100 bronze cannon on three decks. Monstrous
'Royal' ships such as* Sovereign *and* Vasa *embodied
the wealth and fighting power of the kingdoms that
launched them - the last arguments of kings.*

Philip II had hoped to send against the English had
been in Flanders to reduce the obstinate,
Protestant Dutch, and Dutch ships and sailors had
done what they could to assist the English and
damage the Spaniards in the campaign of the
Armada and previously. Dutch ships had tried to
prevent the mustering of the invasion fleet, but
were outmanoeuvred through inland waterways
by the duke of Parma.

A half century after Medina Sidonia had sailed
to wreck and ruin, neither of the two antagonists
at Gravelines were what they had been previously,
and nor were the Dutch. Spanish power had had a
lofty height from which to decline. And so,
declining, Spain was still a force to be reckoned
with, despite the destruction of the Armada and
other setbacks. The English had set the world an
unmistakable example of their own proficiency at

sea, and trade routes and markets previously
unexploited were opening before the bows and
cannon of English seafarers. They had rivals. The
best efforts of Philip II and his successors had not
been enough to subdue the resourceful and
tenacious Dutch, who had preserved the
independence of their original seven provinces
since their revolt from Spain in 1568. In 1628 they
inflicted a blow upon the Spaniards sufficiently
staggering to compare with the Armada. Piet Hein
took revenge for his four years as a Spanish galley
slave by capturing the entire *flota* of that year, the
whole of the gold and silver treasure from the
New World, intended to sustain Spanish efforts
against the Dutch. Now it would go to sustain the
Seven Provinces' efforts against the Spaniards.

The vindication of Atlantic ships and cannon in
the defeat of the Armada was not lost upon the
watching nations of Europe. Europe's shipbuilders
drew two lessons from the battle, both of which
were evident in the three fleets that drew together
off the straits of Dover at the anchorage called the
Downs. Modern understanding of the battle has
somewhat obscured the fact that there were two
great lessons learned from Gravelines, not just one.
Faster and handier ships were indeed the result of

234

Elizabeth's battles in the channel, and the shallows of the Dutch coast produced a seaworthy middleweight that would evolve into the famous frigates and 'Seventy-Fours' of the great days of sail. *Triumph*'s two stands against the galleasses would spawn the first in a long line of leviathans.

Medina Sidonia had used light sailing pinnaces for his communications. Howard had a string of them picketed along the Armada's line of advance as scouts, and Drake had used them in his inshore raiding. The Dutch pirates found slightly enlarged versions of these earlier ships useful in reconnaissance and piracy, so much so that by the reign of Charles I, the English and the French were buying or copying them. The wreck of one, the English *Swan*, provides much valuable detail about this class of ship. The Dutch term for them, *sloep*, was taken into English as sloop, signifying in the king's navy a fast, light vessel with a single deck of guns.

It was a tax law that led the Dutch to the design of their famous *fluyt* and victory over Spain at the Downs. The duty taxed vessels by their upper deck area, which was the deck that was easiest to measure. The thrifty response was to build long, narrow, shallow draught vessels with arched sides and upper decks smaller than those below. What resulted was a seaworthy ship of strong construction that required a smaller crew than the earlier designs and yet could carry a great weight of cargo, or guns, and fight them in a heavy sea. The middleweight ships Maarten van Tromp would send against

POWER AND PRESTIGE *gleamed in* Sovereign of the Seas' *gilded stern carvings with which Charles I's shipwrights bedecked the stern of his prize warship. Carvings such as these proclaimed a nation's wealth and fostered pride in the vessel and the fleet at sea, also allowing identification of a given vessel at close quarters. French vessels protected their carvings with matting.*

the Spaniards in terms of rig and armament much resembled those of Howard and Drake: but they had stronger hulls carrying much improved armament, and were capable of tremendous endurance. There was more to Tromp's favourite *Aemilia* than met the eye. The Dutch, Spaniards and Portuguese in similar vessels would soon be fighting pitched battles off the coast of Asia.

With deeper harbours and *Triumph*'s success to remind them, the English, Spaniards, French and, notably, the Swedes followed her direction of development, the clearest manifestation being the 'Royal Ship,' a vessel embodying the power, prestige and wealth of the kings who sent them forth. Such vessels proclaimed the wealth and power of their owners in their intricate carvings, elaborate, gilded ornamentation and in the bright colours in and around their heavy canon in long rows of gunports. The salvaged wreck of *Vasa* provides an incomparable look at the seventeenth century's new species of behemoth. Its evolution is not difficult to trace.

> *'Our swiftness in out sailing them, our nimbleness.... carrying more artillery than the Spanish ships...discharging our cannons...double for their single – having better gunners.'*
> — ENGLISH CAPTAIN NICHOLAS GORGAS

Sovereigns of the Seas

Henry VIII's anxiety had produced some successful and some disastrous innovations, manifest in the construction and loss of the *Mary Rose* and the English triumph at Gravelines. Nets on wooden racks meant to make boarding impossible had trapped and killed *Mary Rose*'s own crew as she sank. But the idea of heavy truck guns low in the hull, also found on *Mary Rose,* opened new possibilities for construction in the more successful ships that followed. A man-of-war with her weight well towards the waterline and gunports open might capsize. This happened to the *Mary Rose,* to the Swedish *Vasa* in 1627, and the French *Thesée* at Quiberon Bay over a century later. But the payoff was too tempting to resist such a devil's bargain. A vessel like this could use her own battery as ballast, carry a large number of heavy guns in a hull built to withstand a beating and support a lofty sailing rig that could move her with the grace *Triumph* had shown in twice escaping the menacing galleasses.

Vasa, raised, preserved and restored at Stockholm, is 69m (226ft) long and 11.7m (38ft) wide. She was meant to carry 175 crew and 300 soldiers as well as her 64 cannon, 48 of which were the 24 pounders that became the standard after the battles of the Armada. Her guns, like her hull, had reached the final form that cannon would ultimately take under canvas. They were of standardized size, a great advantage for fleet logistics and to crews trying to load and fire them under the stresses of combat. The *Vasa*'s cannon were made of cast bronze, reflecting one of the failures of English innovation. In their pursuit of stronger weapons with a faster weight of fire the English designers had produced wrought-iron breech-loading guns hammered together from rods and hoops. But the pressures of firing opened the seams and flame spurted from around the removable breech chambers despite wedges meant to hold them in place. The time was not right for the breech-loading gun at sea.

For two centuries the preferred naval artillery would be the stronger one-piece gun, cast bronze if possible, weaker iron, if not, throwing balls of a weight up to 14.5kg (32lb). There had been larger guns before, but these guns had over twice the rate of fire of their predecessors and superior accuracy. Some additional increases in the rate of fire would come from tinkering with the tackle that ran the cannon out, but guns much of this type would still be in service at sea in 1865. Bronze cannon were the mark of luxury of the era. English reports from as late as Quiberon Bay rejoiced in the 'brass guns' found on captured ships.

Charles I of England found his own navy was unable to prevent or even referee the great Battle of the Downs, where Maarten van Tromp

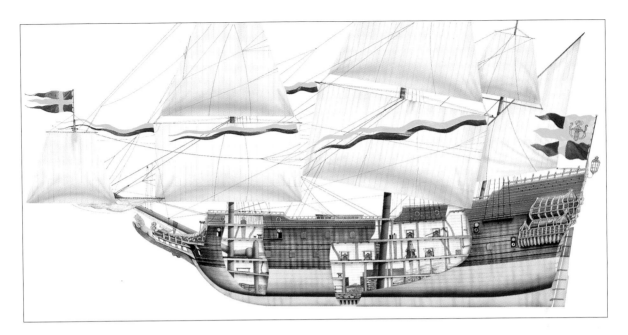

annihilated a Spanish fleet again driven from Calais with fireships, into what they had hoped was to be a secure English anchorage. Charles's frustration found its expression in the name of the 1,500 ton monster 'Royal Ship' Phineas Pett would design and put into the water eight years after the battle. *Sovereign of the Seas* at times carried more than 100 bronze cannon on three gundecks, and used them with a ferocity that she earned the name 'the gilded devil' from the Dutch who bore the brunt of her guns. Royal prestige and the need for decisive firepower produced a ship in the seventeenth century that would not have seemed out of place in the line at Trafalgar, but at a cost Charles eventually paid with his head.

The Battle Begins

The location of the battle itself, which began on 15 September 1639, was the same as that of Gravelines: the English Channel. Tactics and objectives were much the same too. A powerful Spanish fleet was carrying troops, attempting to put them ashore, and the defending squadrons were moving aggressively to forestall the invasion. This time Admiral Antonio de Oquendo led a force of 45 of Spain's remaining heavy warships as escorts to 30 transports conveying approximately 13,000 fresh Spanish levies to the Belgian coast.

SUNK AND SALVAGED, Sweden's Vasa has contributed enormously to our understanding of 17th-century warship design. Advanced features such as standardized armament and improved gun carriages contrasted with primitive living conditions for her unfortunate crew and a beam insufficient for her lofty decks and masts to prevent her capsizing upon her maiden voyage in 1627.

The Dutch judged that cannon at sea were a better counter to such numbers than muskets in the polders and when Tromp found the Spanish fleet, like Howard previously, he would not relinquish contact while his ammunition held out, even though his own squadron numbered a mere twelve besides his flagship.

The Dutch proved better at communication and coordination than the Spaniards. The following day another five ships joined Tromp's squadron and Tromp went for the kill. Tromp unleashed his captains at the Spanish transports like wolves upon sheep. The rapid fire of the Dutch cannon caused horrific casualties among the stunned and huddled Spanish infantry, unable to do anything but suffer and die under the bombardment, some of it from their own defending warships firing blindly in the smoke at what they thought were the foe. Dutch seamanship

Battle of the Downs

1639

A great Spanish fleet of 75 ships, containing 13,000 recruits bound for Flanders from Spain, was intercepted by a much smaller Dutch fleet of 18 ships under Admiral Maarten Tromp. British warnings and shore-based supporting gunfire could not prevail against Dutch warships and a thick fog. Maarten van Tromp's vessels were built to operate in shallow water and skilled Dutch seamanship allowed him to penetrate the anchorage in offensive formation. The Spanish had courage and little else as they found themselves beset on all sides by smaller ships that battered their hulls and massacred the raw army recruits on board. A consequence was that English monarch Charles I began extracting 'ship money' for a navy powerful enough to prevent future flouting of British sea power. Despite the carnage, Spanish power at sea remained formidable enough to prepare yet another great fleet, but the aggressive and enterprising Maarten van Tromp demonstrated conclusively the burgeoning naval might of the United Dutch Provinces.

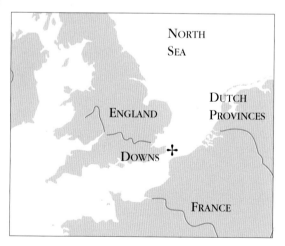

The engagement took place off the coast of Kent, in British waters. The battle destroyed what remained of Spanish naval power, seriously weakened their position in Flanders, and gave the Dutch naval supremacy in the North Sea.

1 Fleeing the Dutch, the Spanish fleet retires into the neutral English roadstead of the Downs.

3 A squadron of Dutch ships prevents Sir John Penington's English flotilla from intervening.

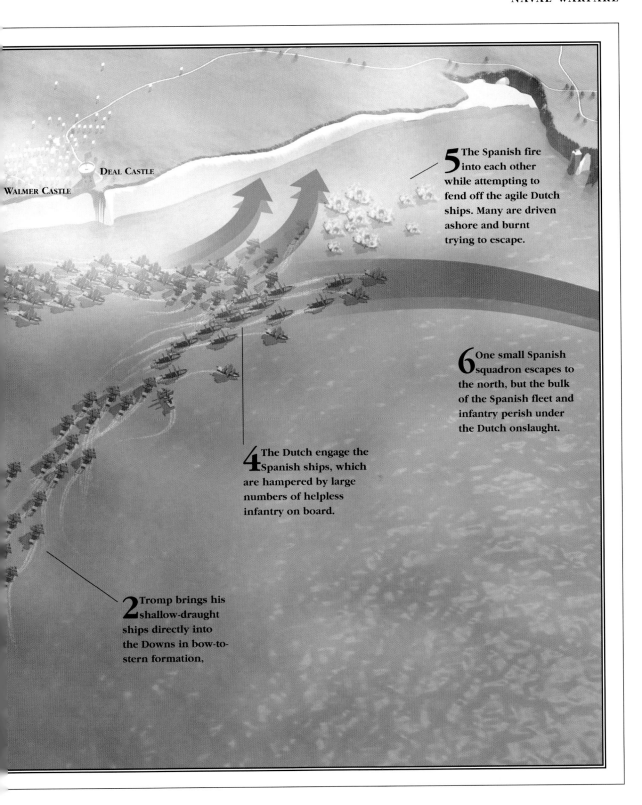

WALMER CASTLE

DEAL CASTLE

5 The Spanish fire into each other while attempting to fend off the agile Dutch ships. Many are driven ashore and burnt trying to escape.

6 One small Spanish squadron escapes to the north, but the bulk of the Spanish fleet and infantry perish under the Dutch onslaught.

4 The Dutch engage the Spanish ships, which are hampered by large numbers of helpless infantry on board.

2 Tromp brings his shallow-draught ships directly into the Downs in bow-to-stern formation,

BALANCE OF POWER *and propulsion allowed the heavy cannon of the later ocean-going warships to ballast the towering array of masts and sails needed to move their increasing tonnage through the water. Stores for extended cruising and the vulnerable powder magazines could be placed well below the waterline, impervious to enemy fire. Ships used less sail in battle, spreading more in the event of pursuit - or escape.*

and aggressive manoeuvring prevented Oquendo from any action but that of attempting to shelter his fleet in a neutral anchorage: this time the Downs. When the Spaniards arrived there an English squadron under Sir John Penington ordered the Dutch to sheer off, at the threat of his own force joining the Spaniards if Tromp initiated battle.

Tromp had made good use of his time, re-supplying with powder by purchase at Calais and sending a report to the Netherlands of the situation, the upshot of which was that the entire naval might of the Seven Provinces arrived to add itself to his flag, bringing the order to engage. Oquendo, repairing the carnage and facing

adverse winds to the north and hostile ships to the south, left the initiative with the Dutch until 10 October, when Tromp blithely ignored Penington's warning shots and sailed in for the kill.

The terrain of the Downs anchorage prompted the tactic of line of battle. Tromp's lighter ships (*Aemilia* weighed only a mere 800 tons with 46 cannon) sailed bow to stern, keeping contact through heavy fog as they bore down upon the Spaniards, clustered around the massive *Santa Teresa*, which contained around twice *Aemilia's* crew and 68 cannon. Tromp had read his history: 96 men-of-war and 12 fireships tore into the Spaniards. Tromp also detached a squadron to attack the English if Penington chose to enforce English neutrality. He did not. Neither international law nor *Santa Teresa's* might could save the Spaniards from the onslaught.

The Spanish flagship caught fire and thunderously exploded, while other Spanish ships were driven aground and shattered or burned. Only nine vessels under a Dutch renegade escaped the slaughter, with 7000 survivors. It was the final collapse of Spanish sea power.

Quiberon Bay, 1759: Forces of Nature

In 1759 ships, guns and tactics at sea were much the same as those Tromp had employed a century previously. One change was the appearance of a new intermediate class of warships to fill the gap between ships the size of *Aemilia*, and behemoths like the *Sovereign of the Seas*. Another was that for the first extended period of time since Sluys in 1340, France had grown to become a major power at sea.

Frigates like the *Aemilia* had the range and cruising ability to project naval power far overseas, and the speed to detect and report upon enemy activities, qualities that gave them a value out of proportion to their size. But if *Aemilia* had engaged Charles I's 'gilded devil' the result would not long have been in doubt. A speedy vessel that could endure or even attack a monster 'Royal Ship' seemed desirable to the Dutch, and also to Cardinal Richelieu of France. When the English supported rebel Protestants on the French coast in 1628, Richelieu realized the French navy was powerless to prevent such interference. There was a need for sea power and an opportunity to take a new direction in acquiring it.

The Cardinal sought to fund his king's role in the Thirty Years' War by expanding trade, but French merchant vessels would need protection. With the Seven Provinces politically well disposed, Richelieu purchased vessels small and great from the Dutch. Most notable of these was the beautiful and functional *Saint Louis* of 1626, built in Amsterdam by the de Groot brothers, the same master shipwrights who had designed the *Vasa*. The Dutch favoured spacious gun decks where cannon could be served to best advantage, and *Saint Louis* had these for her 60 cannon. They had also made improvements in the sailing rig from which this great French man-of-war benefited. Gratings protected her crew from falling debris, and allowed ventilation and light to the decks below. Having purchased this prototype,

French shipwrights began to copy the design, incorporating notions of their own as the new French navy expanded.

The new design of warship, later mounting rather more guns, came to be named after the standard number of guns it carried, and was called 'the seventy-four.' While the French were innovating, the English were standardizing, and in the reign of James II a system of 'rates' was introduced to categorize the Royal Navy's vessels. Under this system *Sovereign of the Seas* was designated 'first rate', until her accidental destruction by fire (after being renamed *Royal Sovereign*) in 1696. A ship like *Aemilia* was labelled as a 'fifth rate', barely able to take a place in the line of battle. The 'Seventy-fours' and their imitators, so eagerly incorporated into the fleet by English captors, came into the system as 'third rates' – a term that went into common usage and

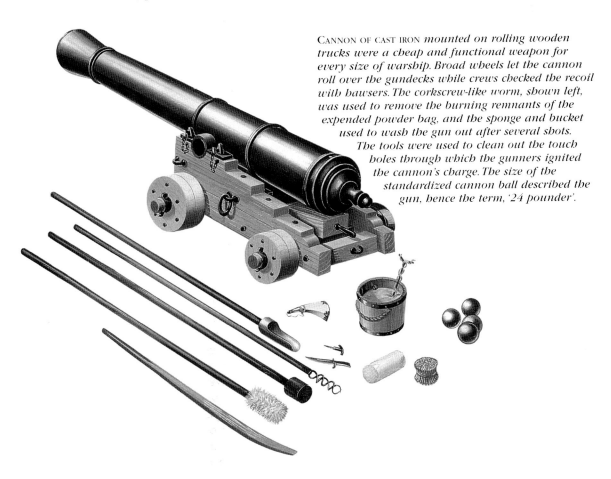

CANNON OF CAST IRON *mounted on rolling wooden trucks were a cheap and functional weapon for every size of warship. Broad wheels let the cannon roll over the gundecks while crews checked the recoil with hawsers. The corkscrew-like worm, shown left, was used to remove the burning remnants of the expended powder bag, and the sponge and bucket used to wash the gun out after several shots. The tools were used to clean out the touch holes through which the gunners ignited the cannon's charge. The size of the standardized cannon ball described the gun, hence the term, '24 pounder'.*

Battle of Quiberon Bay
1759

'Just go at them', was Admiral Edward Hawke's
order to his captains, while weather and audacity
combined to create the most decisive British
victory of the year. Hawke forfeited the use of his
lower gunports in the unexpected attack, but
prevailed. He set an example that Nelson would
follow at Copenhagen and the Nile. Two powerful
fleets off the French coast largely decided the
outcome of the Seven Years' War. The ships, guns
and tactics employed were much the same as, if not
identical to, those Tromp had employed a century
previously at Downs. Shadowed by British frigates,
Admiral Conflans again sought shelter from the
sea's roughness and once again the hostile admiral,
in this case 'The Immortal Hawke', sought the
advantage of surprise by attacking in unfavourable
terrain in unfavourable conditions. Standardized
British tactics and technology prevail despite the
brave resistance of the surprised French vessels,
and French armies and fortresses in the distant
New World could no longer be safely supplied.

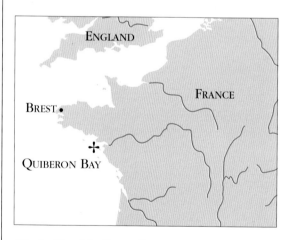

*The battle of Quiberon Bay took place on a
stormy night in November 1759 off the coast of
St Nazaire, on France's Biscay coast. Admiral
Hawke's victory effectively ended French plans to
land an invasion force in Scotland.*

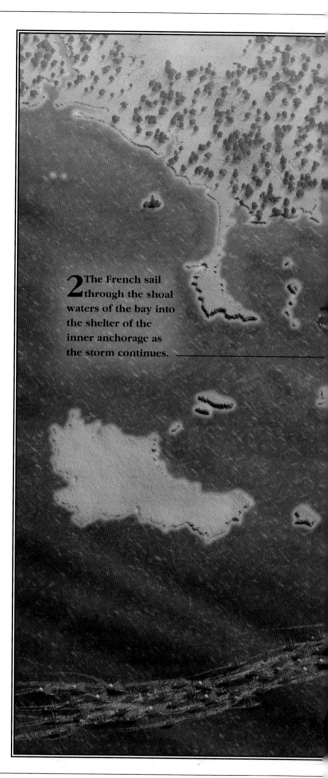

2 **The French sail
through the shoal
waters of the bay into
the shelter of the
inner anchorage as
the storm continues.**

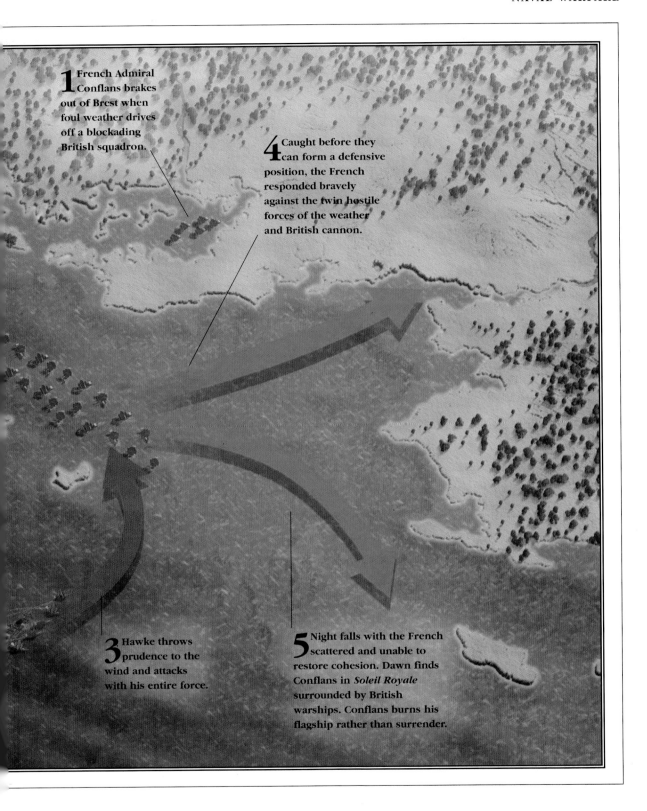

1 French Admiral Conflans brakes out of Brest when foul weather drives off a blockading British squadron.

4 Caught before they can form a defensive position, the French responded bravely against the twin hostile forces of the weather and British cannon.

3 Hawke throws prudence to the wind and attacks with his entire force.

5 Night falls with the French scattered and unable to restore cohesion. Dawn finds Conflans in *Soleil Royale* surrounded by British warships. Conflans burns his flagship rather than surrender.

DEATH FROM ABOVE could come from weapons such as this coehoorn mortar in platforms called 'fighting tops' nestled upon the lofty masts of 18th-century warships. Fire from marine marksman and blasts of shot could clear the upper decks of an enemy warship, rendering her immobile, or 'decapitate' a foe by selective fire at officers. One such shot killed Maarten Tromp in 1653. Nelson would perish from another.

has since come to mean something rather different. These ships were highly effective and valuable fighting vessels, and became the standard in all the world's major navies. The French navy included dozens of these supremely serviceable vessels as early as the 1660s.

The new French designs had the strong, narrow hull built on the Dutch pattern combined with a deeper draught than the shallow harbours of the Netherlands could accommodate. With their guns on two decks instead of three, the French vessels rolled less and fired their guns more accurately in a swell. Dutch, French and English trading voyages to India and the East prompted further refinements of rig and construction, as the hulls became thicker to withstand the rigours of shipworm, rough seas and shot. Speed was a significant factor in long trading voyages and in a type of warfare the French came to favour in the face of powerful English squadrons built rather more heavily of English oak. The *guerre de course*, 'war of the chase,' allowed the fast, powerful ships of the French navy to make war costly to Spain, England and at times even the Dutch. Their frigates

took small prizes and fought off pirates and Muslim raiders, while seventy-fours took on more substantial enemy vessels in the absence of the 'first-rate' Goliaths.

Superior French Design

A factor not to be overlooked in the design of these newer ships was the increasing comfort of their crews. Conditions on board the Venetian galleys at the time of Lepanto could become so dire in any sort of bad weather that one fleet suffered a great many casualties from exposure in crews swamped in wet weather. Disease and malnutrition killed far more Englishmen in Howard's fleet than Spanish cannon, and the salvage of *Vasa* made clear that among the splendour of the great ship's cannon and carvings her crew wore their own thin clothing, still held together with wooden pegs, without so much as an issue hammock to rest bodies weary from the demands of sails, guns and anchors.

The French did things differently: light and air had their advantages in health and comfort, and while English crews were lucky to get a pot of 'slum' cooked over the galley fire in good conditions, the French provided hot meals and baked fresh bread in brick ovens in the place of worm-raddled pork and ship's biscuit. On distant voyages the French grew salad greens in plant boxes, which would have at least reduced the physical and mental consequences of vitamin deficiency among the decision-making officer classes. For the English, things were much worse. Before Gravelines Sir Richard Hawkins had written of oranges, lemons and scurvy that God's great power 'hath hidden such a great and unknown virtue in this fruit, to be a certain remedy for this infirmity'. This insight was forgotten or ignored in the dawning Age of Reason, until rediscovered by Captain Cook, and hundreds of English sailors suffered and perished needlessly as a result.

Imitating the Invincibles

A representative example from just before the time of Quiberon Bay gives an example of the French advantage in ship construction, and the means by which the British learned to overcome it. *L'Invincible*, a seventy-four built in 1744, did not quite live up to her name, but she was formidable nevertheless and successfully repelled three British ships which sought to take her in 1745. Quantity will often, if not necessarily always, defeat quality, and a squadron of 14 British warships under Edward Boscawen later captured her and the rest of her squadron. Towed to Portsmouth, the design of *L'Invincible* provoked considerable interest and admiration. Lord Anson repeatedly recommended that British shipyards should build copies, and eventually the authorities of the navy agreed. The first of these 'clones' hit the water in 1755, just in time for Quiberon Bay.

The English had made their own advances in shipbuilding since the Downs, if not to the same degree as the French. In terms of basic hull design, their shipwrights still had not gone so far from the galleon. When Nelson's *Victory* was first built in 1765, she looked more like Charles I's 'Royal Ship' *Sovereign of the Seas* than she did herself in her final incarnation, as she can be seen today. Over the decades tactics were beginning to influence technology, rather than the other way round.

Howard's line of battle at Gravelines had been essentially 'follow the leader'; Admiral Tromp's at the Downs a calculated formation of a single line of ships designed to keep his vessels in contact in a close formation bow to stern in a fog. The Royal Navy came to the conclusion that all major actions should be fought in line, and built ships to fit that tactical concept. English fleets in line fought it out with lines of like-minded Dutch, and in the end superior English resources, if not seamanship, drove the Netherlands from primacy in both military and civilian seafaring. By that time divisions in separate lines were fighting their counterparts according to orders conveyed by by increasingly complicated pre-arranged signals.

FRENCH SAILORS HAD *enough to do with manning the sails and guns of their ships besides fighting as infantry 'marines', on shipboard. The cutlass they carried was a weapon of strength, not skill, capable of severing limbs or shattering more agile weapons. Flintlock muskets allowed a discharge of shot or ball in a boarding action, in which knives, belaying pins or 'boarding pikes' might also find employment.*

FRENCH SCIENTIFIC DESIGN *manifests itself in* Soleil Royale, *Conflans' flagship at Quiberon Bay. Her spacious decks and hatches allowed more comfort than in darker, closer British vessels, while her cleaner hull allowed for greater speed and long-distance cruising. Decks became increasingly flush and streamlined as design progressed. French vessels were much-desired prizes for England's sea dogs, but Conflans chose to abandon and burn* Soleil Royale *rather than suffer her to fall into British hands.*

The Naval Manual

One legacy from Gravelines the English maintained through the years following was rapid, accurate gunnery, which battered French and Dutch into submission if luck, weather or manoeuvre did not intervene. The Royal Navy also systematized tactics and techniques along with the standardized ships, guns and rigging, creating the dry but vital concept of military doctrine,

which the Admiralty published in manuals of instruction issued throughout the fleet. Captains had no excuse for not doing what was expected of them in a given situation, as Admiral John Byng found when he tried to substitute his own judgement for that of the manual, and failed to relieve the besieged island of Minorca in 1756. A firing squad shot him on his own quarterdeck in Portsmouth, as Voltaire dryly observed, *'pour encourager les autres'*.

The diaries of Samuel Pepys, Secretary to the English Admiralty and its effective civilian administrator, provide a perfect snapshot of the workings of the English naval system as it adopted the technology, tactics and bureaucratic basis that would, in the end, give the British Navy superiority over both the Dutch and the French.

There was a great deal of fighting before that came about. Winston Churchill called the Seven

Years' War of 1756–63 'the First World War', due to its global scope. Frederick the Great and his Prussians fought Maria Theresa's Austrians on the fields of Silesia, and American colonists fought French and Native peoples alongside British Redcoats in the woods of Ohio and Pennsylvania. The British and French East India companies and their surrogates battled among the bemused populations of the Indian subcontinent, and in 1759 a French fleet under the Count de Conflans, Hubert de Brienne, was on its way to rendezvous with yet another fleet of transports being assembled for an attack on the British Isles. The new frigates and seventy-fours could fight anywhere in the world, but to end the war quickly the French could do no better than to take the fighting to the enemy's centre. None of the other battles lost or won would matter if French troops could force a peace in Westminster.

The Commanders

The admiral of the French fleet, Conflans, was a determined and audacious man, as demonstrated by his initiative in breaking out of Brest when inclement weather drove a British blockading squadron away from the coast. A smaller British squadron located his fleet of 21 heavy ships, which Conflans aggressively drove away as he neared the transport fleet awaiting his escort in the large and apparently safe anchorage of Quiberon Bay. The storm still raged on, gathering strength as the French made their way towards the rendezvous that had eluded Medina Sidonia in 1588. A waiting frigate on scout duty sped away with the news of the French fleet's arrival. It was 14 November 1759.

Facing Conflans was an admiral slightly more determined, and rather more audacious. At that moment he was sheltering his squadron in the lee of Belle Isle, at the mouth of the deeper channels that allowed ships to sail where Quiberon Bay's numerous shoal waters did not otherwise permit. Admiral Edward Hawke had taken the opportunity to re-supply when he had lost the French at Brest and had set his own 23 vessels in an ambush at their destination. Conflans and his captains saw the British moving out from the island to confront them. The French admiral

decided to make for the bay's inner anchorage where he could put his fleet in a sheltered defensive position, where he thought he would have the advantage even if the British were foolhardy enough to brave the shoals and wind. Terrain was determining tactics once again.

Doctrine – the manual – required Hawke to wait out the storm and engage in more favourable weather. In the gusting winds and rolling seas he

THE OFFICER'S RAPIER *was a sign of rank and surrender in the formalized combat of the period. It was a deadly weapon, longer and more agile than the heavier, clumsier cutlass. Marines were elite troops on board ship, charged with preserving discipline among the crew and taking or defending a ship in the intense combat of a boarding action. French muskets were lighter and handier than the massive 'Brown Bess' of their British counterparts, hence more useful in the rigging of a warship.*

would lose the valuable services of men stationed in his rigging armed with muskets and short cannon called coehorns or 'murderers' that could rain shot and ball down upon the upper decks of the enemy. One such shot killed Maarten Tromp in 1653: another would do for Nelson at Trafalgar. The heavy seas made it dangerous to open the lower deck gun ports, where the most valuable, heaviest guns were mounted. And ships might run aground on the shoals. But Hawke boldly discarded doctrine and prudence, and signalled his fleet to follow the French and engage ship by ship. In doing so he staked his career, his nation's safety and possibly his life upon the prospect of success.

'Toujours l'audace'

An American admiral, when asked what made the difference between a good and great admiral responded, 'Thirty seconds.' Hawke had more time than that to assess the situation and make up his mind as the storm and wind raged on. What seems to have decided him to 'go at them' was the same judgement Nelson would make at the battle of the Nile: that where the enemy could go, so could he. At 2.30 in the afternoon the British sailed past the second ring of islands within the bay and began a

general engagement with the French. A check at the outset and a reminder of the purpose of the discarded instructions came when three of Hawke's ships collided with each other in driving rain soon after his order to engage. One element of conflict at sea was a constant from Lepanto through Gravelines, the Downs and in this instance: the leader led. Hawke in his own *Royal George* worked his way through the rest of the fleet until he found Conflans poised, if not entirely ready, to receive him in his flagship, *Soleil Royale*.

What damaged the French the most in the struggle was their apparent amazement that Hawke had chosen to fight in such hostile conditions, and in treacherous shoal waters. Conflans had not managed to get his defensive formation organized before the British were firing upon the rear of his fleet, and, unprepared to fight

HAWKE DEFEATS CONFLANS *in stormy weather in the Bay of Biscay. British ships driven before the wind roll low into the waves, allowing their shots to shatter French hulls and gun crews, a favoured British practice. French vessels likewise employ their own preferred tactic in response, 'firing on the up roll' into British sails and rigging - forestalling the twin unpleasant possibilities of escape, or pursuit.*

THREE-TIERED GUNDECKS *marked the 'First Rate' capital ships of the Age of Fighting Sail. On the top deck the loaded cannon is run out on its truck through the open gun port, ready to fire upon the approaching enemy. The middle deck depicts a fired cannon rolling back into ship from the recoil of its shot, where it will be cleaned and reloaded by the gun crew in the relative safety of the inner hull. The lowest deck shows a gun secured against the closed gun port for sea. A 'loose cannon' was more than metaphorically dangerous in a ship rolling and pitching in heavy weather.*

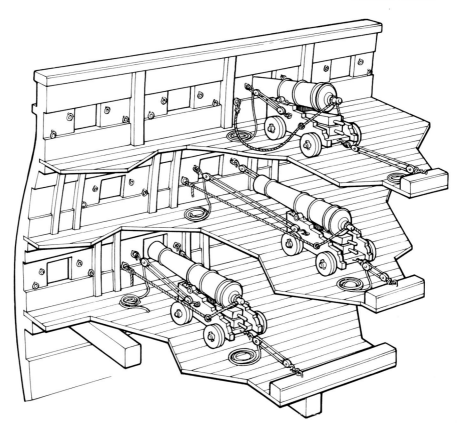

in such a storm, the fire of the French gunners was much less accurate than the cannonade the British unleashed upon them. Courage was certainly not confined to one side or the other – the French *Thesée* gamely opened her lower rank of gun ports for more firepower as *Torbay* blasted away at her, and immediately sank as the furious sea poured in through them into her hull. The French *Formidable* endured a battering from three British ships in succession before finally lowering her colours in surrender.

Conflans apparently vacillated, manoeuvring *Soleil Royale* as if to lead the fleet back into open water, and then making for the shelter of the inner bay as darkness fell. Hawke had no other choice but to anchor and hope that the wrought iron and cables could withstand the demands made upon them. For two of his ships, they did not, and these vessels were driven upon shoals and destroyed during the night. Next morning the rest of the British fleet found *Soliel Royale* anchored in their midst. Refusing to surrender, Conflans tried to

disengage, but ran aground and burned his flagship rather than let it be taken as a prize. Two French ships escaped southwards to Rochefort, and eight fled into the estuary of the River Viliane after jettisoning stores and guns. By sheer audacity and outstanding gunnery, Hawke had fought a successful battle of annihilation. British casualties were two ships and 300 sailors. The French lost three ships sunk, two captured and one burnt. The rest were dispersed and the French invasion plan was completely scuppered.

Despite the evolution of doctrine, the greater tactical sophistication of the commanders and the systematized artillery and signalling, this battle was fought in a general melee less organized than in any of the other three battles outlined above. Terrain, tactics, technology and, above all, weather were all significant, but the human factor was the dominant one at Quiberon and ultimately decided both the fighting techniques employed and the outcome of conflict in the early modern era.

Select Bibliography

Adams, Simon. 'The Battle that Never Was: the Downs and the Armada Campaign' from M. J. Rodriguez-Salgado & Simon Adams, eds., *England, Spain and the Gran Armada, 1558-1604*. Rowman & Littlefield: 1991.

Allen, Paul C. *Philip III and the Pax Hispanica, 1598-1621: The Failure of Grand Strategy*. New Haven: Yale University Press, 2000.

Armstrong, Richard. *The Early Mariners*. New York: Frederick A. Praeger, Incorporated, 1968.

Anderson, Fred. *Crucible of War: The Seven Years' War and the Fate of Empire in British North America, 1754-1766*. New York: Alfred A. Knopf, 2000.

Andrews, K.R. 'Elizabethan Privateering,' from *Raleigh in Exeter X: Privateering and Colonization in the Reign of Elizabeth I*. London: David Brown: 1985.

Archibald, E. H. H. *The Wooden Fighting Ship in the Royal Navy AD 897-1860*. London: Blandford Press, 1968.

Barker, Thomas, *Double Eagle and the Crescent: Vienna's Second Turkish Siege*. Albany, NY: SUNY–Albany Press, 1967.

Black, Jeremy, ed. *European Warfare, 1453-1815*. New York: St. Martins Press, 1999.

Black, Jeremy. *European Warfare, 1660-1815*. New Haven: Yale University Press, 1994.

Bradford, Ernle. *The Sultan's Admiral: The Life of Barbarossa*. New York: Harcourt, Brace & World, Incorporated, 1968.

Bruijn, Jaap R. *The Dutch Navy of the Seventeenth and Eighteenth Centuries*. Studies in Maritime History Series. Charleston: University of South Carolina Press, 1993.

Brumwell, Stephen. *Redcoats: The British Soldier and the War in the Americas, 1755-1763*. Cambridge: Cambridge University Press, 2001.

Chandler, David. *Marlborough as a Military Commander*. London: Spellmount, 1989 (reprinted).

Chandler, David. *The Art of Warfare in the Age of Marlborough*. New York: Hippocrene Books, 1976.

Chandler, David, ed. *The Military Memoirs of Marlborough's Campaigns, 1702-1712*. London: Greenhill Books, 1998.

Corbett, Julian. *Fighting Instructions, 1530-1816*. London: Naval Records Society, 1906.

Davis, James C., ed. *Pursuit of Power: Venetian Ambassadors' Reports*. New York: Harper & Row, Publishers, 1970.

Delbrück, Hans. *History of the Art of War, Volume IV: The Dawn of Modern Warfare*, trans. Walter Renfroe. Lincoln: University of Nebraska Press, 1990.

Duffy, Christopher, *Frederick the Great: A Military Life*. London: Routledge, 1988.

Duffy, Christopher. *Instrument of War: The Austrian Army in the Seven Years War, Vol. I*. Chicago: The Emperor's Press, 2000.

Duffy, Christopher. *Military Experience in the Age of Reason, 1715-1789*. New York: Barnes and Noble Books, 1997.

Duffy, Christopher. *The Army of Frederick the Great*. London: Hippocrene Books, 1974.

Fuller, J. F. C. *A Military History of the Western World, Volume II: From the Spanish Armada to the Battle of Waterloo*. New York: Da Capo Press, 1955.

Gerhartl, Getrud. *Belagerung und Entsatz von Wien 1683*. Militärhistorishe Schriftenreihe, Heft 46, Wien: Österreichischer Bundesverlag, 1982.

Gilkerson, William. *The Ships of John Paul Jones*. Annapolis: United States Naval Academy Museum and the Naval Institute Press, 1987.

Glete, Jan. *War and the State in Early Modern Europe: Spain, the Dutch Republic and Sweden as Fiscal Military States, 1500-1660*. London: Routledge, 2002.

Guilmartin, John Francis. *Gunpowder and Galleys: Changing Technology and Mediterranean Warfare at Sea in the Sixteenth Century*. Revised edition. Annapolis: Naval Institute Press, 2004.

Hall, Bert. *Weapons and Warfare in Renaissance Europe: Gunpowder, Technology, and Tactics*. Baltimore: Johns Hopkins University Press, 2002.

Hakluyt, Richard (Jack Beeching, ed). *Voyages and Discoveries: The Principal Navigations, Voyages, Traffiques and Discoveries of the English Nation*. Harmondsworth: Penguin, 1987 edition.

Harding, Richard. *The Evolution of the Sailing Navy, 1509-1815*. British History in Perspective Series. New York: St. Martin's Press, 1995.

Hatton, R.M. *Charles XII of Sweden*. New York: Weybright and Talley, 1968.

Hale, J. R., ed. *Renaissance Venice*. Totowa: Rowman and Littlefield, 1973.

Hough, Richard. *Fighting Ships*. New York: G. P. Putnam's Sons, 1969.

Kelsey, Harry. *Sir Francis Drake: The Queen's Pirate*. New Haven: Yale, 1999.

Kemp, Peter, ed. *Oxford Companion to Ships and the Sea*. Oxford: Oxford University Press, 1976

Kennett, Lee, *The French Armies in the Seven Years' War*. Durham: Duke University Press, 1967.

Lane, Frederic C. *Venice: A Maritime Republic*. Baltimore: The Johns Hopkins University Press, 1973.

Lavery, Brian. *The Arming and Fitting of English Ships of War 1600-1815*. Annapolis: Naval Institute Press, 1988.

Lloyd, Christopher. *Ships & seamen*. London: Weidenfield & Nicolson, 1961.

Luvaas, Jay, editor and translator. *Frederick the Great on the Art of War*. New York: Di Capo Press, 1999 (reprinted).

Lynn, John A. *Giant of the Grand Siècle, The French Army: 1610-1715*. Cambridge: Cambridge University Press, 1997.

Lynn, John A. *The Wars of Louis XIV*. New York: Longman, 1999.

Mahan, Alfred Thayer. *The Influence of Sea Power upon History 1660-1805*. Englewood Cliffs, New Jersey: Prentice Hall, 1980.

Mallett, Michael. *Mercenaries and their Masters: Warfare in Renaissance Italy*. New York: Rowman and Littlefield, 1974.

MartinezHidalgo, Jose Maria. *Columbus' Ships*. Barre: Barre Publishers, 1966.

Martin, Colin and Geoffrey Parker. *The Spanish Armada*. Manchester: Manchester Univ Press, 2002 (revised edition).

Mattingly, Garrett. *The Armada*. London: Mariner Books, 1974.

McNeil, William H. *The Pursuit of Power: Technology, Armed Force and Society Since A.D. 1000*. Reprint edition. Chicago: University of Chicago Press, 1984.

Nolan, John S. 'English Operations Around Brest', *Mariner's Mirror*, 1994.

Nosworthy, Brent. *Anatomy of Victory: Battle Tactics 1689-1763*. New York: Hippocrene Books, 1991.

Oman, Charles. *The Art of War in the Sixteenth Century*. reprint London: Greenhill, 1987.

Paret, Peter. *Makers of Modern Strategy: From Macchiavelli to the Nuclear Age*. Princeton: Princeton University Press, 1986.

Parker, Geoffrey. *The Dutch Revolt*. London: Penguin, 1988.

Parker, Geoffrey. *The Grand Strategy of Philip II*. New Haven: Yale University Press, 1998.

Parker, Geoffrey. *The Military Revolution: Military Innovation and the Rise of the West, 1500-1800*. 2nd edition. Cambridge: Cambridge University Press: 1996.

Phillips. T.R., ed., *Roots of Strategy: Sun Tzu, Vegetius, De Saxe, Frederick, Napoleon*. Harrisburg, PA: Stackpole Books, 1985.

Rodger, N.A.M., *The Safeguard of the Sea: A Naval History of Britain, Vol I, 660-1649*. New York: Harper Collins, 1997.

Rodger, N. A. M. *The Wooden World: An Anatomy of the Georgian Navy*. New York: W. W. Norton & Company, 1996.

Rodgers, William Ledyard. *Naval Warfare Under Oars, 4th-16th Centuries; A Study of Strategy, Tactics and Ship Design*. Annapolis: Naval Institute Press, 1967.

Royle, Trevor. *The British Civil War: The Wars of the Three Kingdoms 1638-1660*. London: Palgrave Macmillan, 2004.

Showalter, Dennis E. *The Wars of Frederick the Great*. New York: Longman, 1996.

Stoye, John. *The Siege of Vienna*. New York: Holt, Rinehart and Winston, 1964.

Unger, Richard W. *The Ship in the Medieval Economy: 600-1600*. London: Croom Helm Limited, 1980.

Stradling, R.A., John Elliot, et al., eds. *The Armada of Flanders: Spanish Maritime Policy and European War, 1568-1668*. Cambridge: Cambridge University Press, 1992.

Tunstall, Brian, and Nicholas Tracy. *Naval Warfare in the Age of Sail: The Evolution Of Fighting Tactics 1650-1815*. Annapolis: Naval Institute Press, 1990.

Villiers, Alan. *Men, Ships, and the Sea*. 2nd ed. Washington: National Geographic Society, 1973.

Wedgewood, C.V., *The Thirty Years War*. New York: Routledge, 1987 (reprint).

Weigley. Russell. *The Age of Battles: The Quest for Decisive Warfare from Breitenfeld to Waterloo*. Bloomington: Indiana University Press, 1991.

Wernham, R.B. 'Elizabethan War Aims and Strategy' pp. 340-368 in *Elizabethan Government and Society: Essays* presented to Sir John Neale. Bindhoff, Hurstfield and Williams, eds. London, 1961.

Wilson, Peter H., *German Armies, War and German Politics: 1648-1806*. London: UCL Press, 1998.

Wingfield, Anthony. 'The Counter Armada of 1589' from *The Expedition of Sir John Norris and Sir Francis Drake to Spain and Portugal, 1589*, ed. R.B. Wernham. London: Naval Records Society, 1988.

Winton, John. *An Illustrated History of the Royal Navy*. San Diego: Thunder Bay, 2000.

Index

Picture and Illustration Credits

All maps and black-and-white line
artworks produced by **JB Illustrations.**

Aerospace/Art-Tech: 14–15, 37, 58, 75,
172, 186, 198, 209, 214, 217, 219, 224, 226,
233, 234, 237, 241, 245, 246, 247;
AKG-Images: 6–7, 16–17, 34–35, 66–67,

78–79, 117, 122–123, 130–131, 168;
Bridgeman Art Library: 208
(Biblioteque Nationale/Giraudon),
210–211 (The Berger Collection at the
Denver Art Museum), 218 (Museu Maritim
Atarazanas), 248 (Spin & Son Ltd.);
Corbis: 28, 88–89, 106, 147, 170–171;

MARS/Art-Tech: 22–23, 26–27, 30, 36,
49, 59, 64, 68–69, 71, 74, 82, 84, 93, 94,
118, 134, 139, 140, 155, 162–163, 191,
196, 197, 199, 245, 247;
Topham: 97, 101;
TRH Pictures: 47, 52–53, 60–61, 76, 83,
232, 240.